Death March to Bataan

As the days passed, the horrors mounted. By now virtually every prisoner had been stripped of everything he owned save the tattered clothes on his back. Anyone found with Japanese money, photographs, or souvenirs in his possession was executed . . . Beheading was the favorite mode of execution.

Already starved, beset with malaria that produced alternating chills and fever in the 100-degree temperatures, without water and no idea where I was going, I thought my chances of surviving much longer on the march so slim that there seemed little to lose . . . By now I had witnessed so many atrocious deeds that I was consumed with a venomous black hatred for every Japanese. I grew determined not to die as a prisoner, not to fall in the dust and be run through with a bayonet . . . not to be shot in the head in some jungle with my hands tied behind my back. I must try to escape, no matter how long the chance, for only if I got away would I ever have a chance to avenge myself on my tormentors . . .

BEHIND JAPANESE LINES

AN AMERICAN GUERRILLA
IN THE PHILIPPINES

Ray C. Hunt and Bernard Norling

POCKET BOOKS

New York   London   Toronto   Sydney   Tokyo

POCKET BOOKS, a division of Simon & Schuster, Inc.
1230 Avenue of the Americas, New York, N.Y. 10020

Contents

Foreword

WHEN BATAAN AND CORREGIDOR FELL TO THE JAPANESE IN the spring of 1942, all the U.S. and Philippine troops in the Philippine Islands were supposed to surrender to their conquerors. Many of them refused. Sometimes contrary to the orders of their commanding officers, sometimes with the connivance of those officers, sometimes entirely on their own, hundreds of them slipped into the mountains and jungles of various of the Philippine Islands. On Luzon their numbers were augmented by men who, in one way or another, managed to escape during the infamous Death March that followed the fall of Bataan.

Many of these men died soon of hunger or diseases, or they were captured by the enemy, or were murdered by bandit gangs. Of those who lived, some organized bands of guerrillas or attached themselves to such bodies.

These guerrillas were a forlorn lot. Most of them had no authorization from anyone to recruit troops of any sort for any purpose. They had no clear objectives. Common sense indicated that they should try to defend themselves, to collect information about the enemy, and to harass the Japanese if they could, but essentially they were on their own. Their enemies were legion: the Japanese; Japanese spies; several Filipino organizations friendly to the Japanese; the Hukbalahaps, who were impartially hostile to both Japanese and Americans; and those remorseless enemies of partisan forces anywhere—hunger, privation, disease, danger, and discouragement.

The guerrillas never knew how the war was going to turn out. Much of the time they knew little even about how it was going overall. They never knew when they might be ambushed and killed by the enemy, or betrayed by subordinates or civilians, or detected by spies, or awakened at night with bayonets at their throats. Many a guerrilla was killed after some such development. Others, taken alive, often experienced a worse fate: a slow death at the hands of their brutal conquerors.

If a guerrilla managed to survive the war, what then? If the Japanese won, he would surely be killed, most likely in some lingering, painful way. If the Americans won, would he be welcomed back into their ranks as a hero? treated as a traitor? court martialled for desertion? tried in a military or civil court for murder or other crimes committed in the course of his guerrilla activities? Perhaps he would be tried for crimes committed not by himself but by various of his subordinates who might or might not have acted under his orders? perhaps turned over to a postwar Philippine government to be honored or punished as might seem fit to whichever of several Filipino factions happened to come to power? Both the present life and the postwar prospects of guerrillas were distinctly precarious. To espouse life as an irregular in such circumstances required unusual qualities of character and personality.

This book is primarily an account of the activities and experiences of one such guerrilla, Ray Hunt; secondarily, that of several others. Originally from St. Louis, Ray Hunt joined the peacetime army, went to the Philippines just before the outbreak of World War II in the Pacific, survived the Bataan campaign, escaped half-dead from his captors during the Bataan Death March, was nursed back to health by friendly Filipinos, organized a troop of guerrillas, survived an amazing array of hardships and narrow escapes from death, made a noteworthy contribution to the eventual Filamerican reconquest of the Philippines, and was personally decorated with the Distinguished Service Cross by Gen. Douglas MacArthur near the end of the war. He stayed in the U.S. Air Force after World War II, became a fighter pilot, served again during the Korean War, and retired in 1959. He now lives in Orlando, Florida.

The book is based primarily on his own account of his wartime experiences written in the early 1960s but never published, on a longer and somewhat embellished version of the same material penned a few years later, on many conversations I have had with now long-retired Colonel Hunt, and by extensive correspondence with him.

Wherever possible, I have checked his memory and interpretation of events with recollections of his wartime associates and with published literature in the field. Every reasonable effort has been made to assure factual accuracy, though it is unlikely that this has been achieved in every instance, since people's memories notoriously play tricks on them with the passage of time. Moreover, the guerrillas of Luzon were contentious. Those of them who have written memoirs often differ sharply in their descriptions of events; even more in their estimates of each other. Several species of critics and partisans of various "causes" have muddied the waters further. And, of course, many of those who took part in Philippine guerrilla activities in World War II have long since died.

This book is a collaborative work in the full sense. While some of the material dealing with such subjects as prewar American unpreparedness, guerrilla warfare in past history, European partisans in World War II, Filipino collaborationists, and the rise of the Hukbalahap movement in the Philippines has been introduced mostly by myself, this has been done to place Colonel Hunt's experiences and problems in historical perspective and to make the narrative more interesting and meaningful to readers. Likewise, some of the books listed in the bibliography have been read by both of us, some only by myself. Whichever the case, they have been used primarily to make comparisons between the experiences, responses, and thoughts of Colonel Hunt and those of others in comparable circumstances. The finished product has been read and reread several times by both Ray Hunt and me and is justly chargeable to both of us.

Though I "wrote" *Behind Japanese Lines* in the ordinary meaning of that word, the book has been done in the first person throughout. Thus, everywhere save in this foreword, the words "I," "me," and "mine" refer to Ray Hunt. The only exception to this rule concerns the citation of "personal communication to the author" in the notes. Sometimes other ex-guerrillas or associates of Colonel Hunt talked to or corresponded with me, without reference to him. Sometimes they communicated with him, but not with me. Sometimes he passed along to me what they said or wrote to him. Sometimes they communicated with both of us. Thus footnotes of this sort are initialled to indicate who received the information.

Readers may be puzzled, even exasperated, by many seemingly inconsistent references to the military rank of various individuals. This condition arises from an insoluble problem. Soldiers in the American regular army had a permanent prewar rank but also a temporary, and normally higher, rank during the war. Most officers and men were promoted several times during the war. Finally, those who became guerrillas often promoted themselves or were promoted by others without reference to regular military procedure. Sometimes these informal promotions were later recognized by higher authorities during the war, or afterward; sometimes not. Thus, it was quite possible for an individual to have as many as three different ranks simultaneously: regular army, wartime army, and guerrilla. Hence, reference to anyone's rank, below that of General MacArthur himself, is only approximate.

I would especially like to thank Albert S. Hendrickson, Robert B. Lapham, Walter Chatham, and Vernon L. Fassoth, all fellow guerrillas or close wartime associates of Ray Hunt, who provided me with much firsthand information, graciously answered many questions, and saved me from falling into a variety of errors. I also profited from conversations or correspondence with James P. Boyd, Leon O. Beck, Robert Mailheau, William H. Brooks, and Frank Gyovai, all ex-guerrillas who did not know Ray Hunt but who provided me with useful background information about guerrilla life.

I am indebted to those in the University of Notre Dame Interlibrary Loan Office who secured many books for me, to Dr. Jack Detzler of St. Mary's College, who read the manuscript and suggested numerous improvements, and to Mrs. Catherine Box, who helped me greatly by typing the manuscript.

My particular thanks are due to Morton J. Netzorg of Detroit, who generously allowed me to use his extensive private library of Philippiniana, whose annotated bibliography of his own collection proved an invaluable aid to research, whose own knowledge of Philippine affairs straightened me out on various occasions, and who, with Mrs. Petra Netzorg, showed me many personal kindnesses.

BERNARD NORLING

Preface

ALL MY TRIBULATIONS IN WORLD WAR II DERIVED, ULTI-
mately, from my resolve not to be a combat infantryman. In the
mid-1930s, in the depths of the depression, when I was earning
$15 for working a seventy-hour week in a grocery store in my
native St. Louis, I gradually became aware that war clouds were
gathering in Europe and sensed that a major war there might
eventually involve the United States. If war came, I wanted to
be in the air corps rather than in the infantry. Though only the
aged recall it now, in the 1930s memories of World War I were
still fresh among people in early middle age, and that conflict
was still avidly discussed. Aviation had a lot of glamour in the
1930s, but slogging in muddy trenches under shellfire, vividly
remembered from the Western front and recounted endlessly,
had absolutely none. I yearned to be a military pilot, but I lacked
the required two years of college; so I lowered my sights and
aspired to become an aircraft mechanic instead.

These sentiments assumed tangible form on a cold, sunny
day in January 1939 when two friends and I climbed into a
boxcar in a St. Louis freightyard and headed south. We hoped
to get to Randolph Field, an air base near San Antonio. A couple
of weeks later we enlisted there in the army air corps. Training

was prosaic, and life as a KP and latrine orderly was dull. One day I tried out for the camp baseball team but got no response from the coach. Then I went over to the St. Louis Browns training camp in San Antonio for a tryout with the pros. This time those in charge showed some interest in me, but my first sergeant refused to give me time off to go back for a second session. Thus ended whatever chance I might have had to be enrolled one day in the Baseball Hall of Fame.

But, as gamblers know, neither good nor bad luck lasts forever. By the end of 1939 I was assigned to the Twenty-first Pursuit Squadron, then stationed at Hamilton Field, California. Even better, I was sent to school for a six-month course in aviation mechanics, from which I returned a staff sergeant.

It seems to me that draftees, who are usually reluctant soldiers at best, never have any idea of the esprit de corps that can exist in a first-class regular outfit composed of men who know what they are doing and like it. In the Twenty-first everybody—cooks, clerks, mechanics like myself, and pilots—took pride in what they did, got on well with the others, and never worried about doing more than someone else. No doubt this happy condition owed much to our commanding officer, Capt. William E. (Ed) Dyess, a splendid flyer and a man whom we all liked and respected.

For more than a year at Hamilton I worked on the latest U.S. fighter planes (P-40 Tomahawks) and other aircraft, assembling and disassembling them, inspecting the work of others, managing repair crews, and getting in some flying time. But despite the pleasant surroundings and the satisfaction one feels when doing something worthwhile, I grew restless and began to look for adventure. Once I volunteered for service as a civilian mechanic in Gen. Claire Chennault's famed "Flying Tigers" in China, only to be turned down because I had applied after the quotas were filled. Then, on November 1, 1941, our outfit was sent to the Philippines.

Soon after the war began five weeks later, I was swallowed up in the battle for Bataan. Ironically, immediate needs compelled me to become an infantryman and to learn to fight with a rifle, precisely the fate I had taken such pains to avoid by joining the air corps.

Preface

Before the struggle for Bataan commenced, I lost all contact with my family. They did not know I was one of the thousands of Americans who surrendered after that struggle, or that I endured the Death March that followed. Fortunately, they were also unaware of the atrocities visited on me by the enemy, much less the savagery I witnessed as a prisoner which led me to escape and fight as a guerrilla until the American liberation forces returned to Luzon on January 9, 1945. The many hardships I endured were insignificant when compared to the anguish of my parents and sisters. They were left to wonder, day by day for three long years while I was listed as missing in action, whether I was dead or alive. It would be six and a half years before I would actually see any of them again.

Somewhere along the line my father, swayed by the opinions of his friends, decided that I was dead; but this my mother never accepted. She wrote to me repeatedly, disregarding each returned letter marked "Undeliverable." She wrote to one government office after another, to the Red Cross, and to a fighter pilot in the Twenty-first Pursuit Squadron, Maj. Samuel C. Grashio, following his escape from a Japanese prisoner-of-war camp in 1943. Finally, on November 24, 1944, my parents received an official War Department message informing them that I was alive and safe with guerrilla forces.

No matter how tough it was on me, it must have been worse for my folks. How much, I never realized until my own son Gregory spent two tours of combat in the air over Vietnam. Though he was never wounded, I imagined him aboard every American aircraft reported shot down. I wanted so badly to trade places with him because I realized it would be easier fighting than worrying.

To those today who have relatives or loved ones missing in action, maybe it would be best to assume as did my father and to proceed with your lives. If at some later date you are proved wrong, you will be forgiven as I forgave those who assumed I had been lost forever.

RAY C. HUNT

BEHIND JAPANESE LINES

1

The War Begins

AT MIDDAY ON DECEMBER 8, 1941 (DECEMBER 7 IN Hawaii, east of the international date line), I was sound asleep on a camp cot at Nichols Field just outside Manila in the Philippine Islands. Suddenly my slumber was interrupted by a horrendous racket. Bullets were coming down like hail, interspersed with bombs that shook the ground like a series of small earthquakes. I sprang into a half-dug foxhole. A second later a bomb buried itself in the ground no more than thirty feet from me. Providentially, it did not explode. Nearby a friend was buried alive by another bomb burst, but his luck was running: he was dug out after a third man buried up to his neck yelled for help. Still another soldier close to me had a canteen shot off his hip. Thus did World War II begin for me, as it did for the American people, with a shattering surprise.

There was no excuse whatever for our people, or our political and military leaders, or myself personally, being caught so dramatically off guard. The explanation is simplest with regard to the whole country. Most Americans are blithely ignorant of other peoples and nations, most of us are bored by foreign affairs much of the time, and we have a national addiction to utopian hopes for perpetual peace. It is a ruinous combination that no amount of experience, no succession of disasters, has ever shaken out of our people. In the 1930s, specifically, it left our national defenses woefully deficient everywhere, but worst of all in the Pacific.

After we had "won" the first World War, our European allies reneged on their war debts and remained as quarrelsome as ever, so we had lapsed into disgruntled isolationism, vowing never again to be drawn into their disputes. At the Washington Naval Conference (1921–22) we limited our fleet and agreed not to upgrade our military installations in the Far East. This left the Philippines, only 600 miles off the coast of Asia, defended mostly by naval bases 5,000 miles eastward in Hawaii and 7,000 miles away in California. In 1934 we promised the Filipinos their independence twelve years later. Soon after, we declined to fortify Guam. Tokyo observed this sequence of events and, not surprisingly, concluded that America was withdrawing from the Orient. The British, the Dutch, even the Chinese nationalist leader Chiang Kai-shek, regarded our heedlessness with foreboding since their colonies and their interests now lay, thinly defended, beneath the shadow of Japan. Meanwhile the depression had descended, distracting the attention of Americans even more from foreign affairs and strengthening the voices of all those who always want to spend money on domestic programs and trust to good luck for national defense.

In the Philippines money for defense was chronically short, so all things were done late and in a half-hearted, slovenly manner. To be sure, this dismal situation began to improve in 1941. On July 26 the Philippine army was reincorporated into the U.S. Army. Gen. Douglas MacArthur was soon named supreme commander of these combined forces, and he began to assemble a capable staff. By then, too, a few thousand Philippine Scouts, who were part of the regular American army, had been made into effective soldiers.

Nonetheless, these reforms came too late in the day.

The bulk of the Philippine army was still virtually untrained, badly armed, and almost impossible to command since the men spoke something like seventy different dialects. Airfields remained too few, their runways too short and unpaved. Intelligence was poor everywhere. Ominously, thousands of Japanese "tourists," "fishermen," "merchants," even bird fanciers, roamed the archipelago at will. They mapped everything, purchased land, bought into businesses, and smuggled in more of their countrymen. To top off this amalgam of heedlessness and folly, West Point was able to find room for cadets from many countries, even Japan, but for a long time could accommodate only one Filipino per year. Even in 1941 there were only a handful at the Point; thus, a permanent shortage of well-trained top-ranking Filipino officers was insured.

Manuel Quezon, the president of the Philippines, was keenly aware of these deficiencies, but he was as heedless as Washington in dealing with them. In fact, he made the situation worse; in 1939 he visited Japan and returned convinced that Filipinos could never defend their country successfully. Soon after, at his behest, the Philippine legislature stopped military construction, cut the defense budget, deemphasized ROTC, halved reserve training, and postponed the mobilization scheduled for 1940, though money was found to build new roads, bridges, and public buildings, and especially to begin construction of Quezon City, adjoining Manila, to immortalize the Philippine president. Quezon justified this course, which in retrospect looks suicidal, by declaring that defense of his homeland from foreign aggression was the responsibility of the United States.[1] Informed Filipinos hoped that somehow General MacArthur, whom they virtually deified, would see that everything turned out all right.

The failures and derelictions of our military leaders on December 8, 1941, are harder to account for than are those of the American people or even the Philippine government, since our professional soldiers *had been expecting* war. Yet many hours after the Japanese attack on Pearl

Harbor half the American Far Eastern air force was wiped out by bombing and strafing as the planes sat in rows on the runways at Clark and other fields on Luzon Island. Ultimately, of course, all military catastrophes are laid at the door of the commander in chief, in this case General MacArthur; but attempts to fix responsibility more precisely long ago disappeared in a morass of divided authority, selective memories, conflicting testimony, and missing records.

Personally, I was caught sound asleep with no more justification than either my military superiors or my countrymen generally. Two months earlier, back at Hamilton Field in California, our commander, Capt. Ed Dyess, had told the whole Twenty-first Pursuit Squadron that war was virtually certain in the near future. He had added that since we were the most fully prepared combat unit in America we would soon be sent overseas.

Though Ed admonished us not to reveal this news to friends or relatives, in my case he need not have bothered. When I wrote to my parents three days later, I merely expressed regret that I would not be home for Christmas. I added that I was not sure what I would do when my three-year enlistment ended three months later. I had recently half-planned to become a pilot in the Canadian air force but that scheme, like comparable precursors, had come to naught.

On November 1, 1941, the Twenty-first Pursuit Squadron and twenty-three P-40 fighter planes left San Francisco on the USS *President Coolidge*. I had no idea where we were going. I did recall that a few months before I had seen a number of B-17 Flying Fortresses land at Hamilton Field and had been told by a crew member that they were on their way to the Philippines. Thus, I was not particularly surprised when we eventually reached the channel that separates the Bataan Peninsula from Corregidor Island at the entrance to Manila Bay. I wasn't alarmed either, for Mike Ginnevan, an old sergeant only two years away from retirement, assured me that he had once done duty on Corregidor and that the Rock was impregnable. Mike's

4

fate was as sad as his judgment was faulty: he died in a Japanese prison camp.

Once ashore, I found nothing that seemed to have anything to do with imminent war. Downtown Manila seemed a typical modern big city. Sunsets over Manila Bay and the Zambales Mountains on Bataan Peninsula were the most gaudily brilliant spectacles I had ever seen, like the canvases of an impressionist painter gone beserk. A second lieutenant with a heavy red beard startled me momentarily, but I was told that American soldiers thereabouts often grew such beards to impress Filipinos, who have little facial hair. The jai alai building seemed particularly modern since it had air conditioning and gambling apparatus similar to pari-mutuel machines at U.S. racetracks. Equally memorable, if less happily so, was the pungent smell of native villages (barrios) without facilities to dispose of sewage.

Most striking of all were the women. Like most red-blooded American boys of legend, I had a keen interest in girls. It had not been dulled by nineteen days at sea with a shipload of men. Now small, dainty Spanish-Filipina girls with incomparable complexions seemed inexpressibly beautiful. Not far behind were white Russian girls, refugees from Singapore and Hong Kong. Even the straggly-haired *lavenderas* (washerwomen), sitting on their haunches and pounding their dirty clothes with large wooden paddles, would have looked at least moderately enticing if only their lips and teeth had not been stained a ghastly, almost neon, red from chewing betel nut.

Even on the day the war began I remained as carefree as ever. Early in the morning our base cannon was fired. This was a prearranged signal to indicate that war had broken out, but it still took several minutes for its significance to sink in. Through the morning hours that followed, scattered news about Pearl Harbor began to reach us. Even so, Hawaii was thousands of miles away, and I, like so many, did not *feel* any different or suddenly acquire any sense of urgency.

Our superiors, who had plainly been expecting action

for some time, had told us several days before to dig foxholes; but I had attached little importance to this onerous task and had dug only nonchalantly. Though it may seem incredible to the reader, even after the war alarm all I did was dig a little more in my foxhole, knock off for a rest and a cigarette, then fall asleep on a folding cot under a nearby tree. That was where I was when the bombs began to fall.

Warfare is not funny, but most wars do have zany interludes. In far-off Washington, D.C., I've read, an American civilian, maddened by the news of Pearl Harbor, seized an axe and chopped down one of the famous cherry trees once given to the American people by the government of Japan. His action was about as constructive as a good deal that took place all around me that December morning. Several people shouted that the attacking planes were Messerschmitts, though they were in fact "Bettys" (Mitsubishi twin-engine bombers), Zero fighter planes, and other Japanese aircraft. The nearest Messerschmitts just then were about eight thousand miles away, being flown by Germans somewhere in European Russia.

One of our airmen jumped into an unmanned machine gun revetment and began to blast away at the enemy planes. This was sensible enough, and he even hit a couple; but for reasons unknown he cursed and swore wildly at the top of his lungs throughout. Conventional AA batteries blazed away at everything that flew—but all they managed to hit was one of our own Seversky P-35s. At that, they were better gunners than their brethren at Clark Field sixty miles to the north. There the AA batteries missed all the Japanese planes on December 8. Next day they fired furiously at Lt. Sam Grashio, a P-40 pilot in my outfit, but could not hit him either.[2] Some individual soldiers rushed into the open and fired rifles, even sidearms, at planes overhead. While such action spoke well for their courage and martial spirit, it was about as useful as firing BB guns at elephants.

Dogfights erupted overhead in several places. I saw portions of the only one that yielded anything for our side.

Lt. Jesus Villamor, a brave and skillful Filipino fighter pilot, led a flight of antiquated P-26 Boeings in a desperate attack on a squadron of Betty bombers. Though outnumbered 54 to 6, and outgunned, the P-26 pilots were not outflown. They scattered one enemy flight and may have shot down several Bettys.

Uncertainty about this is due to the inexorable exigencies of aerial combat. Oftentimes neither pilots nor observers on the ground can be sure that a given enemy plane or a given number of them have been shot down. A plane is clearly hit; perhaps it even trails smoke; then it disappears over the horizon or into a cloud bank. Did it crash and kill all on board? Did the plane crash but pilot and crew bail out safely? Was the pilot able to fly back to one of his home bases? Did several of our planes successively shoot at a single enemy craft and bring it down, and afterward each pilot report that he had destroyed an enemy plane? Often, after an air battle nobody knows the answers to such questions exactly. Officers, however, like to encourage those they command, and governments believe that the public needs to hear good news, so one's own pilots are usually given the benefit of any doubts and reports of victories easily become exaggerated. In this case, whatever damage he and his comrades did to the Japanese, Villamor became an instant Philippine war hero and was decorated with the Distinguished Service Cross by the U.S. government.

As abruptly as it began, the Japanese attack ended. Only smoke, dust, and the smell of gunpowder lingered amid the wreckage and the American corpses. Among the survivors, pandemonium prevailed. Planes that could get off the ground were flown away to other locations. Men who were separated from their units, or simply bewildered, gravitated to this or that public building in or near Manila. Gradually our officers found some of us and got us regrouped. Though I don't remember how I got there, when my unit was regrouped I was at LaSalle College in downtown Manila. Many other GIs were there, but I cannot now recall a single name or face. From time to time, between Japanese air raids, groups of us were sent back to Nichols Field to remove anything that might be useful either to ourselves or to the enemy. From one of these jaunts I returned with a Springfield .03 rifle packed in Cosmoline, a .45 automatic pistol, and a World War I "tommy" helmet, to add to my collection of souvenirs. I didn't keep any of them long.

In an effort to save civilian lives and prevent the needless destruction of Manila, General MacArthur declared the metropolis an open city. In a response typical of their conduct throughout the war, the Japanese ignored the gesture and bombed the city freely. Soon its streets were filled with rubble of every sort, and the air hung heavy with the stench of countless human and animal corpses.

On December 23, 1941, I sent a commercial cablegram to my parents, wishing them a Merry Christmas and a Happy New Year and enclosing $50. It was the last they were to hear about me until July 28, 1942, when they received a brief message from the War Department that I was missing in action. It was the last they were to hear *from* me for more than three years.

The next night all of us at LaSalle were packed into trucks, with little more than the clothes on our backs. We had barely gotten out of the city when the victorious Japanese came swarming in. All night we travelled in a convoy, arriving next morning at a sugarcane field in Pampanga province just north of Bataan Peninsula. Though I had no idea why we had come to this particular place, I soon found out: it would make our next move, into Bataan itself, short and easy.

Though General MacArthur had attacked Philippine defense problems with his habitual intelligence and energy, he never had either the time or money necessary to repair twenty years of neglect. When the war broke, for example, he had to abandon his own half-matured plans and fall back hurriedly on Washington's old Orange Plan, which called for making a major defense effort in Bataan Peninsula, a steep, rocky tongue of tropical jungle about thirty miles long and fifteen miles wide, stretching along the west side of Manila Bay. He barely succeeded. In the first days of the war the Japanese landed both along Lingayen Gulf in northern Luzon and south of Manila. In both areas the best the Americans and Filipinos could do was to undertake haphazard delaying actions long enough to allow the bulk of their troops to flee into Bataan ahead of the onrushing enemy. Moving the Twenty-first Pursuit Squadron into our sugarcane field in southern Pampanga was a hastily improvised portion of this overall design.

As soon as we arrived, we began to build an airstrip. To avoid detection by the enemy the work had to be done at night. Before daybreak we would string a chicken wire roof over what had been done and stick sugarcane tops through it vertically as camouflage. Since the cane wilted rapidly, a fresh supply had to be cut every night. Meanwhile, day and night the sweat poured off us, swarms of mosquitoes tortured us without mercy, and we dreaded that the Japanese would soon find us. But they didn't. Instead, one by one our scattered "birds" came home to roost. Each returning plane was rolled under the chicken wire roof and given a maintenance check.

This was a touchy business in the best of circumstances, as I had been reminded unforgettably only a few weeks before at Nichols Field. There we had all been working steadily uncrating and assembling our planes, which then took to the air in twos and threes for their shakedown flights. More pilots die in routine flying of this sort than are ever killed in combat. Right off I had gotten one of the worst scares of my life: I thought I had killed a pilot. On each side of the runway where our planes took off, there was a row of trees, and at the end of the runway, with macabre appropriateness, loomed a cemetery. One day one of our planes had risen just above tree level. Then it sputtered, fell silent, and disappeared. The awful thought flashed into my mind that perhaps I had not checked the gas strainer. A lump rose in my throat and my body tensed as I waited for the horrible sound of the crash. Suddenly a loud roar filled the air instead. At the last second the engine had caught, and the plane climbed gracefully into

9

the sky. So thin is the line between life and death even in preparation for war.

Now, in the sugarcane field all our maintenance work had to be done at night in semi-darkness, because in the daytime the metal on the planes was too hot to touch. Perhaps worse, since we lacked many ordinary maintenance tools we mechanics had to ignore inspection guides and make repairs largely from memory and intuition. I never envied the pilots who had to fly planes that had been "serviced" thus. Nonetheless, our luck held, and our minuscule contingent of P-40s flew many missions from this makeshift base.

One day I was sure I was going to die. A Japanese Betty flew over our strip and was hit by our AA guns. (Our gunners had improved considerably since December 8 and now occasionally hit something.) The big bomber slipped sideways briefly, then nosed straight down, engines screaming. I would have enjoyed the sight save that the bomber seemed to be heading straight for me. I learned from later experience that a falling plane anywhere near a person always looks thus, but this was the first time around, and I was certain the Betty was going to hit me right between the eyes. I rushed madly into the sugarcane, which was fully grown. The stalks were high and tough, and they sprawled in all directions. After falling down half a dozen times I flopped flat on my face and awaited death. The rising scream of the plane's engines ended abruptly in a resounding thuuuummmmmp, accompanied by a sharp earth tremor. Pieces of the plane and pieces of its crewmen whizzed about in all directions. Slowly I began to breathe again and to recover my wits. The doomed bomber had crashed about a hundred feet from me.

Soon after this memorable experience we moved southward to Cabcaben and Bataan fields, both situated at the extreme south end of Bataan Peninsula, only three or four miles from Corregidor Island across the north entrance to Manila Bay.

The overall plan for the defense of Bataan became increasingly clear in the early months of 1942. Lines were to be established and held as long as possible. It was expected that they would be breached by the Japanese eventually, but we would then retreat to another line and the process would be repeated. In the actual event, American and Filipino troops were told that we were holding until reinforcements could arrive. Like many Americans, and nearly all Filipinos, I believed this until the very end of the campaign. I simply could not imagine that our government would just leave us there to delay for as long as possible a feared Japanese assault on Australia while the main American war effort was directed toward Europe. Forty years later I still don't know exactly what to make of it. The fierce sacrificial struggle of the Filipinos and ourselves on Bataan and Corregidor is thought by many to have been crucial in saving Australia, but the cost in lives and suffering was heavy for us and frightful for the Filipinos. Had I been General MacArthur, I don't believe I could have swallowed the deception and given the orders, though it must be admitted that since 1945 nearly all military analysts have supported the grand strategic decision of Franklin Roosevelt and Winston Churchill to concentrate on defeating the Axis powers in Europe before Japan in the Pacific.

2

The Struggle for Bataan

MOST OF MY WORKING TIME ON BATAAN WAS SPENT REpairing airplanes. Most were P-40 fighters, all that remained from an original motley array of Seversky P-35s, obsolete B-18 bombers, a couple of B-10s, a few A-27 attack bombers, a handful of observation planes, and some P-26 antiques still used by the Philippine air force. We in the ground crews worked day and night, engulfed by stifling heat and clouds of mosquitoes, to keep our steadily dwindling force airworthy. We not only patched bullet holes but cannibalized disabled aircraft for any parts that might possibly be usable on other planes. Engines, even wings, were transferred from planes of one type to another. Somebody even figured out a way to alter gasoline tank brackets on fighter planes so they could hold 500-pound bombs. After one such operation I heard one skeptical pilot ask a crew chief, "How can I be sure that son-of-a-bitching bomb you attached to my plane won't shake loose during takeoff?" I didn't hear the reply. An appropriate one would have been, "The age of faith has not passed."

Working constantly with planes and watching them in

action impressed me with the clear initial superiority of the Japanese Zero to any of our fighter planes. As the war lengthened, America gradually developed better planes of all types, which the Japanese, whose industry was far less advanced or flexible than ours, could not match. In 1942, though, the Zero was king of the Far Eastern skies. Its detractors have put it down as cheap and crudely built; but it was also light, fast, a marvellous climber, and remarkably maneuverable. It had a shorter radius of turn than our latest fighter, the P-40, which meant that in any contest involving circular maneuvers the Zero soon ended on the tail of the P-40 with fixed guns. For the American pilot in such a situation that was "all she wrote." Though at least one pilot in the Twenty-first Pursuit Squadron wrote favorably of the sturdiness, strength, and straightaway speed of the P-40,[1] I never liked the plane. It was tricky to handle, and there was always something wrong with it. In my opinion, its sole claim to excellence was that it could dive like a rock. It never surprised me that a lot of our pilots who flew P-40s were killed taking off or landing. Once during training at Hamilton Field I saw six such accidents in a single day.

The only effective tactic a P-40 could employ against a Zero was to gain higher altitude, go into a power dive, fire a burst at the Zero in passing, and then hightail it out of the area—a technique first worked out by Gen. Claire Chennault, commander of the Flying Tigers in China. In fairness, though, I must admit that I once watched a dogfight over Manila Bay between six Zeros and six P-40s in which five of the Zeros were shot down without a loss on our side. Either our pilots were much superior to the Japanese or they packed six months of good luck into that one day.

Whichever the case, it became clear early in the Bataan campaign that most of the fighting would be on the ground. Since we already had far more pilots, maintenance men, and other specialists than our dwindling air force would ever need, it was decided to convert many of us into infantrymen. All we lacked was equipment and

13

training. Not a single one of us had as much as an entrenching tool. Most of us had thrown away our gas masks and had used the containers to carry ammunition or anything else handy. To me a rifle was merely something to hang on a wall. One day a real infantryman assured me solemnly that my rifle was my best friend, adding that I should treat it with tenderness and care. I was unimpressed, but eventually discovered that he was right. At the moment, though, I was given a few cartridges, shown how to load my rifle, and told to shoot at some trees and vines for practice. That constituted infantry training.

It did not take long for us to find out if we had learned anything useful. According to the Japanese timetable, the Philippines were supposed to be conquered in fifty days. By January 17 our foes were far behind schedule, and their high command was growing impatient. On that date they launched a series of attacks on several peninsulas along the southwest shore of Bataan that have come to be known collectively as the Battle of the Points. Many of us were hastily trucked to one of them, Aglaloma Point, and deployed in a line across that small peninsula to fight a reported "handful" of Japanese ensconced there.

Our immediate problem was not the enemy at all but the sheer density of the jungle. Gigantic trees towered up to two hundred feet in the air, grew close together, and were crested with luxuriant intertwining branches. Far below, dense masses of vines and bushes took up most of the space between the trees. The growth was so thick that on the ground it was never really daylight, and there were only about six hours of the day that could even be called twilight. By the end of the afternoon one could avoid getting lost only by hanging onto the belt of the man in front of him. Even so, we spread across the point and slowly negotiated the trackless wilderness until we reached the edge of a cliff about a hundred feet high overlooking a short, narrow beach. We looked about, saw nothing, retraced our steps, and using our hands and steel helmets, dug in for the night. It had been a mere sightseeing tour.

"No Japs here," we told each other, only the usual billions of damnable mosquitoes.

It required only two days to lay this myth to rest. The Japanese had played possum and let us bypass them twice because they had not yet gotten enough troops onto the peninsula to attempt battle. As soon as they were prepared, they let us have it so vigorously that we had to call for reinforcements. We got some Philippine army men, who were no help at all because they were virtually untrained, and then some Philippine Scouts who *were* trained and who shored up our ranks at once.

In the next few days, locked in combat in that stinking jungle, I learned a lot about some of the different kinds of men who make up this world. In particular, I learned not to judge a person prematurely. Many a rear area loudmouth fell silent and cringed when he knew a deadly enemy might be only a few feet away yet completely hidden. Conversely, some of the most unlikely men quietly took initiatives and performed far beyond expectation. I saw one young farm boy, praised for having killed several enemy soldiers, remark quietly that he had just done his duty; while another soldier of equally tender years cried and trembled and pleaded that he was sick. He was sick only with fear, but since he was useless to us I could only send him back to the rear. Our squadron commander, Ed Dyess, accepted his temporary demotion to the infantry with good grace. He observed wryly that he would rather be on his father's farm staring at the south end of a northbound mule; nevertheless, he led his men on the ground with the same bravery and skill that he showed in the air. By contrast, another soldier whose rifle stock had been shattered by Japanese bullets fell into hysteria and shouted over and over, "They shot my brother, right in the head."

Among such varied responses to danger the most inspiring was that of one of my buddies, Sgt. Verlon O. Hayes. Once we were strung across the Aglaloma peninsula, one way to insure that the line of men was intact was to pass the words from man to man, "Contact the right flank (or left flank)." The last man at the end of each line

15

would then start the message back with "Right (left) flank contacted." These messages began well but many times failed to return, which caused men to fear that the Japanese had either penetrated our front or outflanked us, either eventuality dictating sudden withdrawal. Verlon fouled up this system repeatedly because he was half-deaf in one ear, the result of being barely missed by a bomb. One day I sent him back to our rear command post with a Japanese prisoner, just to get rid of him. A few minutes later I was surprised to see that he was still with us. He had passed the prisoner on to a lower ranking man in order to stay with us and risk his life in the thick of the fight. This was the spirit that eventually enabled us to kill the "handful" of Japanese in the area—some 850 of them.

I also had my eyes opened about the quality and outlook of enemy troops. To the Japanese, war was not a contest waged according to rules written in Geneva but a struggle to the death in which nothing was barred. Earlier at Cabcaben Field I had been shocked to see Japanese pilots strafe a helpless American pilot as he hung in his parachute. Now I saw something that seemed even more abominable, perhaps because the victims were in my outfit. One day Staff Sgt. William Fowler was killed by a Japanese bullet. Sgt. Benjamin Kerr and a companion went out to remove the body. As they set down the stretcher the Japanese shot and killed Kerr. Because we often saw the enemy thus cruelly use the dead and the wounded alike as decoys, there were times when we had to listen for hours to maimed Americans crying for help while no one dared go to their aid.

I soon learned that Japanese infantrymen were not merely savage and treacherous but also remarkably brave, tough, tenacious, and disciplined. Physically, maybe 80 percent of them could have come from a mold. They were about 5'2" and weighed about 125 pounds. Most were in their early twenties and had only an elementary education. Perhaps a third came from farms. Most had been in uniform a couple of years, and all had passed through the world's harshest military training regimen.[2] Because of the

16

brutality of their training and the thoroughness with which they had been indoctrinated to make any sacrifice for their emperor and their country, they were capable of incredible feats of endurance, not to speak of conduct that seemed insane to Occidentals. In desperate circumstances the Japanese would kill their wounded, even burn wounded men to death in buildings, to prevent the disabled from slowing the pace of military operations.

This grim approach to war did possess a certain macabre "efficiency," but it was also counterproductive. All the support services in the Japanese army, medical included, were meager because Japanese troops were supposed to fight rather than engage in peripheral activities or go on sick call. This meant that many Nipponese soldiers threw away their lives in displays of brainless bravado, while many others sickened and died because they seldom received the medical treatment they needed and deserved. In our army, by contrast, for every man who was actually in combat there were as many as twelve others in training, maintenance, liaison, planning, special services or, above all, generating mountains of paper.

Like soldiers of most times and places, the Japanese were great looters and collectors. Some of their dead wore as many as three or four wrist watches, taken off the corpses of our buddies. The pockets of many of them were stuffed with several different kinds of money. Like G.I.s, most of them kept pictures of families and friends.

Japanese infantrymen were armed with .25-caliber Arisaka bolt-action rifles that weighed about ten pounds with bayonets attached. Both commissioned officers and noncoms carried pistols modelled on the German Luger, and commissioned officers sported fancy samurai swords, which some of them delighted to use for beheading. It is possible that this particular penchant indicated a desire to humiliate the enemy since ordinary Japanese soldiers had a superstitious fear of having their own heads and bodies buried in separate places.

Enemy soldiers usually wore hobnailed boots, with the rough side of the leather outside. Sometimes they wore split-toed tennis shoes which were better suited for climbing rocks, trees, and vines than Western tennis shoes. Oddly, Japanese equipment usually had a disagreeable smell, though I never knew why since most Japanese are clean personally. Such were the opposing troops that I, a rather green young man from Missouri, now encountered for the first time.

Our side instituted action as optimistically as possible. One of our men took up a bullhorn and appealed to the foe to surrender. Back came a reply in perfect English, "Piss on you, you Yankee son-of-a-bitch. If you want us, come and get us." From his enunciation the speaker might have come from Harvard, but the sentiment hardly did.

There was nothing left but to get down to business. We grouped in line to prepare for an advance. There was a clearing dead ahead. On signal (a whistle) I as platoon leader raced across the clearing and jumped into a hole—right on top of a dead Japanese soldier. I was shaken, and repelled, but at least he wasn't alive. With bullets whizzing overhead like hornets I lay low with my distasteful companion until I gradually realized that our entire left flank had failed to advance. There was only one thing to do, however hazardous; race back across the clearing and pull the flank forward, then dash back to the company of the dead Japanese in the foxhole. Bullets whistled about me both ways and I was splattered by bark knocked off trees and vines, but my luck held. Indeed, my good fortune throughout the war was little short of miraculous. Though I came close to death many times from a variety of causes, I was never hit by a Japanese bullet.

The enemy did more than just fire rifle bullets at us. The Japanese had many grenade throwers, which we called knee mortars, that lobbed shells up to seven hundred yards. Though these missiles were no larger than artillery shells, when they sailed overhead they sounded like large ashcans turning end over end. Though the density of a jungle restricts the damage that mortar shells can do, since most of them explode in the treetops, we found them sufficiently unnerving that we called in tanks to root out mortar emplacements. This was a fiasco. The trees were so close together, and the brush and vines so thick, that a tank wallowed as helplessly as a rhinoceros in quicksand.

The Japanese seemed to enjoy nothing about war so much as murderous chicanery. The shooting of U.S. medics I have noted. Another of their unsettling tricks was to send snipers up trees where they tied themselves fast and covered themselves with camouflage. Then, as we advanced against their comrades on the ground and the sound of ground gunfire would hide their own, they would shoot us in the back. This happened so often that we took to spraying trees with bullets indiscriminately during each advance. Even when a sniper was hit, as happened occasionally, he would seldom move or cry out. We would become aware of his presence only if we happened to encounter drops of blood spattering the thick undergrowth.

In these grim surroundings one quickly learned iron self-control or he did not live. Once just before darkness I deployed thirty Filipinos into the center of our line, which had been badly shot up. Soon after this I made the appalling discovery that both our right and left flanks had silently slunk off. If the enemy learned of this, they could outflank us with ease. I feared to tell the Filipinos what had happened, lest they panic. Meanwhile it had become too dark to retreat. So there we sat, motionless, throughout the longest night of my life. I was dying for a cigarette but dared not light a match with the enemy only spitting distance away. But once more our, or at least my, luck held and nothing happened until daylight. Then we had to slip backward into the jungle individually and hope our own troops did not mistake us for Japanese.

One thing that vanished rapidly in this environment was fastidiousness. We learned to eat amid swarms of flies, with cotton stuffed in our noses to lessen the stench of dead Japanese bodies nearby. It was nauseating to discover disabled enemy soldiers whose wounds were filled with maggots, but one soon got used to that too. Actually, the maggots performed a useful service. They ate away the decaying flesh and prevented the onset of gangrene.

Sometimes in war one is torn between duties that seem equally pressing but cannot be reconciled. This happened to me once near the end of the Battle of the Points. There had been a lull in the fighting, and where I happened to be there was a hole in the jungle directly overhead. I looked up and saw two P-40s slip from the top of a cloud bank onto the trail of three unsuspecting Japanese planes cruising below the clouds. Suddenly our planes dove and blasted two of the enemy aircraft, though the third got away. Right away the Japanese retaliated by bombing us on the ground. Two of my close friends were hit. Pfc. John Baker from Illinois was blown in two, and Sgt. Jerry Karlick, a teammate in many enjoyable baseball games back in California, was badly wounded. At this juncture our squadron leader, Ed Dyess, came by and directed me to help him and some others make preparations for an anticipated boat landing along the seashore. I liked and admired Ed, just as everyone else did, and I wanted to go with him, but I could not have lived with myself had I simply abandoned Jerry to die. Ironically, Jerry did die soon anyway, but while I stood indecisively Dyess and his companions passed out of sight. Then I *could not* join them. The whole matter was of no great importance, and I was not even reprimanded for having stayed behind, but it caused me considerable personal anguish. War strains many different kinds of loyalties.

Little by little, almost step by step, for two weeks we pushed the Japanese back through the dense, stinking, steaming, pest-ridden jungle to the edge of the cliffs overlooking the beach below. Here they could be bombed and strafed from the air, shelled by heavy artillery on Corregidor, fired on by Dyess and others in small boats offshore, and pressured from the jungle side by ourselves. Still they fought on with incredible tenacity and fanaticism. A lieutenant once marked their machinegun nests for us and warned us that the last part of our mission was apt to be as tough as what had gone before. His words were tragically prophetic. When we began our final advance, he was the first to die, from a bullet through his heart. Many

20

enemy soldiers leaped off the cliffs to their death below rather than surrender. Others clambered down the cliffs and crawled into caves in their faces. We then lowered boxes of dynamite in front of the caves and exploded them, though how much damage was done thus is questionable.

After we had secured the top of the cliffs, two memorable episodes occurred. One has been recorded by the historian John Toland.[3] I was sitting propped against a tree enjoying the beautiful view over the ocean. I glanced toward the beach and saw a Japanese run across it and jump into the water. "A hell of a long way to Tokyo," I thought idly. Nearby a Filipino machinegunner who was eating his lunch saw the same spectacle. As nonchalantly as if he was target shooting with friends, he set aside his mess kit, picked up a machine gun, positioned himself comfortably, took careful aim, and squeezed the trigger. The swimming soldier stopped abruptly, and a circle of bloody water began to form around his body. The red was brilliant against the emerald green sea. With each wave it grew wider, a sight at once vivid and horrible that I have never forgotten.

The other event occurred a few minutes later. It was embarrassing. I had been sitting close to several hand grenades when I suddenly heard the unmistakable sound of a released grenade pin. The thought flashed through my mind that I must have sat on a grenade and accidentally dislodged the pin. There was no time for a leisurely investigation. I lunged to one side, felling several buddies with a flying block. What had actually happened was that a soldier on the opposite side of a tree from me had pulled the pin on a grenade he intended to toss over the cliff. Having seen him while I had not, the victims of my "human missile" performance were not amused.

The most spectacular phase of the Battle of the Points took place February 1, 1942, two weeks after the campaign started. This time I was only a spectator. Long after darkness the enemy tried to put ashore about one thousand reinforcements from landing barges. Our intelligence had found out about it, and plans were made to give the invaders a warm reception. As the barges began to come in, our shore parties turned searchlights on them, making them ideal silvery targets against the black ocean. Our P-40 pilots roared down on them and strafed them from end to end, shooting them full of holes. Strictly as a spectacle, the operation had a certain weird beauty as the gaudy tracer bullets flashed wildly in every direction when they ricocheted off the water. More to the point, nearly all the occupants of the boats died, either from the gunfire or from drowning. It was one of the most sweeping small victories in the whole war, and it did much for our morale at a time when we had little occasion to feel cheerful about anything.

Though I can't prove it, and have never seen any reference to the matter in any book, I am utterly convinced that on that fateful night, because of one of those incredible foulups that have always haunted warfare, the Japanese helped destroy their own invasion force. By February 1942 I had been repairing American airplanes for two years, and in these last two months I had gained more experience than I wanted in listening to Japanese engines. Every motor has a distinctive sound, and I am not being boastful when I say that I could tell each type of American and Japanese plane from every other without seeing them. I could tell by sound when something was wrong with a particular engine, sometimes even *what* was wrong. On this night, as planes roared back and forth over the doomed barges, I would have sworn that I heard the distinctive sounds of Japanese engines.

In honesty, I must admit that Sam Grashio, one of the pilots who strafed the Japanese landing barges on this occasion, insists that it is impossible that Japanese planes could have taken part along with U.S. planes and remained undetected.[4] Of course, he was better situated than I to judge the matter. All I can say is that my ears never deceived me about the identity of planes on any other occasion.

If the Japanese debacle at Aglaloma Bay was indeed partly suicidal, such events are by no means uncommon in the armed forces of any nation. One of the wildest mix-ups I ever heard of took place on a dark night in 1944 off the north coast of Luzon. A surfaced U.S. submarine there sent boatloads of supplies ashore for guerrillas while a Japanese ship anchored nearby was similarly unloading equipment for Nipponese troops. Small American and Japanese boats crisscrossed near each other for hours. Fortunately, the submarine skipper was the first to realize what was happening and departed hastily before the enemy knew he was there.[5]

Clark Lee, an American war correspondent, describes many other such foulups, which were often fatal, in both the Pacific and European theaters. Some of them, he thought, while not deliberate, nonetheless owed considerably to the intense rivalry among American soldiers, sailors, and airmen, and were regretted but lightly when those who perished were from a different branch of the service.[6] Whether Lee's depressing judgment is justified about Americans, there is no question that the Japanese committed as many blunders of this sort as we did and that in their case the primary cause was persistent rivalry and mistrust between their army and navy, complicated by lack of overall direction of operations.[7] An observant Filipino who saw Nipponese army and navy officers regularly was amazed that they seemed genuinely to hate each other. They seldom associated, and they habitually belittled one another in public. On one occasion he saw a Japanese army ambulance refuse to help a naval officer who had suffered a heart attack, on the ground that the navy had its own ambulances.[8] One of Japan's greatest fighter pilots related that when Japanese naval planes were flying toward Clark Field to begin the war in the Philippines, he and eight others dropped out of formation to attack nine bombers flying *toward* them, only to discover that the latter were Japanese army planes on a routine training flight. The two services simply did not inform each other about anything.[9] I suppose it validates the old saw that nobody *wins* a war: one side out-blunders the other and eventually loses.

After the Battle of the Points was over, we had time to

think about what we had just been through and, hopefully, to draw some useful conclusions. Our casualties had been high because of our inexperience as infantrymen. We had discovered that our foes were ferocious fighters but not necessarily invincible ones. We had been fearful at the outset but had grown less so as we became better acquainted with our weapons and learned to distinguish their sounds from those of enemy arms. We had gained a new appreciation of the necessity to follow orders, and of the value of the hated foxholes—even if we had to dig them with knives, helmets, and bare hands. As the fighting had grown grimmer and the casualty lists longer, we had become calloused, accustomed to death, even that of our best friends. This ability to adjust to circumstances was, I believe, one of our most valuable assets, one of the few areas where we clearly excelled Japanese troops on an individual basis. They tended to be much better at set pieces than at improvisation.

After our brief careers in the infantry we airplane mechanics turned once more to keeping up our steadily dwindling air force, the only one left in all Luzon. It beat infantry fighting, but not by much. Every day the insolent Bettys, that resembled nothing so much as giant silver fish, came over at 25,000–30,000 feet to bomb us. Lower flying planes supported them with periodic strafing, and Japanese observation planes, which we called Photo Joes, added insult by roaming the skies unmolested to take pictures of what their brethren had wrought. Since the enemy pilots and bombardiers had little idea where their bombs would land, one individual in one foxhole had about as much chance of being hit as he did of hitting the jackpot in Las Vegas. Even so, I never felt secure. A 500-pound bomb falling through the air made a whoooosh like a huge swing. Even if it landed five miles away, it sounded like it had hit the front porch, and it shook the ground like a minor earthquake. Every time I dove into a foxhole, I had to go to the latrine, no matter how recently I had been there, and I was not alone. It was a relief to see the Bettys

24

fly away after a raid but discouraging to know that we had no way to prevent them from coming back the next day.

All we could do was curse the bombers and hope for our long awaited reinforcements. For weeks men climbed trees to look for American ships, and everyone prayed that they would come soon. One high ranking West Point officer even made elaborate plans for what to do when the reinforcements arrived. He must have graduated at the bottom of his class.

Maybe we were sustained, ultimately, by our sense of humor, not the least valuable quality of American troops. Even on the blackest days when the fighting was most fierce, if there was a break in the action somebody usually thought of a joke that picked up our spirits a bit. One I still remember. It was told by one of our planeless P-40 pilots about a U.S. navy pilot who could never do anything right. During a mission one day luck was with him and he shot down five Japanese planes. Elated, he flew over a carrier doing victory rolls and followed this with a perfect landing. Jumping to the ship's deck, he shouted, "I'm an Ace! I shot down five of those yellow sons-of-bitches." A uniformed listener bowed politely and replied, "Ah, so! Ah, so!"

Another such story was related to me one day by an old-timer. God, he said, had seen fit to create two kinds of mosquitoes for the Philippines: large daytime mosquitoes that caused dengue fever, and small nighttime mosquitoes that carried malaria. Unhappily, he wasn't joking: I soon contracted both maladies. Of the two ailments, malaria was worse. It could be, and often was, fatal. Its victims endured severe chills, followed by vomiting, fever, and paralyzing headaches. Dengue fever was not accompanied by chills: it merely caused every joint to ache and prevented one from remaining in one position for more than a few minutes at a time. It was rarely fatal: it just made a person wish he was dead.

Medicines to deal with these and a dozen other tropical ills were always in short supply, and no substitute was left untried. Since quinine pills were lacking, I was once dosed with liquid quinine for my malaria. The stuff made everything else, even the air I breathed, taste bitter for the rest of the day.

Even so, one is never so badly off that he cannot find someone else in a worse state. One day I went to the Bataan General Hospital, which was entirely out of doors, to visit some of our wounded airmen. One was a young sergeant who had lost a leg. He told me he didn't mind losing the leg that was now gone, but his voice broke when he added that the doctors were thinking of amputating the other one as well. He was nineteen.

Every effort was made to secure desperately needed medicines, especially to combat gangrene, which developed easily in tropical ulcers. On occasion planes were sent hundreds of miles south to search for drugs and medical paraphernalia. On one such flight the pilot had gotten into the cockpit while others packed all available space around him with small packages and boxes of medicines. Because he was thus laden like a Christmas tree, he could see only directly forward on his return flight. Near home he was jumped by a pair of Zeros he had been unable to sight. He raced for his life and managed to land his oil-streaked plane. Understandably excited, he threw open the canopy and fairly erupted from the cockpit like a dancer from a birthday cake, showering medical packages in every direction before anyone could even tell who he was.

The medicine helped, but there was never enough, particularly to deal with gangrene. Doctors learned to do the best they could with whatever they had—or lacked; in the case of gangrene simply to slash the infected flesh and let air get to it.

We had one burden that was even worse than disease: the threat of starvation. During the month of muddle that followed the onset of the war, a variety of snafus resulted in far too little food being moved into Bataan. During the flight into the peninsula we got a break of sorts when large numbers of Philippine Constabulary troops simply abandoned their units, hid their guns, "resigned" from the war, and went home to plant rice. They would have been of little use in combat anyway, and when gone they no longer depleted our skimpy stock of food. Unhappily, their numbers were more than replaced by some 20,000 panic-stricken Filipino civilians who fled into Bataan and who then had to be fed along with the 80,000 or so assorted American infantry, airmen, and sailors, together with Philippine Scouts, regular army, and Constabulary remnants. When the Bataan campaign began, there were about three thousand tons of canned meat and salmon on the peninsula, supplemented by inadequate supplies of rice. Altogether they constituted regular rations for 100,000 men for a month. Since the siege of Bataan was expected to take much longer, we were put on half rations (approximately 2,000 calories per day) on January 8. This was cut to 1,500 calories on February 1 and to 1,000 calories on March 1 in circumstances where men needed at least 3,500 calories per day to maintain health and strength.

Of course, we were never entirely without food, just condemned to inadequate and diminishing quantities of it. This had physical and psychological repercussions that any doctor might have expected but which seemed odd to us at the time. There is a joke that has been endemic around logging camps for generations to the effect that lumberjacks stay out in the woods all week and talk about women, then go to town Saturday night and talk about logging. In normal times the thoughts of soldiers also run heavily to women, and so they did during January 1942 on Bataan before the insidious effects of semi-starvation made themselves felt. By February ruminations about women had given way almost entirely to preoccupation with food. Some men talked so much about menus and food preparation that they sounded like delegates to a convention of chefs.

We grasped at every expedient imagination could devise to add something to our shrinking daily ration of watery rice mixed with canned salmon. The best one was to make rice cakes and pour a little Eagle Brand condensed milk on them, but this could be done only occasionally because the milk was chronically in short supply. Then we did the next best thing, undertook "moonlight requisitioning" of whatever pigs and goats could be found on Filipino farms. We also hunted deer and small game in the jungle. We tried eating carabao, the huge water buffalo Filipinos use as draft animals, though carabao meat is better suited for making saddles than for steaks. Before long we butchered and rationed all the cavalry horses. Even General Wainwright's favorite horse, Joseph Conrad, ended his military career not in battle but on a menu. Toward the end of the Bataan campaign we were eating anything that walked, ran, crept, swam, or flew, and much that did none of these.

The creatures I hated most to eat were monkeys. It was bad enough that monkey meat was so tough and stringy that it seemed to grow right out of the animal's bones. The worse part was killing the monkey in the first place. I shot one out of a tree for food once. It fell at my feet, still alive, and looked at me in the most pathetic way imaginable, seeming to say, "Why did you do this to me?" I am not sure what it proves, but after seeing and experiencing the malice and ferocity of the Japanese I could kill one of them without a qualm, indeed I became eager to kill as many of them as possible, but I could never kill another monkey.

An animal I did try hard to kill was the iguana, a large lizard with a forked tongue and a hide like a crocodile. Though iguanas are ugly, repulsive creatures, their meat is sweet and tasty, much like the white meat of chicken. One of my bitterest disappointments on Bataan came when hunting iguana at a time when I was famished. I spotted a big one, sighted in carefully on its head with my Springfield .03, pulled the trigger—and the gun misfired. The lizard had also sighted me, meanwhile, and flicked its tongue about menacingly. As quietly as I could, I ejected the faulty cartridge, slid another into the chamber, sighted in just behind the animal's front leg this time, and slowly squeezed the trigger. The iguana crumpled. Without bothering to reload, I stepped forward to pick up my victim. Alas! it was only playing possum. It scrambled off abruptly and disappeared into the jungle. Many a broken heart has been due to disappointment in love, and I've had a few; but heartbreak due to hunger is worse.

By early March some of our pilots had gotten so weak from lack of food that they could no longer fly. Our senior air officer, Gen. Harold George, then interceded with Gen. Edward P. King, at that time General MacArthur's chief of artillery, to get some food from Corregidor for them. Before the supplementary rations were given to the pilots of the Twenty-first Pursuit Squadron, Ed Dyess called in several of us sergeants, explained the situation to us, and asked us how the men would respond to such an arrangement. We replied that they would accept it. Dyess later wrote in his book that he had never been more proud to be an American. No doubt that was the way it seemed to him; and I will say for us that we did understand the necessity of the action, but inwardly we were resentful. The pilots were officers and we were enlisted men. They had decent quarters while we slept outdoors on the ground amid mosquitoes so thick that by dawn our eyes were often swollen shut from their bites. Now, when we were all half-starved, the officers were to get extra food as well.

Each day the enemy crowded us into a smaller area. Scores of thousands of hungry, sick, weak, and increasingly dispirited American and Filipino troops, burdened additionally by hordes of hapless Filipino civilians, milled around in the stifling heat, clouds of dust, and numberless mosquitoes. Bombs fell among us day and night by now, often starting fires in bamboo thickets, for it was then the dry season. Artillery, both American and Japanese, roared incessantly. No literary description of hell could have exceeded it. It was evident that the end could not be far off.

It has been charged that the fall of Bataan was not inevitable, but was due to Allied bungling and slackness: to endless confusion because officers did not know what their subordinates were doing and one unit was ignorant of the intentions of others; to inadequate defenses, lax discipline, and hordes of inexperienced Filipino trainees; to the hijacking of rations by both Americans and Filipinos; and above all to the greater will of the Japanese to fight and absorb losses. The enemy, after all, was also short of food and medicine, also had thousands of men in hospitals and, contrary to legend, did not outnumber us.[10]

There is considerable truth in this indictment, but it underrates the most important component of war, which is psychological. An army is defeated, after all, if one of two things happens; it is physically exterminated, or it no longer believes that victory is possible. The Japanese might have been sick and hungry, but we were more so, as the dreadful toll on the subsequent Death March showed. More important, our foemen knew they could eventually get additional food from Japan, while we had no such assurance of outside succor. They also knew they could get troop reinforcements if these were needed, while we were reduced to *hoping* for reinforcements, and our hope grew dimmer with each passing day. By now our air force was virtually gone, and few experiences in modern war demoralize ground troops more than constant pounding from the air when they know retaliation is impossible. Finally, in every other theater of the war the Japanese were winning, while we were losing. Numbers or no, by April 1942 the Bataan campaign had become a mismatch, both materially and psychologically.

A few days before the final collapse there occurred one of those curious events that could take place only in the American army, though it was not without dismal practicality. We were asked if we wanted to take out $10,000 GI life insurance policies. Given the circumstances, I would have taken out $100,000, but $10,000 was the limit. Nobody quibbled over premiums. Later I discovered that the names of policy subscribers were radioed out.

We were also told that if we wrote letters to our loved ones these would be sent out. I wrote many. Though not one of them got through, my own outlook brightened after each letter. It was a good way for a scared soldier to get some things off his chest.

April 8, 1942, was the last day of the Bataan campaign for the Twenty-first Pursuit Squadron. By now our air force consisted of four patched up, mongrel planes. Ed Dyess ordered Lt. Jack Donaldson to take one of them, mostly a P-40, load it with thirty-pound fragmentation bombs, and look for some Japanese troops who were reported to be near the Bataan airstrip. If he was unable to find them, he was to return and land. If he found them, he was to bomb them and then fly on to Cebu about three hundred miles south. Jack dropped his bombs, rocked his wings to us on the ground, and headed south. Capt. O.L. Lunde also flew south in a Seversky P-35 with another pilot stuffed into the baggage compartment. Dyess then ordered Capt. Hank Thorne and Lt. Ben Brown into the remaining P-35, one on the other's lap in the pilot's seat, with another pilot in the baggage compartment. They also headed south. We in the ground crew then changed a cylinder in the last plane, a beat-up collection of scraps that had originally been an old civilian Ballanca. Aboard it were Lieutenants Barneke, Robb, Coleman, Short, and Boelens, and General MacArthur's propaganda chief, Carlos P. Romulo. The overloaded relic barely got off the runway, flew right over the heads of Japanese troops advancing down the main road on the east side of Bataan, and was able to limp across the strait to Corregidor only when those on board threw all their baggage into Manila Bay. It was the end of the line.

Most of us then retreated a short distance south to Mariveles Bay. There we threw away the firing pins from our rifles, stacked the neutered arms, and awaited the arrival of the new rulers of Luzon. I was bewildered. I had never gotten much information about anything pertaining to the war in my three months on Bataan. For a much longer time than was reasonable, I had expected that we would eventually be rescued, mostly, no doubt, because I wanted so badly to believe it. Like so many Americans, in uniform and out, I had simply assumed that no matter what the situation the United States was bound to prevail in the end. The thought of old-time regulars near retirement and fuzzy-cheeked pilots, not to speak of myself, becoming prisoners of the Japanese, had simply never entered my consciousness. It was also to be the last time I was to see most of the men in my outfit. Ed Dyess, then a captain, was to survive an incredible array of hardships and escape from a prison camp on Mindanao, only to die in a training mishap in California a few months afterward. Lt. Sam Grashio survived and escaped with Dyess, and I regained contact with him years after the war; but most of the others were gone for good.

Though I did not know it at the time, when General King surrendered the American army on Bataan on April 9 some American officers complied to the letter, others encouraged their men to escape into the hills, and still others looked away and left the decision to each individual. Most of us around Mariveles had no choice. We did not relish the idea of capitulating, and we did not know what to expect, but the Japanese were all around us. We could only watch their dive bombers blast away at Corregidor, and wait.

The last free action of the U.S. command was in some ways a grimly appropriate finale to the campaign. They broke out the few remaining food stores and told us to eat whatever we wanted. After being starved for so long we stuffed on corned beef, canned peaches, and hard shell Christmas candy—and promptly came down with diarrhea.

3

The Bataan
Death March

BY NOW (1986) THERE IS NOTHING NEW THAT EVEN A survivor can say about the Bataan Death March. The travail of some 75,000–80,000 beaten, bewildered, sick, and hungry Americans and Filipinos who were bullied, badgered, taunted, stabbed, starved, and shot by their Japanese captors on a hellish march of some eighty miles in stifling tropical heat has long since passed into history as one of the most spectacular and revolting atrocities of World War II. It was also one of the most important events of the Pacific war, for the shared sufferings of Americans and Filipinos strengthened the bond between the two peoples and heightened the animosity of both toward their brutal conquerors.

For many reasons, there will never be anything better than general estimates of how many died on the march. Nobody among either captors or captives attempted to keep records. Thousands of Filipinos and a much smaller number of Americans managed to escape during the march, but nobody knows how many of them died alone in the mountains and jungle, or how many of the Filipinos made it home and quietly became civilians again. Thousands of

33

both peoples died in O'Donnell and Cabanatuan prison camps after the march was over, but it is impossible to distinguish between those who expired from the belated effects of the Death March and those who perished from the cruel regimen in the camps themselves.[1]

More than forty years after the event my own memory of it is as inexact as the guesses that have been made about casualties. I was weak, sick, and confused then, and my predominant impression was that the rest of the world was as muddled as myself. Discipline had broken down completely in the last days before the surrender. Men either milled about aimlessly or sprawled in the dust like dogs, too tired to move.

When the Japanese found us thus, they seemed only slightly better organized than we were. Moreover, armies have always found it difficult to handle prisoners of war, especially large numbers of them. The Japanese had expected to have to deal with about 25,000 military prisoners around May 1. Now, suddenly, three weeks earlier, they had at least three times that many on their hands, with perhaps a quarter of these civilians. No proper preparations had been made to deal with such numbers. At least as important, the Philippine campaign had already taken much longer than the high command in Tokyo had anticipated, so the minds of General Homma, the Japanese commanding officer on Bataan, and his subordinates, were primarily on the rapid reduction of Corregidor, which blocked the entrance to Manila Bay and compelled postponement of their plan to invade Australia. The disposition of prisoners they regarded as a minor matter. Various portions of the task were given over to several different Japanese officers, no one of whom coordinated the activities of the others.

In this atmosphere, just short of chaos, one group of prisoners would start walking from a certain place one day, another group would set out from somewhere else ten hours later, still another from a third locale the next day, and so on. As we tramped along the only road up the east coast of Bataan, we were joined at irregular intervals by small bands of men coming down through jungle trails to surrender, and continually impeded by a steady stream of Japanese tanks, trucks, and soldiers pouring southward to begin the assault on Corregidor. These southbound Japanese took up much of the road, kicked up a horrendous cloud of dust that seemed to hang forever in the humid heat, and frequently struck at the heads of staggering prisoners with their rifle butts or bamboo sticks. Thus, when I say that I don't know how long I was on the Death March it indicates more than personal loss of memory; it was symptomatic of the whole enterprise. In the most straightforward sense, I endured twelve days: we surrendered on April 9 and I escaped on April 21; but I don't remember how many of those days I actually spent marching down the road accompanied by Japanese guards: seven or eight most likely, possibly ten.

Because we prisoners were scattered along so many miles of road and had started the trek in so many different places at different times, the experiences of a given group were often considerably different from those of others; hence the widely varying accounts of survivors. To me, the first days of the march were distinctly easier than those that followed. We started off in what army wits used to call "a column of bunches": small groups of soldiers and Filipino civilians, mingled indiscriminately, sauntering down the road, sometimes with Japanese guards nearby, sometimes not. Now and then a guard would search a prisoner and take whatever possessions he happened to fancy. I was stopped once by a guard who took my sunglasses. Later others successively took my ring, my watch, and finally my canteen, though another Japanese, for reasons unknown, then gave me back a canteen—which still another guard promptly took away from me again.

This was typical of Japanese unpredictability. Any Westerner who had much to do with the Japanese was invariably struck by how their psychology differed from that of Occidentals, and by their abrupt changes of mood. One moment they would be calm, smiling, reasonable, even generous: the next, storming in some inexplicable rage and acting like savages. An American Jesuit who spent the war years at a college in Manila wrote a perceptive book about the Philippines under Japanese occupation. He ascribed the sudden shifts in mood among the Japanese to their lack of an underlying philosophy or fixed religious faith. Some of their philosophical and moral ideas came from Confucianism and Buddhism, which are more truly *attitudes toward existence* than religions in the Western sense; and some have been derived from Shintoism, which is basically a mixture of animism and ancestor worship without either a rational view of the cosmos or a moral code. Then, in modern times, this variegated ancient legacy has been overlaid lightly by a mixture of Christianity and rationalism, a combination that has never been entirely reconciled and digested in the West itself much less in the non-Western world. The vast divergences among all these traditions, not to speak of what resulted when they were muddled together, he thought, had produced fundamental instability in the Japanese character.[2] Needless to remind the reader, I never tried to analyze the Japanese at this level, but I can testify that they were extraordinarily capricious.

Examples of their unpredictability abounded during the first days of our captivity when everything was still wondrously disorganized. Robert Mailheau, a fellow survivor of the Death March, was once near a Japanese battery that suffered a direct hit from an artillery shell fired from Corregidor. The battery and its whole crew were blown to bits. Perhaps a hundred American and Filipino prisoners nearby let out a spontaneous cheer. While this was great for their morale momentarily, one would expect that it would have been followed by some swift and terrible retribution. Yet, for whatever reason, the Japanese did nothing.

Where I was, a guard would sometimes stop us periodically and take one or more men out of a group to fix a stalled truck, drive pack animals somewhere, or do some other menial chore. Once while we were still in the extreme south of Bataan, I was picked, with half a dozen other men, to dig some foxholes. While we were busy at it, the heavy mortars on Corregidor opened up on us. All we American diggers hit the dirt at once, as we had been trained to do, but the Japanese just laughed at us and stood unconcernedly in the open, seemingly confident that none of the shells had their names on them. Apparently they had never heard the admonition that the shell to fear is not the one with your name on it but the one addressed "To whom it may concern." Their bravado in such cases also helps to explain why Japanese casualties were so much higher than American.

Another time I was removed from the road and forced to help a Japanese company prepare a bivouac. Here one of the guards spoke to me in English. I asked him where he had learned the language. He said he had been trained in Yokohama to be a teacher of English. I then asked him which side he thought would win the war. He replied thoughtfully, without the customary Japanese menace or boasting, that he believed Japan would. He added that the training he had undergone in Japan was tougher than anything he had experienced so far in combat, so rough in fact that some of his fellow trainees had committed suicide rather than endure it. He said he hated the British, but about Americans he was silent. From this manner I guessed that he was opposed to the war and not sanguine about its ultimate outcome.

After a few days the guards got better control of things and our regimen became appreciably tougher. Instead of straggling in small groups or even alone, we were now marched in large groups, three abreast, on the left side of the road, so southward bound Japanese vehicles to our right would not be impeded. It was now, too, that the real atrocities began, at least where I was. Guards trotted up and down the columns clubbing men into line with rifle butts, stabbing laggards with their bayonets, and shooting or bayoneting to death anyone chronically unable to keep up, all this accompanied by a fusillade of verbal abuse. Our captors, who had been taught that to become a prisoner of war was a disgrace, repeatedly taunted us with accusations of cowardice and sneered at our inability to keep pace. Heartbreaking acts of savagery multiplied. One poor fellow behind me jumped into a stream as we crossed a bridge. A guard raised his rifle to his shoulder and waited. As soon as the man surfaced, he was shot in the back. Another time I saw what was left of a human body after it had been run over by a tank on a hard-surfaced roadbed. It looked like a wet sack. I saw many men bayoneted and then abandoned to suffer a slow, agonizing death in the dust. I watched a general being clubbed until he was a bloody, unrecognizable mess. As for myself, I was clubbed many times for no reason other than sheer malice.

So we stumbled along, mile after mile, through heat and dust, tortured by hunger, thirst, diseases, and the accumulated effects of three months on short rations. The popping of .25-caliber Japanese rifles grew more frequent as more and more men proved unable to maintain the pace of the march. After a while nobody even looked back to see who had been shot this time. Only once did I see a Japanese officer so much as reprimand a guard for brutality. In that case the guard had deliberately crushed the glasses of a man whom I happened to know, a forty-five-year-old sergeant, William T. Moore. The officer grabbed the guard and knocked him down with a blow from his fist—one of the commonest modes of enforcing discipline in the Japanese army.

Night was, if anything, worse than daytime. We would simply be herded into a field and enclosed with barbed wire. It resembled nothing as much as putting cattle into a corral, save that our plight was sorrier. Since it was near the end of the dry season, the fields were mere bare ground and dust, without grass. Here thousands of men, without food or water, were packed in so closely that one could not shift his body without causing discomfort to others. Worse, there were no toilets, and by now maybe a third of us had dysentery. There we lay in mind-numbing squalor, soaked in our own body wastes and those of others, waiting for dawn to resume the man-killing march.

Judging from what I have heard and read since World War II, our captors must have handled the distribution of food more humanely in other parts of the march than where I was. Bob Mailheau says that on a couple of occasions he and a few others simply walked up to a Japanese cook and made motions indicating that they were hungry, after which they were given some rice. I was not so lucky. I was fed a little rice on the day I was put to work digging foxholes. For seven days after that the Japanese offered us no food at all in regular chow lines. All of us would have died had not the general disorganization that prevailed for three or four days enabled us to scrounge a little food in various ways. When the guards were few and otherwise occupied, we could sometimes dig up a few *camotes* (Philippine sweet potatoes) in fields. Now and then a friendly Filipino would furtively hand or toss us something from along the roadside. Once in a while a person could grab something edible off a bush or tree along the road. It is possible that an individual Japanese guard might have handed me a rice ball on an occasion or two, though I don't remember it. I did go three days in one stretch with no food at all, and later as a guerrilla also went three or four days without food on a few occasions. The sensation is odd. The first day one is hungry, the second much more hungry, and the third ravenous, but on the fourth day the process begins to reverse itself.

Lack of water was worse than lack of food. Though we passed many artesian wells and clear streams, the guards would rarely allow us to fill our canteens. The only places from which they let us drink freely were muddy, slime-covered carabao wallows, probably because it afforded them an opportunity to humiliate us.

Just why the Japanese should have treated us with such unrelieved and unnecessary brutality has been the subject of much learned and unlearned conjecture since 1945. Some have ascribed it mostly to Japanese administrative incapacity and unpreparedness, and to the foulups that are inseparable from war; some have attributed it to sheer Japanese savagery, regarding it as proof that the Nipponese are not yet civilized; some have seen it as Japanese retribution for the racial discrimination to which they have been subjected by white people, noting in particular how the Japanese never missed a chance to humiliate Americans in the presence of Filipinos; others have charged it to the samurai tradition in the Japanese army and to the brutality of its training methods; still others have claimed that it was due merely to the guards on the Death March being the dregs of the Japanese army. People with considerable knowledge of Japanese history and culture have maintained that, while Japan has drawn abreast of the Western world in science and technology, it is still centuries behind in the development of humanitarian attitudes. It has even been suggested that the cruelty of the Japanese on the Death March and in prison camps was due to nothing more complex than a desire to avenge their own heavy casualties in the Bataan campaign and to work off their frustration at having been compelled to postpone their projected invasion of Australia.[3]

I believe there is some substance in every one of these explanations. Even so, I think the most important factor was different, and simpler. Most of the guards seemed to me to be ignorant farm boys, no doubt irritated by our inability to understand and respond quickly to commands given in Japanese, but at bottom concerned mostly to demonstrate how tough they were, to show off in front of their buddies, to let everyone know that they were real men who shrank from nothing.

As the days passed, the horrors mounted. By now virtually every prisoner had been stripped of everything he owned save the tattered clothes on his back. Anyone found with Japanese money, photographs, or souvenirs in his possession was executed. The guards appeared to assume that such items must have been taken off dead Japanese soldiers. Beheading was the favorite mode of execution, and the guards began to show us posters graphically illustrating our fate should we be caught attempting to escape. A typical poster showed a Japanese soldier, both hands on the handle of a samurai sword moments after it had passed through the neck of a kneeling prisoner. As I trudged along, rage and hatred welled up from the depths of my soul and engulfed me. I resolved to escape, or die trying.

Had I been cool and rational, I might have weighed my prospects somewhat as follows: though my regular weight was 150–160 pounds, I was now down around 100, perhaps even less. Already starved, beset with malaria that produced alternating chills and fever in 100-degree temperatures, without water most of the time, and with no idea where I was going, I thought my chances of surviving much longer on the march so slim that there seemed little to lose by trying to escape. All along the road I had seen brave and compassionate Filipinos of both sexes and all ages risk their lives to slip food to prisoners. Surely some Filipinos would help me if only I could get away. Moreover, the Japanese did not know my name, as became apparent when it never appeared on an official prisoner of war list. I suppose I gave them a false name, though I don't remember doing so. I do recall telling them I was in the quartermaster corps, hoping that they would be less likely to hate me. On the opposite side of the ledger were such considerations as these: I knew nothing of the geography of Luzon, and I would be setting off, without food, money, or medicine, amid a people of whom I knew little, whose language I could not speak, and who might easily turn me back to my captors to be tortured and killed.

But the truth is, I never calmly weighed such pros and cons at all. By now I had witnessed so many atrocious deeds that I was consumed with a venomous black hatred for everything Japanese. Now I understood why some men had refused to surrender and had fled instead into the forbidding jungle that covered the Zambales Mountains or had set off, weak as they were, to swim three miles through shark-infested waters to Corregidor. I grew determined not to die as a prisoner, not to fall in the dust and be run through with a bayonet because I could not stand the pace of the march, not to be shot in the head in some jungle with my hands tied behind my back. I must try to escape, no matter how long the chance, for only if I got away would I ever have a chance to avenge myself on my tormentors.

Once this entirely emotional resolution became fixed, I then did begin to plan rationally. With great care I watched both sides of the road, and the guards. As we approached a bridge over a small stream near Dinalupihan on the north border of Bataan province, I saw my chance. We were nearing a deep ditch covered with dense foliage. I slipped from the right marching column to the center, then to the left. When a guard looked away I dove head first over the bank into the ditch. There I lay rigid, terrified that the pounding of my heart must be so loud that the guards on the road above could hear it. But they did not, and as the footsteps faded away I heard an American voice say something like, "Don't look. Do you want to get him shot?"

When the detachment of prisoners above me had passed on, I crawled a short way along the ditch and discovered two others like myself. I touched one of them on the leg. He was too frightened to move. Only when I spoke softly did he look around. He was Corp. Walter D. Chatham, Jr., of the air corps. Ahead of him, lying flat on his face, was a Captain Jones from the artillery. My arrival must have scared them half to death.

Like myself, Walter Chatham should have been killed several times by now. He had gone through the Bataan campaign and had started the Death March from Mariveles at the extreme southern tip of the Bataan peninsula. Near Cabcaben Field, a few miles northwest, an artillery shell from Corregidor, intended for the enemy, had landed in the middle of the group in which he was walking, blowing bodies in all directions. A few days later Walter, by now staggering from hunger, thirst, and fatigue, had grabbed hold of a bridge to keep from falling only to have a Japanese guard unconcernedly flip him over into a ravine some forty feet below. Miraculously, he had landed between two huge boulders and was not seriously injured. Two other Japanese soon came by from under the bridge, but they were headed for an artesian well to get water and ignored him. Eventually Walter clambered back up onto the road and managed to keep moving for another five days until he and Captain Jones had leaped over the bank into the same ditch I chose, maybe ten minutes before I did.

I wanted to leave our abode, but my companions did not. At length I arose alone and began to call out. Across the stream some Filipino farmers heard me, and one started toward us. He walked up onto a log that lay across the ditch, with his eyes turned downward. I asked him if there were any Japanese around. Fortunately, he understood some English. He told me to stay down, and slipped into the underbrush. A few minutes later he returned and motioned for us to follow him.

4

In and Out of the Fassoth Camps

OUR FILIPINO SAVIOR TOOK US A SHORT DISTANCE TO A *bahay,* a house on stilts. It was close enough to the road for us to watch the Death March through slits in the woven bamboo walls. When I saw an American run through with a bayonet by a Japanese guard, it added nothing to my sense of security.

The house already contained another escaped American, a Lieutenant Kiery. His fate was tragic, yet similar to that of all too many in the war. He managed to avoid capture for another two and a half years, only to drown off the east coast of Luzon late in 1944 when he took one chance too many. Al Hendrickson, with whom I was subsequently closely associated, told him to follow a difficult foot trail down the coastline to meet a submarine. Rather than hike through the mountains and jungle, Kiery decided to try a rubber boat in a rough sea. He never made it.

As always throughout the war the Filipinos here treated us warmly and generously, at dire risk to themselves. Various of them brought us rice, water, and crude sugar several times a day. One boy begged me to let him hide me amid fishponds in Manila Bay, promising that he would make me well again and would keep me safe until the Americans returned in perhaps three months. Little did he or I realize that it would be three years. Another Filipino told us that an American civilian owned a nearby hacienda and said he would take us there. This offer we accepted.

The Death March, it must be recalled, did not usually consist of an unbroken string of marching men but of different groups of about four hundred men, each with two guards, separated by a quarter to a half mile or more. Thus, it was sometimes possible to slip away safely when one contingent had passed and another one had not yet arrived. We waited for one of these breaks about nightfall and started off. As soon as we had put a few sugarcane fields between us and the road, we were loaded onto a cart that had two solid wooden wheels. Then we were covered with rice straw. In this conveyance, pulled by a carabao, we rode all night northwestward toward the Zambales Mountains. I could not have made it on foot. All my previous life I had been strong and healthy, but diseases and starvation had so sapped my flesh that when I looked at my emaciated body I could hardly believe it was my own.

We had a great stroke of luck on the way. Three times our Filipino driver was stopped by Japanese who questioned him in English about whether he had seen any escaped Americans. Since he could not speak English, he was able to answer only when the Japanese questioner happened to be accompanied by a Filipino interpreter who knew the Tagalog language. The Japanese never searched the cart, apparently on the assumption that anyone who could not speak English would be unlikely to harbor Americans. Finally we reached our destination, a cluster of grass-roofed houses under some shade trees. Here some Filipinos fed us and washed our clothes. They also offered us a haircut and shave. I accepted both eagerly, but soon regretted my zeal to be shaved. The barber was a Filipina who commenced operations by dipping her fingers into a coconut shell filled with cold water and patting this on my whiskers. Then she took up a straight razor that had clearly been put to many uses other than shaving. It pulled out at least two hairs for every one it cut. As she scraped away unconcernedly, the tears rolled down my cheeks and I prayed for survival.

While I was undergoing this memorable shave, a muscular, bronzed man entered the house. He was Vincente Bernia, a Spanish mestizo (half-Spanish, half-Filipino). Vincente and his brother Arturo were wealthy sugar planters who lived nearby. Vincente was soon to take me to William Fassoth. He and Fassoth were two of the finest, most selfless men I have ever known. Between them they saved my life.

Fassoth came from a family of Hawaiian sugar planters. In 1913, as a young man, he went to the Philippines where he purchased a 1600-acre rice and sugar plantation. Soon after the war began in December 1941, Japanese planes bombed his house, sugar mill, and rice mill, and shot all his cows. With his family, his twin brother Martin, and a number of Filipino employees and friends, William Fassoth retreated about ten miles back into the foothills of the Zambales Mountains and built a camp. At first this was intended only to be a refuge for the Fassoth family, who had sufficient food and medicines for their own use. Soon, however, American soldiers began to arrive, sometimes singly, sometimes in twos and threes. Some of them had escaped from Bataan before it fell; some, like myself, had escaped during the Death March; a few had simply wandered aimlessly in the jungle ever since the initial Japanese invasion of Luzon.

Before long the sanctuary became so crowded that Fassoth and Vincente Bernia decided to build a bigger camp some six miles farther back in the mountains. It would be a semi-permanent rest camp for stray Americans. Fassoth would do the building while Bernia expressed assurance that he could get enough money and supplies from his wealthy friends to help maintain it.

This was not an idle boast. Long afterward, William Fassoth's son Vernon acknowledged that without the help of the Bernias maintenance of the Fassoth camp would have been impossible.[1] Moreover, during the first few months of the war, before the Japanese occupation could be consolidated and made systematic, the Fassoths themselves could still purchase ordinary foods and medicines in nearby villages. The Bernias stimulated the whole operation by offering fifteen pesos to any Filipino who would bring an American into the camp.

I was one of the first to arrive at the first camp. I started toward it riding a horse, with Vincente walking beside me and holding me aboard. Eventually I grew so weak I could no longer sit on the horse, so I had to be carried the last three hundred yards on the back of a Filipino.

The camp itself was built astride a small stream, completely concealed under tall trees. The only guests when I arrived were a few escapees as sick and exhausted as myself. Some of them had suffered such agony from tramping barefooted or in disintegrating shoes on the Death March that they had begged Japanese guards to shoot them and relieve their misery. The Japanese, usually only too glad to oblige in such cases, had refused, apparently in the belief that the Americans would soon die anyway and that they might as well do so painfully. The men had subsequently been rescued by Filipinos and now lay in the Fassoth camp with their raw feet swelled so badly that they could not put on shoes, much less walk.

Vincente spoke to us expansively of his plans. After we had been nursed back to health, he was gradually going to form an army of irregulars from people like us and carry the fight to the enemy as guerrillas. He talked of his contacts in Manila that would enable him to get food and medicine through Japanese lines, and of the cruel invaders whom he longed to destroy. I yearned to fight and kill the Japanese as much as he did, and certainly welcomed the food and occasional medicine I received, but for five months I could do nothing but try to recover my health. I was cursed throughout with malaria, beri beri, and jaundice. At times the beri beri was so severe that I was partially blind. It was in this state that I was told that Corregidor had surrendered. I thought grimly of old Mike

Ginnevan's assurance to me that the Rock was impregnable.

Of course, the Japanese soon got wind of what was going on. There was nothing to do but move the camp six or seven miles farther back and higher into the Zambales range, which runs along the west coast of central Luzon. William Fassoth, who wrote a brief history of his camps after the war, pays tribute to the famished and weakened Americans who helped him lug everything from the first camp up narrow, slippery mountain trails to the second. I can say only that I will never forget dragging myself to the second camp.

The new camp consisted of one large building about fifty by a hundred feet and several smaller ones, all made entirely of bamboo and without nails. Filipinos are geniuses with bamboo. They make everything out of it: cooking utensils, drinking cups, woven baskets, animal snares, fish traps, scabbards for bolo knives, bridges—anything from tweezers to houses.

The locale of the new camp was ideal, isolated high in the mountains and so near running water that a bamboo pipe carried water into the camp and a nearby waterfall provided a continuous and convenient shower. Nonetheless, the whole enterprise had a near-fatal flaw. If the camp was not to be spotted by enemy reconnaissance planes, it was necessary to do something that was mad, medically. The undergrowth was cleared away but all large trees were left intact for camouflage. Thus, the natural habitat of the mosquito was left substantially undisturbed. Soon the rainy season commenced. Nobody has seen rain until he has seen it in the Philippines. Many downpours would have been called cloudbursts in the United States, yet they went on for hours, day after day. The mountain streams swelled into torrents. While this had the incidental benefit of keeping the enemy away, it made it much harder to procure food or medicine and it allowed the mosquitoes to multiply. This stifled what little progress many of us might have made in our constant battle with diseases. Several times our rice supply was so seriously depleted that we boiled rice husks and ate them. They were tasteless, but they did combat beri beri somewhat.

One incident during this era of semi-starvation I will never forget. Vincente managed to get us a considerable quantity of navy beans, the sort universally reviled in World War I but now regarded as manna from heaven by those of us who had eaten little but rice for months. Mrs. Catalina Dimacal Fassoth, William's Filipina wife, who gave unselfishly of her time cooking and trying to care for us, prepared the feast. We lined up with our bamboo tableware in ardent anticipation. With my first bite I was astounded. Judging from the looks on the faces of the others, so were they. Filipinos like sugar and prepare many of their foods with it. Mrs. Fassoth, knowing nothing about navy beans, had thrown a lot of sugar into the water when she boiled them. But we ate them.

Something should be said here of the Fassoth camps in general, for they have been the subject of markedly different postwar accounts. At one time or another there were three of them, each situated farther back in the mountain fastness than its predecessor. It has been claimed that as many as three hundred American soldiers were in and out of one or another of the camps at various times, with anywhere from sixty to ninety at any one time, though these numbers are probably inflated.[2] As many as seventy-five Filipino porters were employed to carry in food at different times. I lived in the first camp for a few days and in the second for five months.

A particularly dark description of the second one is given by Forbes Monaghan, who never saw the camp and who must have derived his information from two Jesuit scholastics from his Manila college who once spent a day and a night with us. Monaghan says we were fed regularly, but were so undisciplined, demoralized, and wolfish that we were little better than animals. He asserts that a West Point captain, Samuel Dosch, was the only sane man among us. He says the two scholastics organized a musical program at the camp, followed by a sermon and some prayers, and then went to Col. Peter Calyer, the highest ranking American officer still free in Luzon, and persuaded him to appoint Dosch commandant of the camp, after which order and discipline were restored.[3]

Col. Russell Volckmann, with whom I had serious trouble later and who eventually became the leader of all the guerrillas in north Luzon, spent some time in the camp. He agreed with Monaghan that some men there had sunk to the level of beasts, but he thought they were only a small minority, much outnumbered by two other groups: the despondent, pessimistic, and listless; and a band of heroic types who had grown in adversity, had become imaginative, resourceful, optimistic, and resolute. The thoughts of the latter were on recovery, for they wanted to get well and form guerrilla bands to harass the Japanese.[4] Volckmann's sidekick, Maj. Donald Blackburn, largely agrees with Monaghan. He says that when he and Volckmann arrived the camp was unbelievably filthy because it was dominated by renegade enlisted men who refused even to dig latrines, and was rife with dissension of every sort. He claims he made friends with the disagreeable leader of the place, a Sergeant Floyd, following which he and other officers began to do the needed camp chores and gradually led the enlisted men, out of shame perhaps, to join in. Even so, he thought most men in the camp just wanted to hide out in the mountains and await an eventual American reconquest of the Philippines.[5]

William Fassoth's own account, written soon after the war, contrasts sharply with all these. He describes food as plentiful and morale as high throughout. My friend Walter Chatham, who was lying in the ditch when I jumped off the road on the Death March, and who spent five months in the Fassoth camp with me, says (1985) he remembers morale as generally high, especially on July 4 when pieces of bamboo were joined together to make a flagpole on which to hoist the American flag in defiance of possible Japanese observation planes. He says food was more plentiful than on Bataan, and claims he never heard of the renegade enlisted men who allegedly ran the camp. I would be inclined to accept Walter's assessment, save that he acknowledges that he was out of his head with cerebral malaria for at least ten days on one occasion, that he was so sick he could scarcely move for many days at a time, and that once he was so near death that he saw another man buried in a grave that had been dug for himself. Thus, one cannot be sure how much he knew of what went on, or how accurate his memory was.

Vernon Fassoth, William's son, spent part of his time in the camps, part of it searching for Americans, and part of it scrounging the battlefields of Bataan for arms, dynamite, TNT, or anything else potentially useful. He echoes his father's claim that food was plentiful and medical care was as good as could be expected in the circumstances. He acknowledges that, despite this, camp morale was frequently low and that at least one inmate committed suicide from despair. Some of the malaise he attributes to trouble that developed between his father, who wanted the camp to be simply a place of rest run on a civilian basis, and some of the commissioned officers in it who wanted to run it as a regular military encampment. Most of the latter eventually left after repeated arguments with the elder Fassoth.

Henry Clay Conner, whom I never knew but who had escaped from Bataan and was in the Fassoth camp for a time, wrote an account of his experiences soon after the war. He blamed most of the trouble in the camp on two considerations: (1) Most of the men were hungry, sick, and still frightened or shocked by their recent experiences, and so were extremely "edgy"; (2) Worse, some of the officers insisted dogmatically on the prerogatives of rank, while the enlisted men took the view that since all hands were now in the same fix, rank should cease to mean anything.[6]

My own recollections do not jibe with any of these exactly. Because I was sick in bed so much of the time that I eventually acquired several bedsores, it is certainly possible that much went on that I knew nothing about and that my impressions of life in the camp are not to be taken seriously. Be that as it may, I will record what I can remember. It seemed to me that nearly everyone was sick and dispirited much of the time. Barbarities there may have been, but I don't believe they were nearly as commonplace as Monaghan indicates. I certainly wanted to live to kill Japanese one day, and this may well have been true of Volckmann too, but I also remember his friend Blackburn telling me one day that Volckmann was frequently so despondent that he, Blackburn, feared that Volckmann might do something foolish. I do not recall food being plentiful, as the Fassoths indicate: quite the reverse.

One conclusion about it all is obvious: human memories, especially after the passage of years, are highly fallible. Another is that what seems shameful, intolerable, or unprecedented to one person may seem to another only what has to be expected in extremely trying circumstances. For myself, I remember the Fassoth camp as a place where I suffered from something or other constantly but for which my predominant sentiment is deep gratitude.

Fassoth himself had good luck for that time and locale. After establishing the third camp he finally surrendered to the Japanese in the spring of 1943, perhaps from resentment at the laziness and ingratitude of so many of the men he had befriended.[7] The Japanese imprisoned him for the rest of the war at Cabanatuan with military POWs rather than with civilian detainees at Santo Tomas in Manila. Surprisingly, he was treated humanely. The Bernia brothers were not so fortunate. Vincente was killed by the Japanese while helping to defend another camp established by Colonels Merrill and Calyer of the Thirty-first Infantry. It was said that his brother Arturo was wounded, then captured by the Japanese, who trussed him to a pole like a pig and carried him into the jungle to an unknown fate. Both Bernias were as truly heroes as any Filipino or American in uniform.

In the late summer of 1942 my prospects looked dim indeed. I still lay in bed much of the time, beset each day by the alternating chills and fever of malaria. Vernon Fassoth and others would carry me outdoors periodically in the hope that sunlight might do me some good. My malaria was complicated by beri beri, which swelled my hands, feet, and face to such a degree that when they were touched indentations remained in the flesh as they might in putty. Finally, I had yellow jaundice, which activated my kidneys eight or ten times a night.

Whatever food we had fell into two categories: that which made the bowels inoperative and that which made them uncontrollable. The best one could do was alternate the intake. I felt like the man who sat with one foot in a bucket of hot water and the other on an ice cake and who, when asked his temperature, answered "average." It is incredible what the human body can bear; marvellous how hard it is to kill a strong young person, short of cutting off his head. My personal resiliency still amazes me, in retrospect. By the time the war ended I felt strong and healthy again. I decided to stay in the Air Corps and resolved to try to realize my onetime ambition to become a fighter pilot. I succeeded in passing the stringent physical and mental examinations required, and survived in a pilot training program in which one-third of the aspirants washed out. If someone had asked me, in 1942, if such a metamorphosis was possible, I doubt that I could have summoned sufficient strength even to laugh at him.

Filipinos had a lot of intriguing medical beliefs and practices. Their effects varied from bizarre to lethal. Henry Clay Conner, who like me owed his life to friendly Filipinos, relates that early in 1942 a Negrito tribesman once brewed an herb called *dita* and gave it to him for his malaria. In two days the chills and fever abated and Conner felt vastly better. When he tried to secure more *dita* on his own, however, he was warned by an educated Filipino, the brother of a doctor, that while *dita* did not harm Negritos it often caused people less tough to end up deaf, dumb, blind, or dead.[8]

In my case, one day a Filipino around the camp commiserated with me and told me that if I wished to recover I should drink the blood of a black dog. The thought was sickening, especially since the blood was to be secured by cutting the dog's throat, but numerous Filipinos regarded it as a sure-fire universal remedy. I was so desperate to recover that I had become willing to try anything, so I agreed. When some of the repulsive stuff was actually brought to me in a coconut shell, I could down only one swallow. Nothing beneficial happened. Maybe my faith wasn't strong enough.

Then I was told that work would help me. I did not believe I had the strength to do even ordinary camp chores until I saw the man who slept next to me, Lt. Bob Reeves of ordnance, breathe his last. We rolled his body in a bamboo mat and held services. Soon three others died, and it was obvious that more were sliding downhill inexorably. I decided I had to work, no matter how I felt. So I did a few chores, vomited, and repeated the sequence.

How this personal medical experiment would have turned out I will never know, since it was cut short by the enemy on a bright moonlit night, September 26, 1942. What happened was surely inevitable. The camp itself was at an elevation of at least four thousand feet. Just to bring in sufficient food to keep us alive was difficult and required many porters. Eventually the Japanese caught one, an Igorot tribesman. They tortured him fiendishly and learned the location of the camp. Then they put a white shirt on the man and tied a rope to him so they could keep track of him in the dark. They caught the Filipino guard at our outermost outpost fast asleep. They tied a rope around his neck too, and forced him to guide them the rest of the way. The guard at the outpost nearest our camp they slashed to shreds with a samurai sword as he clutched desperately for the field telephone. Having thus achieved complete surprise, about two hundred Japanese, each with a miner's lamp mounted on his head, descended on the camp, screaming like banshees and shooting wildly.

Oddly, I now owed my freedom, and likely my life, to the diseases that had heretofore nearly killed me; specifically, to what they had done to my kidneys. When the raid came, I was outdoors, on the opposite side of the barracks from which the attack was mounted, urinating for perhaps the twentieth time that day and rolling a cigarette from home-grown tobacco. The tobacco I had cut carefully and carried in a small bamboo tube. When the attack came, I panicked and started to run, but I was so weak I fell, in the process dropping my tube of tobacco. So treasured in miserable circumstances are even the smallest pleasures that I fumbled about to retrieve the tobacco before I even tried to run again. Small difference: at once I fell again and lost my tobacco for good. This time I realized that I was simply too weak to run, so I walked to the brink of a nearby creek, dropped over the bank, followed the meandering stream bed for some time, then crawled out on the other side and melted into the primeval forest. As I worked my way through bamboo thickets, I could hear the ping of Japanese rifles behind me.

Back at the camp the Japanese broke into the barracks, with their head lamps shining, and ordered everyone out. One GI broke and ran, simultaneously striving desperately to wrestle his .45 out of the musette bag on his back. He barely reached darkness outside when a Japanese soldier hit him over the head with a bayonet. The .45 fell out of the American's hand into the camp garbage pit, unseen by any Japanese. Six other Americans indoors were caught in bed. Like me, they survived by a fluke. The Japanese, finding them unarmed, spared their lives. Three Filipino men and a baby were not so lucky. The invaders butchered the men with bayonets. When the baby began to cry, one of them seized it by the feet and struck off its head with one slash of a sword. Then the victors set fire to the camp and burned it to the ground.[9]

Before the Japanese onslaught we had gotten two advance warnings that the enemy had learned of our whereabouts. We had, as a consequence, moved farther back into the mountains. Writing years afterward, William Fassoth said sixteen of us then came back to the camp, believing that the Japanese would not raid us after all, that ten of us escaped during the actual raid, and that six were taken prisoner by the enemy.

Walter Chatham, who was one of the six seized, remembers only seven of us left in the camp and thinks I was the only one who escaped. Walter should know the straight of it, since the invaders took him away after they burned the camp; yet I believe he was mistaken on two different counts. I distinctly recall hearing several shots from a .45-caliber pistol well before daylight. The most likely explanation for this would be that some sort of Japanese-American gunfight took place, perhaps out of Walter's sight or hearing. Second, I don't believe I was the only one to escape, as I will relate shortly.

Only many years later did I learn how fortunate I had been to get away. Those captured were turned over to the Kempeitai, the Nipponese equivalent of the Russian NKVD or modern KGB. All six of them were promptly put in one four-by-four cage, from which they were let out only once a day to relieve themselves. There they were kept for three weeks. Walter Chatham, though only a corporal, was the highest ranking man, so he was interrogated. His captors grilled him interminably about the Bataan campaign, but since he knew nothing important about U.S. dispositions or plans he could tell them nothing. Enraged, they beat him repeatedly with a blackjack, then with a baseball bat. Then they clamped his hands to a table, shoved bamboo slits under his fingernails, and lit them. The splinters and the heat split all his nails, and he passed out from the pain. The Kempeitai men then doused him with water to revive him, after which they repeated the tortures. At other times during the three weeks they stepped on his bare feet with hobnailed boots, split his skull with a baseball bat, and threw him down a stairway.

Had I been captured at the Fassoth camp, almost certainly I rather than Walter would have been put through this ordeal since I was a staff sergeant and outranked him. Weak and wasted as I was, a mere wraith of perhaps one hundred pounds, I doubt that I would have survived.

For the next several weeks I lived much like a man who has just broken out of prison: hurt, hungry, hunted, and hiding. After managing to get some distance from the Fassoth camp in the middle of the night, I stopped on top of a ridge and slept until dawn. All that remained of the camp was a thin wisp of smoke that drifted upward in the still of early morning. As I sat gazing at it pensively, there was a sudden thrashing sound in the underbrush nearby. My pulse leaped, then subsided, as I spotted another survivor from the camp, a man named Mackenzie. I have long since forgotten whether, like myself, he escaped when the Japanese attacked or whether he was one of those wiser individuals who had retreated into the hinterlands when we had been warned that the enemy knew of our whereabouts. I called to him softly. He froze until he located me, then came forward joyously.

Mackenzie had some tobacco and matches, so we began our day by smoking a cigarette and pondering our next move. We decided to go down into the lowlands. We crossed a cogon grass field and then a stream that ran down a deep ravine. As we made our way down hillsides, I thought increasingly of the shoes I had been compelled to leave behind at the Fassoth camp. My feet were so swollen from beri beri that my toes were cracked open underneath. I walked on my heels to avoid the short, sharp grass shoots that grow at the base of the six-to-seven-foot cogon grass, but the uneven terrain and my weakness caused me to stumble frequently and bring my torn feet down heavily on the spiky grass. Then I would sprawl awkwardly to escape the intense pain, and grab frantically at clumps of cogon grass to ease my fall. For some time we proceeded thus, Mac walking and I staggering, until we came to an inviting mountain stream full of *suso*. A *suso* is something like a freshwater oyster, a creature that lives in a shell stuck to a rock. We pried some off rocks in the stream, built a little fire, put some water in a bamboo joint, and boiled them. When cooked, *suso* can be popped out of their shells with a sharp rap of the heel of one hand against the other, or by banging them against a rock. We ate ours with relish, but inadvisedly topped off our dinner with some green papayas, which promptly produced diarrhea.

Farther on we came to a deserted hut where we decided

to spend the night. By now a different kind of foot trouble was developing rapidly. Back at the Fassoth camp, at the time of the Japanese attack, when I had stumbled away in the dark, I somehow acquired a deep gash on the top of my right foot. It is possible that I was grazed by a stray enemy bullet, though I so hated even to think that a Japanese might have hit me that long afterward I refused the offer of a Purple Heart. It is more likely anyway that I simply cut my foot somehow when running or falling. Whichever the case, by now the wound had begun to fester, usually the prelude to a tropical ulcer unless treatment was prompt. This was not a trivial prospect. Tropical ulcers are slow to heal even if treated, and we had no medicine of any kind.

Mackenzie and I were awakened at dawn by the crowing of a rooster. This meant that there had to be some people around, so we headed in the general direction of the sound. Soon we came to a house occupied by an old Filipino man and a young girl. Once more, as was to be the case so many more times during the war, I was the beneficiary of the friendliness and generosity of ordinary Filipinos. Though these two had never seen us in their lives and could communicate with us only in sign language, they fed us rice and venison and then, for reasons unknown to us, probably fear of the Japanese, quietly packed up and left.[10] Long afterward I cannot help but wonder if we Americans would have taken comparable risks and shown equivalent kindness to Filipinos.

Once more Mac and I had to decide what to attempt next. We were still well up in the mountains. I wanted to stay a while where we were, if only to nurse my sore feet, but Mac was adamant about going down into the lowlands and so departed alone. My guess proved bad. The next day a typhoon, which the natives call a *baguio*, roared through the area. It swept the roof off the house, put out my fire, and crisscrossed all the mountain trails with fallen trees. Now I was out of both food and fire, and my feet were deteriorating visibly. A life insurance salesman would have rated my prospects close to zero. For four days I lived on guavas and green bananas, the latter ranking second only to green papayas as a loosener of the bowels. Then my luck turned. In a nearby outbuilding I found a pair of rubber shoes. The tops had rotted away, but the soles were still substantial. After tying them onto my sore feet with vines I could walk again, so I headed off for the valley below.

After a time I came to a village inhabited by Baluga pygmies, a mountain people dressed chiefly in G-strings but whose men were armed with American rifles. If they seemed strange to me, I must have looked quite as outlandish to them. Back at the Fassoth camp my head had been shaved to combat lice, and my chief garment now was a pair of extra large overalls that hung limply on my cadaverous frame. Though the Balugas were frightened momentarily at this apparition appearing suddenly in their midst, they soon recovered and fed me some *camotes* and green papaya soup. By now an ulcer had indeed developed in the wound on my foot, and had eaten a deep hole in it. The Balugas treated my malady by grinding a red rock into powder, pouring this into the wound, and then covering it with a white paste produced by chewing some leaf. Then they took me to a trail that led downward into the lowlands and left me.

That evening I came to a house nestled against a hillside where foothills disappeared into lowlands. Here I was greeted hospitably by two Filipino couples and offered a choice of food or cigarettes. Incredible though it must seem to a reader, my addiction to tobacco then was so great that I opted for cigarettes and smoked three or four of them. Later my hosts fed me anyway and let me take a bath, after which I felt refreshed and restored, save only for my throbbing foot.

By now it was in bad shape. The ulcer had eaten a hole an inch across right down to the bone. Little beads of decaying flesh honeycombed its sides and stank atrociously. In fact, as soon as I sat down in the house the family dog picked up the smell and kept coming towards the foot, sniffing inquisitively. I kept driving him away. At length one of the Filipino women, who spoke English, noticed what was taking place and urged me to let the dog lick the wound clean. The mere thought disgusted me, but there was nothing to lose by trying. The dog eagerly worked its tongue into the festering cavity and began to lick away the rotting flesh. The pain was excruciating, so bad that I had to stand and hold my foot down to endure it; but when the dog had finished its loathsome task the foot felt better. I stayed there a week. The dog continued its treatments every day, and my foot began to heal. How easily civilization causes us to forget simple things, that from time immemorial animals have healed themselves by licking their wounds.[11]

5

Daily Life with Filipinos

RECEIVING UNORTHODOX MEDICAL TREATMENT FROM A
Philippine dog began a process that came close to making
me a Filipino. William Fassoth had not been caught when
his camp was raided by the Japanese because he had been
away in the lowlands. From there he began to make arrangements for selected Filipino families to assume the
dangerous task of hiding and feeding one American each.
I was inherited by Mr. and Mrs. Louis M. Franco, who
lived in the village of Tibuc-Tibuc near Gutad at the extreme western edge of Pampanga province, about ten miles
north of the northwest corner of Manila Bay and close to
the route of the Death March. The Francos did not know
a word of English, but they treated me splendidly all the
same.

They built me a low hut with a grass roof near a small
river that meandered through a flat field covered with cogon grass. This made it possible to supply me with food
and other commodities twice a day by wading in the stream
and thus avoiding formation of a trail that might betray
my hiding place. They also presented me with a .16-gauge
shotgun pistol for protection, a weapon I was afraid to

61

shoot lest it blow up in my hands. Later they gave me a Lee Enfield rifle, in which I reposed more confidence.

Here I settled down and tried to regain my health. I swam in the stream a great deal, both for enjoyment and for exercise. During the heat of the day I lay in the sun for long periods. Everyone has heard cynical observations to the effect that if one does not like a given medical opinion he has only to wait five or ten years and the opposite one will come into fashion. At the present time (1985) medical orthodoxy has it that long exposure to the sun is harmful to the skin. Maybe so, but it didn't seem true to me in 1942. Sun, swimming, rest, and ample food gradually healed my foot and restored my health. In the process I turned as brown as the Filipinos themselves. Save for my beard, which I could shave, and my Occidental nose, about which I could do nothing, a casual observer could hardly have distinguished me from a Filipino, no mean asset in the life I was to lead for the next two and a half years.

Much of the time, of course, I had to stay under cover to avoid being spotted by Japanese planes or passing patrols. These days were, I believe, the longest of my life. I soon discovered that the best way to pass the time was to read and study. The Francos brought me what books they could. Most of them were elementary school texts, but since they were all I had I read and reread them many times. From them I learned much about the history, government, religion, and customs of the Philippines. With some amazement I discovered that more than seven thousand islands comprise the Philippines, that at least eighty-seven dialects are spoken by their inhabitants, that Spanish was still the official language of the Islands, that Americans had made English compulsory for school children, and that Tagalog, a smooth, flowing tongue that is pleasant both to speak and to hear, would probably replace both Western languages eventually.

I became acquainted with the Philippine national heroes José Rizal and Emilio Aguinaldo, the former considered the father of his country and the latter celebrated as the leader of Philippine resistance to American occupation after the Spanish-American War of 1898. I became acquainted with the details of the U.S. occupation, and of the insurrection that followed it; with the excellent record made by Gen. Arthur MacArthur as governor-general of the Philippines; with the career of Manuel Quezon, the first president of the Philippine Commonwealth; and of his close relations with Gen. Douglas MacArthur, the famous son of the able governor-general.

Not least interesting were descriptions of how the habits of particular Filipinos had caused the U.S. Army to replace the .38 automatic with the .45 as standard issue. The Moros, fierce Moslems who inhabit Mindanao and some small southern islands, hated the Christian and pagan Filipinos and fought them periodically. They also had the disconcerting habit of occasionally running amok. This state was induced either by binding themselves tightly with bamboo or by winding an elastic vine around their genitals. In either case, half-mad with pain and quasi-religious fanaticism, they would race about wildly, killing anyone they met until someone killed them. By hard experience it was learned that a bullet from a .38 did not pack the wallop necessary to stop an amok Moro before he could slash or spear his intended victim. Only a .45 would do it.

I also began in earnest to learn Pampangano, the dialect of the area. For many days I wrote out phrases phonetically, memorized them, and practiced their pronunciation. There is nothing like concentration for learning, and eventually I developed a good command of the tongue. Mastery was not immediate, though. One day I addressed a native boy: "Magandang Hapon." He stared at me quizzically and after some hesitation asked me if I realized what I had said. I replied that I had intended to say, "Good afternoon." He laughed and told me that the meaning of the word "Hapon" depended on which syllable was accented. Ha-*pon* meant afternoon. *Ha*-pon meant Japanese. What I had actually said was "Good (or beautiful) Japanese."

As my linguistic studies progressed and my health improved, I came out of hiding periodically to visit local villages and homes where I could practice my vocabulary and make Filipino friends. As a teenager I had studied the Hawaiian guitar for a time. Now some Filipinos gave me a standard (Spanish) guitar, on which I practiced a good deal. Soon I learned to sing war songs and love songs in Pampangano.

I also learned something about Filipino psychology and customs. The favorite weapon of most Filipino men was the bolo, a long, curved knife carried in a bamboo scabbard and used for a variety of purposes. Most Filipinos were good-natured much of the time but, like people everywhere, they occasionally lost their tempers and got into fights. The aftermath of a fight waged with bolos could be devastating. I have seen survivors of bolo battles reconstructed with as many as four hundred stitches.

Filipinos love to gamble, particularly on cockfights. The owners of fighting roosters often appeared to think as much of their feathered protégés as of their own children, and spent much time and effort training them. The training itself breathed the spirit of boot camp in the Japanese army. A favorite way of "conditioning" an unfortunate chicken was to tie its feet to a wire clothesline and then flick the wire to make it spring back and forth. The terrified rooster had to strain every fiber to stay upright, a process which gradually turned his leg muscles into something like steel wire.

My Filipino mentors did not tutor me merely in their language and folklore. They also taught me various ways to augment my food supply. One such way was to make and set snares to catch wild chickens, which are smaller than American chickens. The roosters are brightly colored and crow their brains out all night long. In the 1940s they were plentiful all over the Philippines and though wild were not hard to catch in a simple noose trap that would snare one by the neck or one foot and hoist it into the air. I also learned to catch birds at night by throwing a fish seine over their roosting places in the tall cogon grass, and to catch fish from the river with the same nets. The Filipinos also taught me another way to catch fish that seemed implausible but was surprisingly effective. They would pile a lot of rocks in a streambed, leave them for a week or so, then cover them with a large net and weigh down its outer edges. Then they would slide their hands carefully under the net and remove the rocks one by one until only fish remained inside.

Coping with Philippine livestock was more challenging than with local birds and fish. Most Philippine animals are midgets compared to their American counterparts. A notable exception is the water buffalo, or carabao. Wild carabao are fierce, and those in the Philippines once experienced the distinction of being hunted by Theodore Roosevelt; but domesticated carabao are huge, patient, docile beasts, so gentle that children can tend them. They pull the plows, wagons, and carts of the Philippines at a leisurely pace with seeming contentment as long as they are fed and get a couple of baths a day in a nearby river or mud wallow. Unlike the skin of a horse, that of a carabao is loose and rolls back and forth across the animal's back when it walks. This, I discovered, makes riding one no mean feat. I had seen natives ride them many times, so one day I climbed aboard with a Filipino boy. The carabao either did not like me or rebelled at the idea of being ridden double. He promptly took off cross-country. The Filipino boy wisely jumped off, but I clung desperately to the critter, jerking on the rope that went to a ring in his nose and shouting at him in English, a language to which he remained obdurately indifferent. With each leap and each tug on the rope, I slipped farther forward on his rippling hide until I was astride his neck, just behind his massive, ominous looking curved horns. Here I had no leverage, so I could not jump; I could only *fall* off. I hit the ground hard and lay motionless. The Filipino boy rushed up to me and inquired solicitously if I was hurt. Fortunately, I was only dazed—and more wary of carabao.

As I had just learned, carabao, despite their bulk, could run with surprising speed for short distances. Sometimes

Filipinos would race them against horses. The carabao held their own admirably in such matches, though they certainly weren't graceful runners. One day I watched a man train a carabao for racing. He held the guide rope with one hand and the animal's tail with the other. The very ground shook as the thundering beast thumpety-thumped across the landscape, his trainer's feet hitting the ground every twenty feet or so behind him. I also observed what it would have been useful to me to have known earlier: that when the animal's skin rolled one way the trick was for the rider to roll the other.

In my many weeks in and around Tibuc-Tibuc, I became acquainted with the considerable array of foods eaten by ordinary Filipinos in that locale. Some were delicious; many more were wholesome and reasonably tasty; some I never learned to savor. Perhaps the best foods were the many varieties of fruit. Mangoes were absolutely delectable. Bananas came in a score of varieties, some of which could be fried in coconut oil. Coconuts could be prepared a dozen different ways—after one climbed a tree and laboriously wrestled the nuts out of the top of it. Breadfruit and guava were good, though, once more, procuring them could be arduous. My worst experience picking fruit came in a guava tree when I was attacked by a swarm of large, pugnacious red ants. They were all over me before I noticed them. It would have required a dozen hands to disperse them, and since I had to use one of my two to hold onto the tree I could only swat them ineffectually. By the time I got to the ground, I was painfully chewed up. Cashew nuts were abundant and tasty but had to be handled with care since the shells exuded a juice that produced an irritating swelling if it touched the skin. The best way to deal with them was to roast them slowly until the shell became virtual charcoal, and then remove the nut.

Because few Filipinos had firearms before the war, carabao, deer, pigs and chickens were plentiful. Chicken and venison were, of course, good. Wild pig was tasty enough, though very fat. Occidental pork producers have carefully bred hogs to reduce their fat content. I was invariably impressed by how much fatter were the wild pigs I riddled with Thompson submachine guns (tommyguns) in the Philippines. (One thinks little about the sporting side of hunting when hunger drives him to stalk animals for their meat.) Carabao meat had an acceptable flavor but was so tough the Devil himself would have been hard put to chew it. Filipinos also esteemed large rats that lived in sugarcane fields, though I must add in their defense that they did not eat rats of the sort that infest garbage dumps. I don't know whether I ever ate "sugar rat" or not. Sometimes one was served stews and soups that were best consumed without asking a lot of questions.

Rice was the staple of the Philippine diet. Because of its starch one could easily gain weight on it, though the weight was as readily lost if one fell sick. Once I subsisted for eight days on rice and tomatoes alone. "Coffee" was made from rice and corn roasted together, then served with much sugar. Cassava, the root of a common tropical plant, was cut, fried, and made into something like potato chips. Small, transparent shrimp were somewhat disconcerting when they jumped around live in a coconut shell just before they were to be devoured, but they were palatable. Fish were sometimes dried and stored for later consumption, sometimes merely cooked as they had come from the water, without being cleaned. The diner ate as much as he chose and threw away the rest. Small fish called *bagong* were often mashed and left to ferment, a process that turned them into a sharp-flavored, smelly seasoning. Cattle intestines were carefully cleaned and much prized. One's craving for sweets was satisfied most easily by chewing sugar cane, though the Filipinos did make a crude brown sugar by pouring boiled cane juice into coconut shells to harden. Sometimes they made candy by boiling sugar and freshly grated coconut together. What resulted made a respectable confection—and a memorable laxative.

Filipino cooking and serving techniques required some adjustment on the part of an Occidental. Most Filipino food was either boiled or roasted, and it ran heavily to soup. Silverware was unheard of. Everything but soup was put on banana leaves spread on the floor and eaten with the fingers. I occasioned much good-natured laughter before I finally mastered the knack of kneading food into a ball before popping it into my mouth. But learn it I did, just as I learned to eat nearly everything put before me. Soon the Filipinos complimented me for not being "delicado" (choosy).

There were times, though, when I drew the line. I never became reconciled to the delicacy called *balot,* a fertilized egg that had been buried in manure for some time, and I never developed a taste for Philippine jerky after watching clouds of flies blow it while it was being dried in the sun.

But the worst was dog. The first time I ate it, I didn't know what it was. When I was told, I promptly vomited my entire dinner. It was not that the flavor was repellent; it was just that I had always liked dogs and the thought of having eaten one gagged me. Maybe devouring Man's Best Friend would not have seemed so bad had I not learned of the barbarities that preceded a dog's appearance as the main course in a dinner. The usual procedure was to tie the poor beast to a tree, starve it for several days, then stuff it with all it could eat and batter it to death with a club. The carcass was then cut into small pieces, cooked with rice, and served with wine. Eventually I got so I could force myself to eat dog if I didn't have to watch the butchering, but I always drank a lot of wine with it.

Later in the war I heard tales about famished Japanese soldiers who allegedly resorted to cannibalism. Though I am not so ill-balanced that I think more of dogs than of human beings, somehow the prospect of cannibalism never seemed as repulsive to me in those days as devouring a dog, and I sometimes wondered idly if I could ever become so starved that I would sink to cannibalism. Fortunately, no test case ever arose.

Usually I was alone in my grass hut, but now and then I had visitors. The least welcome one appeared one day while I was lying on my side with my ear to a bamboo floor. I heard something near my foot and looked down.

There was a good-sized snake crawling alongside my leg toward my head. Momentarily I was frozen with terror: I even stopped breathing. Gradually I recovered my senses sufficiently to decide that I must grab the loathsome creature with my hands if it came much closer, since it might bite me and the closer a bite is to the heart the more dangerous it becomes. Perhaps the snake also had a premonition of impending disaster: when it reached my waist it abruptly made a ninety-degree turn and vanished into the cogon grass. My heart resumed beating.

Other visitors were more agreeable. Nobody will ever know exactly how many American soldiers escaped into the hills and jungle during the Bataan campaign or on the Death March. There must have been several hundred. Many died soon of starvation or diseases, and the Japanese caught quite a few. Others tried to live out the war in wilderness hideouts, or moved furtively from one Filipino settlement to another for months or years. Some sought a way out of the Philippines, others looked for guerrilla forces to join, still others tried to melt inconspicuously into the Filipino populace. Periodically one or more of these footloose fugitives passed through the small village of Tibuc-Tibuc. One such was a Maj. John E. Duffy, a Catholic priest whom I was to meet again in San Antonio, Texas in 1946. He had graduated from Notre Dame and enjoyed talking about his namesake, the famous Father Duffy of World War I, who had reputedly said to his troops, "May the Good Lord take a liking to you, but not too soon." I remember him chiefly because he had what seemed to me a remarkable vocabulary of profanity for a clergyman. I used to wonder if he could swear as impressively in Latin as in English.

Another visitor was a Brooklynite named Louis Barella. Because Japanese patrols were known to be close by, he and I were moved one night into the center of a large cogon grass field. Here we were covered with a mosquito net secured at the corners by tying it to the cross stems of the grass. This arrangement foiled the Japanese and the mosquitoes but not a large rat that somehow made its way in but could not find an exit. It kept us busy until I lifted the whole net in desperation and let it scurry away. Needless to say, the mosquitoes promptly exploited the situation; but one thing you learn in war is that life is not a series of clear-cut decisions between good and evil: it is a succession of choices among alternatives all of which are disagreeable.

Another time I had several visitors rather than one. They turned out to be Hukbalahaps, Philippine communist guerrillas. I was to have much more to do with the Huks later on, and my introduction to them on this occasion was not auspicious. Their leader had a parrot which he insisted that I take in trade for my rifle. The bird was beautiful but of doubtful utility to a fugitive from the Japanese, so I declined. A couple of his armed companions then made gestures the import of which could not be misunderstood. I hastily handed over the rifle and accepted the bird.

For unusual people, wartime often provides exceptional opportunities to exhibit resourcefulness. One such individual whom I had encountered in the Fassoth camp and whose path I crossed again at Tibuc-Tibuc in the spring of 1943 was an American soldier who bore the easily remembered name of Johnny Johns. Johnny and a Captain Newman had been captured at the same time by the Japanese. Johnny had persuaded the captain to write a statement calling on all Americans hiding in the mountains to surrender. They were assured that the Japanese would feed them and treat them well, but warned that if they obstinately remained fugitives they would be captured and beheaded. Armed with this piece of paper, Johnny went to the Japanese and talked them into giving him $7 cash, some cigarettes, and a five-day pass, in return for which he proposed to travel about in this portion of Luzon and try to induce American escapees to surrender. To insure that he was serious and would come back, the captain was held hostage. After five days Johnny dutifully returned from his travels without having persuaded me, or anyone else, to surrender. In fact, he proved to be more persuasive with the Japanese than with Americans, gradually convincing them that five days was too little time to accomplish anything. Eventually his captors gave him a pass of indefinite duration and sent him on his way once more.

Before the war Johnny had somehow gotten hold of a considerable sum of money, which he had hidden. Now he promptly dug up his cash, headed for Manila, and began a playboy's life in the big city nightclubs. Before long the hostage captain heard through the grapevine what had happened and, realizing the precariousness of his own situation, tried to escape—and made it. Whether Captain Newman knew where I was, or merely happened to find me by accident, I do not know, but soon after his escape he paid me a visit. Meanwhile the Japanese too had learned how Johnny was abusing their trust in him, and arrested him, but Johnny was a slippery customer and soon got away from them again. I was as hospitable to Captain Newman as I could bring myself to be in the circumstances, for the enemy soon got wind of *his* whereabouts too, and swarmed into the area. The alarmed captain abruptly took off. The conclusion was irresistible that I too needed to change my address without delay.

Though I hated to leave the Filipinos who had protected me and treated me so well, I did not depart a day too soon. At one time, in fact, the Japanese had me surrounded in a field of cogon grass but fortunately did not realize it. I waited until nightfall, then stripped naked, tucked my clothes under my arm, and slipped through their lines. The reader might wonder why I chose thus to offer extra opportunities to the ubiquitous mosquitoes. The reason was that I had become so brown from swimming and lying in the sun that at night I was less conspicuous naked than clothed.

Soon after the Japanese left the area, I met two American soldiers, Sgt. Hugh B. McCoy of the Fifth Interceptor Command and Sgt. Ray Schletterer of the Seventeenth Ordnance. They were accompanied by a Philippine army machinegunner, a tiny Igorot tribesman from the mountains of north Luzon named José Balekow. The three of them were headed north. Having nowhere in particular to go, I joined them. Soon we met another escapee, a fellow alumnus of the Fassoth camp named Fred Alvides. Fred was a short, stocky, fast-talking American of Mexican descent, so dark he could pass easily for a Filipino. Most Americans in the camp had disliked him, in part because of his habit of leaving for days at a time, then coming back and bragging about all the good food and girls he had had. According to Vernon Fassoth's recollections, later in the war Clay Conner thought Alvides tried to set him up for the Japanese, but Conner grew suspicious and left the area, whereupon the Japanese killed Fred as a consolation prize.

Whatever the accuracy of that conjecture, I remembered Fred mainly because we had once gotten into an argument in the Fassoth camp, and he had challenged me to a fight. I was so weak then I couldn't have fought Little Boy Blue, but I told him I would take a rain check. I had fought a good deal while growing up, so when I had my health back I reminded Fred of my earlier offer. He was willing so with McCoy and Schletterer as witnesses, we had it out bareknuckled and barefooted, among the rocks along the river. We fought until we were tired, took an intermission, fought again, and quit by mutual consent. Our two referees did not render a formal decision. I would have called it a draw. Fred had a black eye and blood on his face. I had stone bruises on my feet, a swollen hand, and a sore jaw that prevented me from chewing for a week or so. Thus was honor preserved all around.

The fight over, we resumed our trek northward, wandering through the foothills by day and across flatlands by night, guided by a succession of Filipinos. After going perhaps fifteen or twenty miles we stopped at a house in the hills near Porac in Pampanga.

Ever since my health had begun to improve, I had turned over in my mind the idea of forming a guerrilla army of my own to fight the Japanese. Of course, the guerrilla bands could not hope to do battle successfully against regular army units, but they might be effective against the

Kempeitai, the Japanese military police who terrorized Filipino civilians. More to the point, I knew little about either existing Filipino guerrilla operations or the plans General MacArthur had made for American guerrilla activity before Bataan fell. About the Hukbalahap guerrillas I knew nothing at all save that they had coerced me to trade them a rifle for a parrot who couldn't speak English. I knew so little about communism then that I supposed that if I could raise a guerrilla force of my own I would be able to make common cause with the Huks.

Now, near Porac, we met an old man. I told José Balekow, the Filipino who would soon become my bodyguard, to ask him if there were any Japanese in the vicinity. The two carried on a long, animated conversation during which José, who was barefooted, shifted repeatedly from one foot to the other on the hot noonday sand. Eventually I lost patience and asked José what the old man had said. "Nothing," he replied. The truth of the matter was that there are so many dialects in the Philippines that understanding can easily vanish within twenty miles. José had no idea what the old man had said, but was ashamed to admit it. Perhaps symbolically, in a nearby house a mynah bird chattered incessantly in still another dialect. The whole episode made me realize how much I had yet to learn if I was ever to do anything in the Philippines save skulk about as a fugitive until I was either killed or the war ended.

The next night we crossed the Manila-Baguio highway, only a stone's throw from Camp Dau, just north of Angeles, a town lit by electric lights. By now I had been in the bush nearly a year, and the lights seemed a striking curiosity. We headed on into the central Luzon ricefields near the base of 3,367-foot Mt. Arayat, a spectacular peak because it rises all alone off a level plain just a few feet above sea level.

The area was also the home base of the Huks, with whom my second meeting proved no more propitious than the first. Soon after we were hidden in a house in a small village, at least five hundred armed and menacing men showed up in broad daylight. Here, we thought, were the guerrillas we had set out to meet. This proved true, but misleading. As Americans we had expected to be greeted joyously by any Filipino guerrillas. The leader of this band, however, strode into the grass-roofed hut where we sat on the floor and spoke to us sharply. If he and his followers hated the Japanese, they did not seem to be enamored of us on that account.

Nonetheless, they offered to help us on our way, which was, at that time, just generally north. When night fell, they set off, telling us to walk with them for protection. They assured us that later they would furnish us with guides. Meantime we should not talk. We didn't—but we didn't stop thinking about the cool reception we had gotten or its possible implications. After a time we came to a river, sat down, removed our shoes, forded the stream, and, once across, sat down to put the shoes back on. We exchanged apprehensive looks and made haste slowly, fumbling with the laces until the last barefooted Huk had reached us. His demeanor and actions were hardly reassuring; indeed, they stimulated the suspicions already growing in our minds. First he stopped and stared at us; then he looked toward his companions moving off. After a pause and another look at us, he hastened to the front of his column to talk to his leader. This time we shed our shoes in record time, recrossed the stream, and got out of there.

McCoy wanted to proceed northwestward along the foothills of the Zambales Mountains into Tarlac province and toward Lingayen Gulf, while I wanted to go toward the ricefields of central Luzon northeastwardly, mostly because I had heard that American-led guerrillas operated there. So we split, José choosing to stay with me.

Our guess, or luck, proved better than theirs, for McCoy and Schletterer were later reported to have been captured by the Japanese near Tarlac City. José and I, by contrast, found refuge in a house along the main highway to Manila. A religious service was held in the place almost as soon as we arrived. The sermon was given in Pampangano and then, with unfailing Philippine courtesy, repeated in English for my benefit. The language mattered little to me. All I was aware of was the roaring of Japanese trucks as they passed up and down the road just outside the building. Whenever one stopped, I put my hand on my gun just in case God's Will might need reinforcement. I also noticed that the worshippers' eyes betrayed comparable concern.

We had an even closer squeak a few days later. José and I had intended to stay in a grass hut in the middle of a ricefield, but neighboring people invited us to visit their village. José did not want to go, perhaps because the whole area was infested with Sakdalistas, anti-American Filipinos who at least professed to regard the Japanese with favor. Curiosity got the better of me, though, so I left José behind with all my possessions save a gun. While I was visiting, I learned that the Japanese had raided the place where we were staying. I was broken-hearted at the thought of what I assumed had happened to José, but he was a resourceful fellow and managed to escape soon after the Japanese caught him. He was overjoyed to find me quickly. He told me the Japanese had surrounded our grass hut, thrust guns and bayonets through all the windows, and told him in English, Spanish, and several native dialects that they knew both he and an American were in the house and that it would be wise for both of us to surrender. They had examined my shoes, canteen, and bedroll, after which they had slapped José around briskly when he played dumb and claimed not to know where I was. Now we wasted no time. As soon as darkness fell, we melted into the night and walked northward into Tarlac province. There I would spend the next six months, moving every few days from house to house, village to village, never knowing which day, even which hour, might be my last.

Certain aspects of this existence were not unpleasant. In villages where no American had ever set foot before, I was treated as a demigod, showered with every attention, even observed curiously when I ate and slept. I practiced the guitar and picked up native tongues sufficiently that

Filipinos stopped conversing in dialects in my presence if they did not want me to hear what was said. I fished a good deal, and I learned more than I had ever expected to know, or wanted to know, about rice farming.

The latter was done in a remarkably methodical, even rhythmic, fashion from planting to harvest. When the square paddies were covered with water, carabao broke the ground by pulling one-handled plows. Rice seedlings were then transplanted by hand, by young and old of both sexes, standing in water nearly knee-deep. The young shoots were jammed into the mud with a corkscrew motion, always in a systematic way from left to right as far as the planter could reach. In the tropics people must pace themselves when working to avoid exhaustion. Filipinos did this in a delightful fashion, by having a guitar player set the tempo. I planted rice for eight days once and found that, outside of the work itself being wearing, the hardest part was to adjust to the tempo of the guitarist. Life in the paddies was enlivened by the presence of numerous leeches and occasional small but deadly green vipers. Men ignored the leeches, though their bites would bleed slowly for hours, but girls wrapped their legs as defense against them. The sight of either a leech or a viper invariably provoked much squealing and either real or feigned terror among the girls.

After the rainy season the ricefields dried, the grain ripened, and the farmers harvested it with sharp hand sickles. Completing the harvest was as stylized as planting. During the day rice stalks were spread on the ground, and carabao plodded endlessly in a circle over them until all the grain was trampled from the straw. Evenings women put rice grains into hollowed logs and pounded them methodically until the husks came off. The sound was as rhythmic as that of railroad men alternating hammer blows when driving spikes. The rice was then laid on broad, hand-woven, nearly flat, circular discs and tossed into the air. The wind blew away the husks, and the rice grains, being heavier, fell back onto the discs. Eventually the rice was packed into sacks or large bamboo baskets. The whole procedure was accompanied by much guitar playing and light-hearted talk. Thus did the Filipinos make rice harvesting one of the lesser fine arts. Alas! they were never able to make it an exact science. No matter how much hand picking went on along the way, harvested rice always contained a few tiny rocks. One soon learned to eat rice cautiously; the alternative was jangled nerves and chipped teeth.

Despite these occasional happy interludes life remained in essentials what it was bound to be for a fugitive in a war zone, highly uncertain and always dangerous. I had more close brushes with death in those months than I like to remember. One night I walked up to the back door of the house of a man named José Louis. ("Just like your fighter," he had said to me when we first met.) He had also promised to get me a pair of shoes. Now another Filipino came to the door and whispered to me that the Japanese military police were at that moment questioning "Joe Louis" in an adjoining room. I didn't wait for the shoes.

Another time I sat on the floor in a house, a loaded and cocked .45 in my lap, and peered intently through the weave of a bamboo wall at a Japanese cotton inspector who had stopped to ask for a drink of water. On still another occasion I happened to be in a house alongside a road on a day when the Japanese chose to move troops down the road all day long. The lady of the house, Mrs. Victoriano de la Cruz de Arceo, whom I called Ina (mother), sat calmly on a bench on the porch and smiled at the enemy soldiers as they passed.

The most harrowing such episode I ever heard of had a history of some interest. It was mistakenly attributed to me by an American newsman near the end of the war. I thought it happened to Bob Lapham, with whom I subsequently became closely associated. As I heard it, one day Bob was talking to a few Filipino farmers in a little village near Tarlac City when some Japanese unexpectedly turned up. Luckily, a few of the Filipinos happened to see the visitors before the latter saw Bob. One of them was a Moro girl, a most unlikely person to be in central Luzon, for the Moros' homeland is in Mindanao, hundreds of miles south. Anyway, with amazing presence of mind she grabbed a hollow log of the sort in which rice was pounded, pushed Bob to the ground, and turned the log over on top of him. The Japanese were friendly, made some idle conversation, and asked for a drink of water. Then a couple of them sat down on what likely would have been Bob's casket had he so much as sneezed. Had it been I, my heart would have pounded so loudly the Japanese surely would have heard it. Actually, the whole tale is apocryphal, I learned after the war; just one of those yarns that everyone had heard but which always happened to someone else.[1]

Though I knew the risks involved in moving about, I found it psychologically impossible to stay hidden all the time. Many days I would go out of doors and start conversations with local people, partly as a relief from boredom, partly because it pleased me to practice some dialect I was trying to learn, partly to observe the delighted surprise of a person who is addressed in his native tongue by a foreigner, partly because I was gradually making up my mind to recruit a personal force of guerrillas. Having experienced and witnessed the cruelties of the Japanese on the Death March, I lived in constant dread of being recaptured. Moreover, the last thing I wanted to be responsible for was the death or torture of the brave Filipinos who had protected me and shown me so many kindnesses. Thus, even though I often talked to people of whose antecedents and credentials I knew nothing, I did so with some feeling of guilt and a deep sense of foreboding.

The faithful Filipinos sometimes went to incredible lengths to protect me. It would be hard to imagine a more heartening demonstration of loyalty than that displayed by Mr. Dolfin L. Dizon, the village leader of Matatalaib, a suburb of San José, east of Tarlac City, in Tarlac Province. Mr. Dizon assembled all the people of his barrio, fingerprinted them in their own blood, and ordered them to swear never to reveal my presence among them. He told them they were to die, if necessary, rather than provide any information about me to the Japanese.

By now I talked and acted like a Filipino and was the same color as most of them. A casual observer might or might not have noticed my longer nose and the consideration that while I was of average size for an American I was bigger than most Filipinos. If the Japanese had ever caught me and examined me closely, though, they would surely have discovered the truth, with results likely to have been fatal to me. José Balekow thought it was inconceivable that I could continue to live undetected among Filipinos, so even though he was my "bodyguard" he refused to sleep in the same house with me. José soon grew restless for other reasons as well, the main one being that he longed to go back north to his family and fellow Igorot tribesmen.

His eventual departure was speeded by an incident that was funny to me, though not to him. He had found a girlfriend in a nearby village, and one day he set off to visit her. For the occasion he dressed in his best. He had to cross a river that ran directly behind the house where I was staying, so I offered to ride across it behind him on a carabao and then bring the animal back. All went splendidly on the crossing until we reached the opposite bank. Here the carabao's hind legs slipped. I grabbed at José to keep from falling into the river but succeeded only in pulling him in with me. He clambered to his feet, soaked to the skin and splattered with mud. Outraged as the proverbial wet hen, he took the Lord's name in vain repeatedly and vehemently, then went stamping off in the direction of his beloved. I wanted to laugh but did not dare.

The many weeks of inactivity, interspersed with the narrow escapes detailed above, and climaxed by the departure of José, made me increasingly restless and thoughtful. Ever since the Bataan campaign I had doubted, on the intellectual level, that I would survive the war. Yet I did not want to die, and above all I did not want to die in some anonymous way or place. I thought a lot about my family back home and wondered if I would ever see them again. In fact, I worried about the whole matter so much that I wrote a few brief accounts of my experiences, placed them in bottles and buried them, in each case telling one Filipino where one bottle was in the hope that whatever my fate might be my parents and sisters might learn of it someday. Each slip of paper promised a reward to the bearer, reflecting my hope that at least some of the Filipinos who had done so much for me might eventually receive some compensation. I was the only son of an only son of an only son, and the chance that my name and bloodline would continue seemed slim. Maybe it is a man's ego that dies hardest.

During these months the Japanese were engaged in building an airfield at San José near Tarlac City. When it was finally completed, the first plane to land on it, a big Betty, flew directly over my current hideout on its final approach. My mind was flooded with fantasies. I longed to blast it out of the air. I dreamed of stealing a Japanese plane and flying away, though I was neither a pilot nor a navigator. Of course, I understood the mechanism of planes, I had watched many takeoffs and landings, and I had often ridden in planes piloted by others; but I knew little geography, and had I managed to steal an enemy plane and get it into the air I would not have known where to head. Besides, it would have been just my luck to run out of gas, or encounter Japanese fighters, or even be intercepted by American fighters somewhere. They would see the "flaming meatball" Japanese insignia on the side of the plane and shoot me down. Of course, there had not been an American plane over that part of the Philippines in more than a year, but one day I was certain I heard one, a P-40. I rushed out excitedly to watch it come—and go. No others followed. Most likely the Japanese had captured or repaired one, and one of their pilots was testing it.

The mere sight of the American plane affected me strangely. I began to tell everyone I met that American planes were bombing Tokyo daily and that U.S. ground forces were now scoring victories regularly in the South Pacific. These stories were all fabrications. I hadn't heard a radio broadcast since the fall of Bataan, and I had no idea how the war was going beyond what one could guess from seeing an occasional Manila newspaper printed under Japanese auspices. About all one could glean from that source was where fighting was taking place.

Psychologists have long known that if you tell the same lie often enough you gradually come to believe it yourself. In my case the process was accentuated by the eagerness with which most Filipinos accepted the tales and spread them. Why did I do it? I still don't know precisely. Self-delusion, I suppose. I had never doubted that the United States would win the war someday, somehow. At the moment I wanted badly to hear some good news, and to bring some to the Filipinos too. Maybe war makes us all a little crazy.

Crazy or not, it was at about this time that I began to organize a band of guerrillas; and one of my first discoveries was that spreading news about the war, even though it was spurious, possessed practical utility: it helped recruiting.

I did not undertake my new career lightly. The thought had been in my mind for a long time, and by now I had seen and heard enough about guerrillas to understand what would be involved. The most disagreeable prospect was that I might have to kill people personally and that I would surely be responsible for the deaths of many at the hands of those under my command. Guerrilla life would not be for the squeamish.

My thoughts went back to a time before I fled Pampanga province. A Spaniard had told me he could get me forged papers attesting that I was a Spanish national, and that I could then live and move about freely, even in Manila. I had turned him down for the simplest of reasons: I did not want to go to Manila and wander around in civilian clothes. Moreover, if a soldier is caught doing this in wartime he is usually executed. When the war was over, I was decorated at the same time as Maj. Edwin P. Ramsey, an officer from the Twenty-sixth Cavalry who became a Luzon guerrilla leader and who did spend considerable time roaming from town to town pursuing various personal adventures, though he also managed to lead his guerrillas effectively when he was with them. But I just did not want to do this: I wanted to fight the Japanese.

Now I began to gather my first recruits. They were Filipino laborers whom the Japanese had conscripted to build their airstrip. I talked furtively with various of them whom I trusted and outlined plans for guerrilla activity. They kept me informed of everything that went on among both Japanese and Filipinos. As mutual confidence developed, plans grew more elaborate, and long-hidden guns began to appear as if by magic.

Perhaps the thesis that I had temporarily lapsed into insanity is strengthened by the consideration that precisely when I was simultaneously filled with fears, entertaining fantasies, bemusing Filipinos with imaginary American victories, and trying to recruit a personal army of irregulars, my interest in the opposite sex began to revive for the first time in more than a year. When one is sick and starved, thoughts of romance are remote, but as I regained health and strength the girls began to look prettier. My interest in them had taken an abrupt leap upward one night before I left Pampanga when a beautiful Filipina, accompanied by a guitar player, had treated me to a moonlight serenade on the veranda of a hacienda. Most Filipinos can't conceal their dialect when they sing English songs, but this girl was not only gorgeous personally but a flawless singer in English as well. No matter. Before anything could develop, I had had to leave Pampanga one jump ahead of the Japanese.

My next encounter with romance was strictly as a spectator, and it was considerably more sobering. In most parts of the Philippines then courtship was still patterned on the Spanish model. Young men serenaded girls, and if a meeting took place there was a chaperone. One day in a small village where I was hiding, a handsome young fellow arrived begging for food, lodging, and employment. He was accepted by the local inhabitants and given work cutting sugarcane. One day he either misinterpreted the feelings of a young Filipina or could not control his emotions: he grabbed the girl and kissed her in front of others. Whatever the girl's true sentiments, in the circumstances her only respectable recourse was to complain, which she did by screaming loudly. Soon the entire village had learned of the incident. Barrio leaders took counsel and solemnly asked the boy why he had so rashly bussed the girl. He said he loved the *dalaga* (maiden) and wanted to marry her.

Though this sounds like the prelude to an idyllic romance, it didn't turn out that way. The girl was asked, in private, how she felt about her suitor's unorthodox advances. She said she was unimpressed. The village leaders then told the boy a lie: that the girl had accepted him and that all of them should have some drinks to celebrate the joyous occasion. They took him to an isolated hut, and amid the drinking one of them split the boy's skull with a bolo. He was then buried secretly in an unmarked grave. I learned about the whole matter only later when I missed the boy and asked what had happened to him. It cooled my romantic ardor abruptly.

Love will not be denied forever, though. One day two Filipina sisters came to see me. I was astonished not only by the beauty of their features and complexions but also by their excellent command of English. They belonged to the de Leon family, which was partly Spanish. Their father owned a small roadside store in San José, Tarlac. They were brave enough to invite me for dinner at their home, situated just behind the family store. One of them, whose name was Chinang, I fell for immediately. She obviously liked me, too, and soon I began to pay her almost daily visits, to the distress of her father, who feared that the Japanese would see me. After many lingering conversations I decided I wanted to get married; partly from genuine affection for Chinang but more, I think, from the fear that I would not survive the war and the consequent desire to leave behind some trace of myself: a son, I hoped. Chinang accepted my proposal readily, though I did not tell her that I had no intention of taking her with me on the constant travels that I knew would be an inescapable part of my life if I ever got my guerrilla band organized.

Whoever said the path of true love was never smooth could easily have been thinking about us. While Chinang appreciated the practical necessity of being married secretly, managing this was not easy. The first minister she contacted advised her against the marriage. Considerable time passed before she worked up nerve enough to approach another. This was not just timorousness on her part. There was some risk involved in telling *any* minister about even the existence of an American, not to speak of the danger the minister would court by officiating at a Filipino-American wedding or the risk involved for anyone else having anything to do with the matter. Perhaps equally frustrating, Chinang had the normal feminine desire to tell her friends all about her impending wedding, but she dared not do it.

As if matters were not complex enough on the matrimonial front, I developed a severe toothache that throbbed with every heartbeat, day and night. There were no dentists in the vicinity nor even any dental instruments. In fact the only tool I had seen thereabouts that bore any resemblance to a dental implement was a pair of pliers owned by a Filipino friend, Felix Garrovo. One day I grew sufficiently desperate to try to pull my own tooth. It was no use. A dentist's forceps are curved to fit a tooth. Pliers are not, and squeeze and pry as I might all I accomplished was to chip off enough enamel that my mouth felt like it was full of sand. By now the pain was so bad I began to think favorably of that ancient mode of anesthesia, hitting the patient alongside the head with a flat rock. I even asked Felix if he could gather some strongarm types who could knock me out and pull the tooth before I regained consciousness.

Then Chinang came to the rescue. Somewhere she found a dentist, who was properly armed with the weapons of his trade. He came to see me barefooted, with his pants legs rolled up and his eyes darting furtively as if he feared a Japanese might be lurking behind my door. He gave me a shot of worthless Japanese novocaine, then applied his tools and yanked out the tooth. The pain was excruciating momentarily, but relief was almost as fast. How many people in ages past must have endured horrendous pain that modern drugs and medical procedures alleviate routinely!

Alas! the tooth was still not the end of our troubles. When Chinang at last told her father that she planned to marry me, he burst into such a rage and talked so wildly to village people that they feared he would report my existence to the Japanese. This caused Chinang to grow so despondent that she attempted suicide. That was enough for me. I gathered my meager belongings and headed off northward once more, this time accompanied by a few followers.

But a woman in love is hard to shake off. Chinang followed after and spent a night with me. That was enjoyable in an obvious way, but, more important, we had a long, serious talk in which I gradually convinced her that the best course for her was to return home. I promised to visit her when I could later on, but I never saw her again. It was not that I forgot her utterly, or deliberately avoided her; in fact, I once visited her village in 1945 after it had been liberated by American troops. I came to deliver some food to the local inhabitants. It so happened that Chinang was out of town that day.

This was a major turning point in my odyssey. A fugitive I remained until the end of the war, but from this time forward I was at least a fugitive at the head of a body of armed men.

6

Early Guerrillas of Luzon

AN ENORMOUS AMOUNT OF NONSENSE HAS BEEN WRITTEN about guerrilla warfare, especially since World War II. Much of it is mere hagiography of the political Left. Irregular operations were not invented by Spaniards resisting Napoleon, or by T.E. Lawrence in the Arabian desert, or by Marx, or Lenin, or Mao Tse-tung, or Castro, or Che Guevara or Regis Debray, and none of them had much to say about it that had not been known for centuries. Guerrilla operations have existed since the dawn of history. Basic strategy and tactics have differed according to particular circumstances but have always been the same in essentials, since they are based on common sense and imagination: e.g., when you are the weaker party in a war you avoid major battles and instead harass the enemy. You cut his communications, ambush small detachments of his forces, cut off his stragglers, try to sap his strength and morale, and seek to win civilians to your own cause. Such modes of fighting have been applied by revolutionaries and reactionaries, by peasants and urban rebels, in all sorts of circumstances for all sorts of purposes. In the nineteenth and twentieth centuries guerrilla activities have usually had some strong ideological basis: religious fundamentalism, communism, or, commonest and most important, nationalism.

Many men have found guerrilla warfare attractive. It offers greater opportunities for personal initiative and daring than does conventional war; it appeals powerfully to those with intense ideological commitments; it requires strong feelings of comradeship and personal loyalty to leaders; and it involves less onerous discipline than regular operations.

Most professional soldiers, by contrast, have been impressed mainly by the dark side of partisan operations and so have despised them. Guerrillas, unhappily, almost always attract more than their share of unsavory human types: smugglers, poachers, bandits, congenital haters, and sadists. By necessity, but often by disposition as well, they hide behind hapless civilians, and often plunder and coerce them in the bargain. Their operations run heavily to ambushes and the taking of hostages, and they commonly give no quarter to their foes. They pose as civilians themselves, and do not wear uniforms or distinctive emblems. Thus, no matter how heroic they may seem to those whom they aid, they are criminals in international law and entitled to no quarter from regular troops. To professionals, guerrilla leaders often look like mere undisciplined adventurers, interested in either plunder or promoting a political career at least as much as in fighting. To them guerrilla operations seem amateurish, erratic, irrational, unpredictable, and retrograde; a relapse into the sporadic and uncontrolled violence that so often characterized warfare centuries ago and which persists in the twentieth century primarily among backward peoples in primitive parts of the world. Finally, professional soldiers dislike as innately defeatist the basic assumption of guerrillas, that one's own side is the weaker party.[1]

I agree with the professionals that guerrilla war is a disagreeable way to fight. But neither the considerations enumerated above nor my personal feeling about them diminishes the fact that irregular operations have often been remarkably effective. During the American Revolution

Francis Marion badgered the British relentlessly from the swamps of South Carolina, where they could not use their artillery or cavalry. Napoleon sent 670,000 men and 520 guns across the Pyrenees between 1808 and 1813. Spanish civilians and irregulars fought the invaders savagely, by every means human ingenuity could devise. French firing squads shot them down in reprisal, episodes immortalized in the paintings of Goya. But Napoleon did not conquer Spain, and only 250,000 of his men and 250 guns ever returned to France. Russian Cossacks decimated another Napoleonic army in the famous retreat from Moscow in 1812. By employing guerrillas the Boer generals De Wet and Botha lengthened their war against the British in South Africa by two years (1899–1902). It took the United States three years to overcome Philippine guerrillas at about the same time. T.E. Lawrence and Arab irregulars made endless trouble for the Turks in World War I and set them up for the final decisive blow from the regular British army, an exploit that involved nothing new in the realm of warfare but got much publicity because Lawrence was a romantic figure who could write well. In World War II Russian guerrilla operations carried on in close conjunction with the regular Soviet army cost millions of Russian casualties but had much to do with the ultimate defeat of Germany. Since World War II, guerrilla operations have become close to standard operating procedure for revolutionary groups in underdeveloped parts of the world.

In World War II the eyes of most Americans were fixed on Europe much of the time. Propaganda, either orchestrated by governments or manufactured wholesale by journalists, glamorized European "resistance movements" generally and the French "maquis" in particular. By contrast, the war in the Pacific was viewed mostly as a defensive action against Japanese conquest in 1941–42, and then as a slow process of reconquest, 1943–45, in either case conducted by regular armed forces. Actually, the Philippine resistance was at least as impressive as any of its counterparts in Europe, and it was carried out under more difficult conditions. It was always harder for Philippine guerrillas, whether Americans or native Filipinos, to secure either outside aid or sanctuary, since in the Far East there were no equivalents of the Swiss or Spanish frontiers to slip across when circumstances grew desperate. The tortures and beheadings perpetrated by the Japanese in the execution chambers of Fort Santiago in Manila were lesser in scale than the deeds of Hitler's Gestapo but no less ghastly. Loyalty to America and resistance to the Japanese cost the Filipinos dearly: 5 percent of them were killed; millions were terrorized by unbridled Japanese torture and rape; and scores of thousands were crippled permanently. They were impoverished from wholesale theft and destruction of their resources, and their capital was laid waste more thoroughly than any cities on earth save Hiroshima, Nagasaki, and Warsaw.

If it ever could be written fully and accurately, the history of the resistance in the Philippines would fill many large volumes. It will never be written thus, for several reasons: (1) many of the most important figures involved have long since died; (2) many guerrillas never kept records lest they fall into the hands of the enemy; (3) during the war rivalry between various groups and leaders was rife, resulting in postwar accounts by survivors that vary dramatically, especially in their assessment of individuals; and (4) near the end of the war and afterward hordes rushed to become "guerrillas" or to pay someone to manufacture papers attesting that the bearer had played some heroic role in the "resistance." Gleaning anything like the truth from this mountain of grain and chaff is problematical at best. The present account cannot claim to do more than indicate the general character of guerrilla activity on Luzon, explain my role in it, and offer some personal estimates of others with whom I dealt.

Some Filipino guerrilla units were formed within two or three weeks of the beginning of the war, even before Manila fell to the Japanese, in madly optimistic anticipation of a short enemy occupation. Some of these raided feebly guarded Japanese centers in Manila while the battle for Bataan was going on. The numbers of such groups expanded rapidly, and they attracted all sorts of people, chiefly dislocated people. Among them were bureaucrats who had been dislodged from their jobs by the Japanese, schoolteachers with nothing to do since President Quezon had ordered all schools closed to prevent the Japanese from using them for indoctrination, operators of small boats whose craft had been seized or wrecked by the invaders, former Filipino soldiers who had escaped from Bataan or Corregidor into the jungle and who were now roaming about aimlessly on the lookout for a chance to "reenlist" with former officers or in vigilante groups, college students unable to get home from Manila, adventurous girls who preferred an uncertain life in the hills with native boyfriends to the prospect of rape by the Japanese, and everywhere the chronically unemployed and footloose. Many of these people were ragged, hungry, confused, even half-dazed, concerned mostly to protect themselves or their families. Only a few military men among them had clear ideas about resisting the Japanese. Such pathetic and bewildered people drifted easily under the control of almost anyone charismatic or forceful.

Many of the guerrilla leaders were reasonably sound, cautious, and able men. Others were mere desperadoes, reminiscent of characters from mystery novels and adventure movies. Worst of all were the monomaniacs. As I hope this account will make abundantly clear, I have many reasons for admiring and feeling grateful to the Filipino people; yet, like all people, Filipinos have their faults. One weakness widespread among them is vindictiveness. Many a Filipino "guerrilla" was concerned mostly to take advantage of current confusion to avenge himself on old enemies, destroy some rival family, betray a political foe to the Japanese, or simply to indulge a taste for sadism. Cruel as the Japanese were to everyone else, cruel as some despicable Americans were to suspected Filipino collaborators, nobody exceeded the savageries various depraved Filipinos inflicted on their own countrymen.[2]

Sinister guerrillas of this sort, especially the outright bandit types, struggled among themselves for followers, for territorial jurisdiction, for the opportunity to plunder hapless civilians, and merely for survival. Kidnappings, executions, even lilliputian wars were endemic among these rival bands. In one such case, on the island of Leyte, a pitched battle between the followers of Kangleon and Miranda resulted in the deaths of two hundred men.[3] Also on Leyte, in March 1943, were two other guerrilla outfits, one led by a "Captain" Gordon Lang, and the other by a swashbuckler, "Major" Chester Peters. The latter had a mestiza wife who called herself Joan of Arc. The two gangs spent most of their time fighting each other.[4] When Wendell Fertig proclaimed himself a brigadier general on Mindanao, a worthless "Colonel" Gador on Panay could not bear the thought of being outranked and so promoted himself to "major general," even though he commanded fewer than thirty men and had never fired a shot at a Japanese.[5]

In many ways the most intriguing guerrilla of the "maniac" variety was an ex-radio announcer on the island of Cebu named Harry Fenton. Trying to render a fair estimate of Fenton's role in the war illustrates a common problem in historical research. Both Americans and Filipinos who have written about Fenton have depicted him as a murderous semi-lunatic. They agree that he hated the Japanese with a passion approaching insanity; that he refused to acknowledge that many ordinary Filipinos had to continue to work under the Japanese at the only occupations they knew; that he regarded all such people as Japanese agents and slew so many of them on the slightest suspicion that he eventually alienated his own troops, that he was paranoically hostile to any suggestion that guerrilla leaders from elsewhere acquire any influence on Cebu; that he was an unbridled womanizer whose sexual excesses disgusted his subordinates; and that he was probably plotting to overthrow Maj. James Cushing, his co-leader of the Cebu guerrillas, when he was abruptly seized, court martialled, and executed by one of his subordinates.[6] The main points of contention about Fenton are whether his wild extravagances were due to a cruel nature, an inordinate fear of being captured by the Japanese, or the onset of insanity.

Yet Fenton kept a diary, which survived him. In it there are numerous references to the execution of spies, but these are interspersed with many more notations about guerrilla plans, war rumors, problems of getting food and supplies, familiar references to "Jim" (Cushing), the co-leader he was allegedly trying to supplant, and expressions of concern for his wife and child. The tone of the whole diary is calm, even matter-of-fact. No one reading it alone would assume that there was anything unusual about its author.[7] Of course, Adolf Hitler was kind to animals and loved Wagnerian music. Still, one wonders if Fenton was really the monster of legend. Lots of guerrillas were jealous of lots of others, and only those who survived wrote books.

On Luzon conditions were deplorably reminiscent of those on the other islands. Throughout the central part of Luzon the Hukbalahaps (communists) and USAFFE (United States Armed Forces Far East) irregulars fought each other savagely, with luckless civilians caught in the middle. On one occasion early in the war a conference of competing Filipino bands was assembled. All parties agreed that nobody should come armed, but the conferees were shooting at each other before dinner was served.[8] Even when rival leaders were not quarrelling among themselves, their men were sometimes so trigger-happy that they would do such things as shoot at any car on a highway on the theory that only people who collaborated with the enemy would have cars.[9]

Luzon had its quota of "crazies" too, though separating truth from legend about them is often difficult and sometimes, by now, impossible. One such, about whom many lurid tales were told, was an ex-Brooklyn policeman, John O'Day. Yet Albert Hendrickson, who was to be my commanding officer and friend, and who knew the man, said the stories about him were nonsense circulated by other guerrillas out of jealousy.[10] An alleged criminal lunatic in north Luzon was a Filipino, Lt. Emilio Escobar, known locally as Sagad (broom). This reputed monster, whom one writer calls "The ruthless Attila of the resistance movement in northern Luzon,"[11] boasted of having killed four thousand people, nearly all of them his own countrymen. Escobar was reported to have done such things as leap at the throats of persons he disliked, behead women who gave him wine he did not fancy, execute women procured for him who did not perform to his satisfaction, and murder an eight-year-old girl who refused to go to bed with him. Other less celebrated brutes, some Americans, some Filipinos, were said to have kept harems of the daughters and relatives of accused collaborators, to have slashed at civilians with bolos on the slightest pretext, and to have forced victims to indulge in cannibalism before they were killed. In Pangasinan, where I eventually operated, a Col. Antonio Costas ordered the liquidation of his own father as a Japanese spy.[12] When such ogres unquestionably existed, and grisly tales about others were widely believed, it was little wonder that many civilians feared a knock on the door at night by a Huk or a USAFFE guerrilla more than they did the Japanese.

My own experience with Filipino guerrillas, however, was that most of them were much better men than this motley array of bandits, adventurers, psychopaths, and wastrels. Some of the Filipinos were ex-soldiers who, like myself, had escaped during the Death March, or prisoners who had been released by the Japanese to go home and die but who had recovered and chosen to fight the enemy again. Others, particularly leaders and organizers, were either educated people or local officials, though the rank and file were ordinary folk of little or no education. But whether they were ex-soldiers or civilians, educated or not, they felt humiliated by defeat. They were deeply loyal to General MacArthur and to their own president-in-exile, Manuel Quezon. They believed that MacArthur would return and that the United States would eventually win the war. Meantime, enraged by the savagery of the Japanese, they wanted to strike back.

On several of the southern Philippine Islands it was not difficult to organize guerrillas, for in the south many soldiers never surrendered but just went home, hid their arms, and later emerged as vigilantes in the interiors of islands where the Japanese controlled little more than a few coastal towns. On Luzon, by contrast, there were fewer undefeated ex-soldiers, fewer arms, and because Japanese control was tighter and more pervasive, fewer opportunities to recruit, arm, and train men.

Nonetheless, two native leaders of irregulars on Luzon stood out in the first months of the war. In the far north, a provincial governor, Roque A. Ablan, organized a guerrilla force and even got permission from President Quezon to issue his own currency. As early as January 28, 1942, he ambushed fifty Japanese. In bloody reprisal the enemy bombed several villages, killed twenty civilians, began an extensive mopping up campaign against guerrillas, and put a huge price on Ablan's head. One day he disappeared; the only guerrilla chieftain in north Luzon whose fate was never discovered.[13] The other leader was Guillermo Nakar, a captain in the Philippine army who commanded a battalion of the Fourteenth Infantry in north Luzon when Corregidor fell and who refused to surrender. Early in the summer of 1942 Nakar secured a radio from Capt. Everett Warner before Warner surrendered to the Japanese. Warner had earlier sent a weak radio signal addressed to MacArthur that was picked up in Java and passed on. Now Nakar sent a few other messages, the last on August 22. Few events in the whole war heartened the supreme commander more, for they told him that neither Filipinos nor Americans had given up, that there were still organized units on Luzon raiding actively and distributing propaganda pamphlets. Soon after, one of Nakar's subordinates, Lt. Leandro Rosario, revealed Nakar's hideout to the Japanese. On September 29 Nakar and his whole staff were captured without a fight. They were publicly tortured and executed.[14] Nakar's fate was to be sadly typical of that of many guerrilla leaders. If one alienated a subordinate or the local civilian population, it was usually not long until a Japanese patrol learned of his whereabouts.

Even before the war began, General MacArthur had

made tentative plans for guerrilla operations. Unlike many in Washington and elsewhere in those years, he and his staff believed that Filipinos would continue some kind of resistance to a Japanese occupation, particularly if they received aid, encouragement, and leadership from Americans.[15] Accordingly, his chief of intelligence, Gen. Charles A. Willoughby, had enrolled American miners, plantation owners, and businessmen, along with a larger number of Filipinos, in an intelligence apparatus which was to operate in case Japan overran the Philippines.

How many people were involved in this enterprise is uncertain. Al Hendrickson, the commander of USAFFE guerrillas in Tarlac, for whom I eventually became executive officer for many months, once rescued seven American miners at Lusod, near Baguío, early in the war, and found that none of them knew anything about plans for guerrilla operations. Of the Americans who *were* involved in the scheme most appear to have been killed during the war, though many of the Filipinos were not. It was the latter who formed the nucleus of an "underground."

MacArthur had even made highly optimistic plans for an American-Filipino counterattack near the end of the Bataan campaign. If Japanese lines were breached, Allied troops would then be able to operate on the rich central Luzon plain where food was plentiful. From here they could protect the north approaches to Bataan and Corregidor. Even if they failed, he considered, many of them could escape into the Zambales Mountains and could undertake guerrilla warfare in conjunction with Filipino forces already operating there. In any event, nothing came of this scheme because all the Allied troops near the end of the Bataan campaign were too sick, starved, exhausted, and dispirited to attack anyone.

Also before the fall of Bataan, MacArthur had directed Maj. Claude Thorpe (often spelled Thorp) to lead perhaps twenty Americans and Filipinos through Japanese lines to Mt. Pínatubo in extreme northwestern Pampanga province. Here they were to gather arms, form local Philippine Constabulary men into a guerrilla force, disrupt the enemy from behind and, when American reinforcements arrived in Bataan, fight their way out. Of course, the reinforcements never arrived and Bataan surrendered, leaving Thorpe and his associates abandoned. Still, he had at least been sent out by MacArthur, which was more than any of the numerous freelance operators on Luzon then could say, so for a short time Thorpe assumed command of all irregular forces on Luzon, though his real authority was shadowy. He had with him Lt. Robert Lapham, Sgt. Everett Brooks, Capt. Ralph McGuire, Maj. Charles M. Cushing, Sgt. David Cahill, Pvt. Earl L. Baxter, Sgt. Alfred D. Bruce, Cpl. Stafford, 1st Sgt. Slutsky, Sgt. McCarthy, nine Filipino Scouts, and Herminia "Minang" Dizon, a remarkable Filipina ex-schoolteacher with whom I subsequently became intimately acquainted. Various other American and Filipino escapees from Bataan, Corregidor, and the earlier fighting in north Luzon joined this group from time to time.[16]

Estimates of Thorpe's character and abilities vary widely. William H. Brooks, who had escaped from Bataan and who knew Thorpe, said he was one of the finest men he had ever encountered and that he deserved a Silver Star for his deeds. Clay Conner, who was closely associated with Thorpe, concurred, alleging that "he did a staggeringly great job in a very short time." Robert Lapham, who came out of Bataan with Thorpe, accepted an appointment from him, and understandably felt a sense of loyalty to him, respected him as an American career officer of the traditional sort. Others have depicted Thorpe as cold, aloof, slow of thought, unwilling to take advice, and prone simply to hide out much of the time.[17]

If there was any truth in the last, it was only partial. Perhaps ten days after they had made their way through the Japanese lines, Thorpe and his followers were holed up somewhere east of Olongapo in the foothills of the Zambales Mountains. They had run low on food and equipment but had also observed that every day a Japanese truck convoy passed over a winding mountain road nearby. Thorpe decided to ambush one of the convoys, partly to punish the enemy but primarily in hope of replenishing his depleted supplies. A "Captain McIntyre" (almost certainly Capt. Ralph McGuire), who understood demolition work and who had brought several sticks of GI dynamite wjith him from Bataan, buried his explosives forty to fifty feet apart along a level section of the road. Before long a Japanese staff car was sighted coming up the winding dirt track. It was followed by three trucks carrying Japanese troops.

McIntyre (or McGuire) had rigged his dynamite expertly, and he lit the fuses at just the right times. The first explosion blew up the first truck and killed most of the Japanese troops in it. The others overturned the staff car and the other two trucks, spilling their occupants both onto the road and into the ditches beside it. A wild gun battle broke out immediately. Several Japanese shot the Filipino driver of the staff car as he tried to flee up the side of a hill. An American, Corporal Jellison, narrowly escaped death when a Japanese officer missed him with a pistol at point blank range. Reprieved, he shot the officer in the head with his M-1, and for good measure killed several Nipponese soldiers floundering in the road, too crippled or too shocked to run away. Sgt. Everett Brooks grabbed his tommygun and killed all the half-dazed enemy soldiers who had been blasted or thrown out of the second truck. Thorpe himself fired one burst from his tommygun only to have it jam, but he stayed cool and directed his men as they shot the Japanese who had been blown from the third truck. There were no known enemy survivors.

There were other Japanese troops not far off, though. They heard the explosions and subsequent shooting, and soon directed light artillery and mortar fire into the area. Thorpe and his men at once fled northward farther into the mountains.

Despite this sweeping, if small, victory, and whatever his character or native talents, Thorpe was soon trapped in near-hopeless circumstances. He succeeded in establishing his headquarters near Mt. Pinatubo, and he tried to bring some system into guerrilla operations. Unquestionably, his most inspired action was to appoint Lapham inspector general of various groups in central Luzon. Lapham eventually became the commander of guerrillas in Pangasinan, Nueva Ecija, and northern Tarlac. In the opinion of a Filipino historian of irregular operations in that part of Luzon, Lapham did more than anyone else there to "further the cause of freedom."[18]

Otherwise, things went badly for the whole group. Thorpe himself was captured by the Japanese in the fall of 1942. According to some tales told afterward, he was taken to a Manila cemetery in the dead of night, where his captors cut off his head; according to others, he was decapitated in Old Bilibid prison. Several of those who had been with him were also soon caught and executed.

These developments were heavy disappointments for General MacArthur in Australia. As soon as he had arrived there after his celebrated escape from Corregidor, he had begun to plan the eventual reconquest of the Philippines. To facilitate it he would need regular, accurate information about the size of enemy ground forces and their disposition, the number and location of Japanese ships, the activities of the Japanese military administration, the temper of the Filipinos, and a thousand lesser matters. Well-organized guerrilla units would be ideal collectors of such intelligence. The commander in chief gave the job of coordinating guerrillas for such purposes to his own G-2, Gen. Charles Willoughby, who in turn put Col. Allison Ind in immediate charge of Philippine affairs, a position known among staffers as "the ulcer factory."[19]

Things went reasonably well in the southern islands, where Japanese control seldom extended beyond a few coastal towns. By November 1942 Maj. Macario Peralta had assumed control of all guerrillas (about eight thousand men) in the Visayan Islands and was regularly relaying information of all sorts to Australia. On Mindanao Col. Wendell Fertig gradually established his authority and began to send similar information. On Luzon, by contrast, after the capture and execution of Nakar, MacArthur heard nothing until January 3, 1943, when a radio message came from the Cagayan Valley in the far north. It was signed by

Capt. Ralph B. Praeger, who had escaped when Corregidor fell. He had salvaged a radio transmitter from a mine, and with a Filipino communications worker who had been persuaded to join Willoughby's prewar underground intelligence network, had managed to make halting radio contact with the outside world.[20] Praeger said he was running a local sub rosa government and could organize five thousand Filipino trainees, ROTC students, and intelligence operatives if only he could get arms and ammunition. He received much encouragement from Australia but no material aid, since MacArthur was then short of everything for his own campaigns in the swamps and jungles of New Guinea.[21] In any case, MacArthur wanted the guerrillas to confine themselves to gathering intelligence so as not to provoke the Japanese to wreak reprisals on helpless civilians; but many guerrillas, and civilians as well, were anxious to ambush enemy soldiers and to liquidate spies and Japanese sympathizers. Ultimately the guerrillas did much in all these realms, though gathering information was their most important activity since it enabled American forces to know where to land and what to expect from the enemy when they began the reconquest of the Philippines late in 1944.

Though only Thorpe, Lapham, and a few others had instructions from USAFFE headquarters to undertake guerrilla operations, this did not dissuade a varied array of Americans and Filipinos from organizing their own private armies in 1942.

Around Manila two odd, though not bloodthirsty, bands evolved who quarrelled a good deal among themselves: the Hunters, composed heavily of ex-ROTC students, and Marking's guerrillas. The latter were named after their nominal leader, a Filipino ex-boxer and ex-bus driver, Marcos Augustin; though the brains of the outfit was clearly Marking's mistress, a sharp, energetic, and tenacious mestiza who bore the picturesque name of Yay Panlilio. Before the war she had been a newspaperwoman. During the conflict she displayed sufficient ability and personal magnetism that Marking's guerrillas called her Mammy and named one of their regiments after her, while

99

no less a figure than General Willoughby paid tribute to her contribution to the Allied cause. After the war she wrote one of the most informative and interesting books done either by a guerrilla or about irregulars.[22]

The personal relationship of Panlilio and "Marking" was quite as tempestuous as the guerrilla life they led. Marking respected her talents and knew she was vital to his organization, but he could never stand to be bossed by a woman. As a consequence, they quarrelled incessantly. At the end of the war she left him and came back to the United States, only to succumb eventually to his repeated entreaties and marry him.

Up in north Luzon, when the Japanese landed at Lingayen Gulf in December 1941, nearby Baguio, the summer capital of the Philippines, was declared an open city. Whether for this reason, from bad judgment, or from mere timidity, Col. John P. Horan, who commanded a U.S. battalion nearby, withdrew in great haste southeastward toward Balete Pass, intending to join other American forces in central Luzon. He destroyed most of his equipment along the way but was still beaten to the pass by the Japanese. He then simply disbanded his tired and demoralized troops, and he and they fled into the mountains. Horan himself was lucky not to be killed by Al Hendrickson, whose guerrilla detachment I later joined. Hendrickson had laid an ambush for the Japanese near Balete Pass. Horan narrowly missed being bagged by mistake, only to be ordered by General Wainwright to surrender to the Japanese. Horan's conduct has been described by one stern judge[23] as heartbreaking evidence that much peacetime army experience sometimes seems to ruin men for war. Nonetheless, his actions did indubitably spread the sparks of guerrilla resistance all over north Luzon.

Meanwhile a baroque character named Walter Cushing had raised his personal guerrilla force. Cushing was a small, hard-drinking, cocky mining engineer from Texas who had come to the Philippines in 1933 in a mining boom. Fearless to the point of foolhardiness, energetic, imaginative, self-sacrificing, capable of joining the French

Foreign Legion when drunk and then jumping enlistment when some friends got him interested in a new mining venture, Walter Cushing was the sort of man about whom legends grow. Only two days after the Japanese landed in Lingayen Gulf, he left his mine and began to train his erstwhile Filipino miners to be soldiers. Soon after, to the mingled disgust and admiration of their commanding officer, Lt. Robert Arnold, Cushing simply commandeered thirty American soldiers who had been operating an air warning station on the north Luzon coast and who had been cut off when the Japanese swept through central Luzon.[24] The flabbergasted Arnold went along, helped Cushing train the men Cushing had just taken away from him, and cooperated enthusiastically when Cushing began to ambush Japanese detachments. Once they even captured an enemy general and his whole staff. Though Arnold performed with such bravery in these endeavors that he was eventually awarded a Bronze Star, he was disgusted when Cushing claimed all the credit and so deserted him to join Nakar's outfit after the fall of Bataan.[25] Undiscouraged, Cushing then made common cause with Colonel Horan, who reciprocated by commissioning the civilian Cushing a "captain."

These transactions involving Cushing, Arnold, Nakar, and Horan were all too typical of guerrilla relationships on Luzon. Some of the guerrillas were soldiers and some were civilians; the soldiers came in many ranks; some of them had, or claimed, authorization from MacArthur's headquarters, but most did not or could not; they cherished widely differing plans; and most of them wanted to boss some of the others.

Sometimes obscurity and confusion approached infinity. This was especially the case with guerrillas of the lone wolf genre. One such unaffiliated operator was Henry Clay Conner, who allegedly organized no fewer than three thousand guerrillas and was active in several parts of Luzon for three years. He was sufficiently well known and respected that an assemblage of guerrilla veterans of Luzon was convened in his honor in Indianapolis in September, 1984. Several of those who attended publicly paid tribute to his achievements and memory. Conner was even in the Fassoth camp at the same time I was.[26] Yet I never knew Conner existed, and I wonder if General Willoughby in Australia did either, since he does not mention Conner a single time in the seven hundred pages of materials he assembled and published under the title *The Guerrilla Resistance in the Philippines.*

Be all that as it may, after Corregidor fell Walter Cushing decided that further resistance was useless and so disbanded his organization, though he did not surrender personally. Instead he began to publish a news sheet to counteract Japanese propaganda. Soon he was travelling all over Luzon, even into Manila, to contact other guerrilla groups and to solicit money from wealthy Filipinos in order to buy U.S. weapons and ammunition that the Japanese had captured and were now selling on the black market. He took the weapons back north with him in a truck, but the Japanese caught up with him in Isabela province.

What happened next is uncertain. According to some melodramatic accounts, it was a Hollywood-style shootout that ended when Cushing, riddled with enemy bullets, saved his own last one for himself. According to Al Hendrickson, who had once been a guest of the Filipino landowner on whose veranda Cushing died, a servant of the landowner told Hendrickson afterward that Cushing had been killed by Japanese bullets without having had a chance to fire a shot himself. Whichever the case, the Japanese were sufficiently impressed that, even though he had been responsible for the deaths of perhaps five hundred of themselves, they gave him a formal military funeral. Thus ended the career of ''the granddaddy of the guerrilla forces in north Luzon.''[27]

Two decidedly less flamboyant private operators were Lt. Cols. Arthur Noble and Martin Moses. They had commanded Philippine army units when the Japanese made the Lingayen landings. Their inadequately trained troops had crumpled before the invaders. Moses and Noble had then escaped to Baguio in the mountains, where they joined

Horan. Then they went back down to the central plains, joined the withdrawing USAFFE forces, and retreated with them into Bataan. Here they performed well, then managed to escape from the peninsula after the surrender and make their way north again. Along the way they met several leaders of newly formed irregular groups, but just what they had in mind is uncertain. They are alleged to have reached agreements with at least two of the guerrilla leaders, Robert Lapham and Charles Cushing, that these men and their followers would affiliate with Noble and Moses, now the senior officers on Luzon, whenever the latter should be able to organize the whole area for systematic guerrilla activity. Long afterward, Lapham says he cannot recall any such understanding. Moreover, he doubts that Moses and Noble, in 1942, had any intention of forming guerrilla units at all.[28] In fact, no affiliation took place. The ultimate designs of Charles Cushing, the brother of Walter Cushing, are as cloudy as those of Moses and Noble. Cushing eventually surrendered to the Japanese, supposedly at the behest of his imprisoned wife,[29] though Al Hendrickson relates a different account of the surrender and the motivation behind it, later in this narrative.

Whatever their earlier intentions, Moses and Noble eventually claimed control over perhaps six thousand men heretofore scattered throughout a dozen lesser partisan groups. Through Praeger's transceiver they reported to MacArthur that they had established a unified command, adding that they had also done much damage to Japanese installations at small loss to their own forces, that morale in their units was excellent, that thousands of young Filipinos would join them eagerly if arms became available, and that their most pressing immediate need was for radio communication to keep track of their scattered forces.[30]

Perhaps they exaggerated. Donald Blackburn thought Moses habitually depressed and pessimistic, and considered that both Moses and Noble readily found excuses *not* to undertake significant guerrilla activity.[31] The truth matters little: before any effective response could come from Australia, the luck of Moses and Noble ran out. The Japanese captured their orderly, tortured him until he revealed the whereabouts of his superiors, then captured them June 3, 1943, and executed them three months later. The careers of a high percentage of guerrilla leaders ended either like those of Noble and Moses or like that of Captain Manuel P. Enriquez who assumed command of Nakar's unit after Nakar was captured. Al Hendrickson, who became my commanding officer in the guerrillas in mid-1943, had once been in hiding with Enriquez and had gotten to know him well. He thought Enriquez was more of a playboy and self-conscious local celebrity than a warrior. Be that as it may, the Japanese, with their habitual barbarity, seized Enriquez's wife and children. The poor woman then pleaded with her husband to surrender. He gave way, but unwisely tried to keep up his contacts with guerrillas around Baguio. Eventually he disappeared.[32]

With the demise of Moses and Noble everything in north Luzon fell into chaos for a time. I have read accounts that describe Luzon guerrillas then as poorly fed, clothed, and equipped; often barefooted; lacking medical supplies; uncoordinated, badly led, and mutually hostile; living in constant fear and danger; and susceptible to Japanese propaganda.[33] The description is recognizable but it is overdrawn, especially for central Luzon. Of course, guerrilla life anywhere, anytime, is not like that around a country club. Nonetheless, to say that most guerrillas were barefooted meant nothing. Few Filipinos out in the countryside wore shoes in the 1940s: I myself went without them for a year and a half. More important, these descriptions of ''guerrilla attitudes'' make no distinction between serious, dedicated guerrillas and mere ''paper'' irregulars and gangs of bandits.

The true situation was bad enough. All irregular groups save Lapham's were operating without authority, since everyone was supposed to have surrendered with General Wainwright when Corregidor fell. None of us had any idea what might happen to us in the unlikely event that we survived the war. If the Japanese won, there would, of course, be no uncertainty about the matter. But if America won, would we be hailed as heroes or court martialled for disobeying orders? or, perhaps, regarded as mere bandits and put on trial back in the United States for murder and other crimes? or instead, tried thus in the Philippines before Filipino judges? Nobody knew, just as nobody exercised unquestioned authority over anyone else. Because of the guerrilla practice of leaders bestowing commissions on themselves and each other, there were units that consisted almost entirely of officers. Colonels were commoner than in Kentucky. Anyone who valued military regularity would have thought he was with Alice in Wonderland.

It is in circumstances like these that exceptional individuals rapidly gain ascendancy. They are not necessarily the "best" men, however "best" might be defined, but they are the most intelligent, or energetic, or ambitious, or clearsighted, or ruthless, or charismatic, or some combination of these. So it was here. In north Luzon Capt. Russell W. Volckmann rapidly assumed overall command after the capture of Noble and Moses. Volckmann was a West Pointer who had been intelligence officer for General Brougher's Eleventh Philippine Army on Bataan. He and his friend Capt. Donald Blackburn, Brougher's signal officer, had escaped from Bataan before its fall and were in the Fassoth camp for a time when I was. After an array of hardships, adventures, and close calls at least as impressive as my own, they had eventually made their way north to Moses and Noble.[34] There Volckmann was assigned the task of coordinating the activities of three of their subordinate commanders. Following the deaths of his superiors, Volckmann proclaimed himself a colonel, designated Blackburn as his chief aide, and took over what Moses and Noble had begun. He divided north Luzon into seven districts, tightened operating procedures, and established a regular system of communication between his headquarters and those units he declared to be within his jurisdiction. He appointed Capt. George Barnett to implement this reorganization.

One immediate difficulty was that some of the guerrilla leaders declined to be reorganized. The most important of these was Robert Lapham. Volckmann and Blackburn had already met Lapham on their trek northward in 1943 and had stayed overnight at Lapham's camp near Umingan in eastern Pangasinan province. Their mutual impressions on that occasion are interesting in view of Volckmann's subsequent efforts to incorporate Lapham's organization into his own. Blackburn says he found Lapham uncooperative personally but that Lapham's camp was remarkably well run, an example of what human intelligence and energy could produce even in the most unpromising circumstances. Lapham said long afterward that both Blackburn and Volckmann seemed anxious to get on north into the mountains where they would be safer, and that neither gave any indication that they planned to become guerrillas. He added that he gave them guns and guides through the territory he then dominated.[35]

Eventually I joined Lapham's organization, and though I did not meet Bob personally until near the end of the war, I heard enough about him from others and learned enough from my regular communication with him that I came to appreciate his abilities, just as Blackburn had, and to like him in the bargain. Unlike some of the other chiefs of irregulars, Lapham was not selfish or personally ambitious. At the moment he was a guerrilla major who had taken advantage of the prevailing anarchy to reorganize his own command and strengthen his hold on several provinces in central Luzon. He named as his executive officer Capt. Harry McKenzie, a former civilian mining engineer who had lived in the Philippines for years and who had a Filipina wife and a son. The province of Tarlac he had put under the command of Capt. Albert C. Hendrickson, with whom I was to have much to do later.

Lapham simply ignored Volckmann's overtures and orders, just as he had earlier fended off the attentions of another ambitious guerrilla freelancer, Maj. Edwin Ramsey. Such was the milieu into which I moved when I fled north from Tarlac in mid-1943.

I had heard that Major Lapham had developed an extensive guerrilla organization in Pangasinan, Nueva Ecija, and parts of Nueva Vizcaya to the north and east, and that his influence extended into Tarlac, the province where I had collected a few ill-armed guerrillas of my own. As I moved northward in early fall 1943, I sent a runner to contact him and to offer to place myself and my small force under his command. About three weeks later the runner returned bearing instructions to me to contact Capt. Albert C. Hendrickson, commander of Tarlac province, and to work with him. After several days of wandering and searching I finally found him. Thus began one of my most memorable associations in the war.

Hendrickson was several years older than I and a couple of sizes bigger, 5'11'' tall and weighing about 180 pounds. He was also a colorful figure, habitually bedecked with a nickel-plated .45 automatic and an M-1 Garand. He was of Finnish extraction and, aside from a year in college, had spent his youth working in the mines and living in the tough towns of western Montana and Alaska. He had enlisted in the army in the fall of 1940 and had been sent to the Philippines almost immediately thereafter.

From the first day of the way until the time we met, Al's life had been a virtual nonstop series of hair-raising adventures that exceeded many of my own. Though we did not then know of each other's existence, Al, like me, was at Nichols Field when the war began December 8, 1941. When the first wave of enemy bombers came over, he looked about frantically for shelter and spotted a nearby taxi with its engine running. He sprinted for it, leaped inside—and found the gears locked. He sprang out, raced to a nearby banyan tree, clambered up it a few feet, and was promptly blown out of it by a Japanese bomb which left him unconscious and temporarily deaf. When he regained consciousness, the bombs were still falling, so he dashed for a nearby stream, jumped in, and found himself buried up to his chest in clinging mud. The Japanese then began to strafe the area. With bullets splattering all about him Al managed to work his way out of the mud, crawl up a steep bank, and run toward a nearby church. When another wave of enemy bombers came over, he had a sudden impulse and dashed out of the church toward another banyan tree. Hardly three seconds later the church collapsed behind him, hit dead center by a Japanese bomb.

Al then took off down a road toward a burning building in front of which were several Filipinos gesticulating wildly and shouting that a female member of their family was inside, drunk, but that they were afraid to go in after her. Perhaps steeled, or numbed, by his experiences thus far, Al entered the flaming building, found the woman with a gin bottle, drunk indeed, and proclaiming to anyone within earshot that she did not care if the Japs killed her. He carried her out and surrendered her gladly to her relatives. Next day he volunteered to go up to north Luzon in the hope of embracing a quieter life fighting the Japanese.

He arrived in La Union province in the far north, a pfc in the signal corps, just in time to be cut off by enemy landings in Lingayen Gulf. His unit disintegrated. Officers and men scattered or hid out. Al managed to escape the Japanese and happened to find a telephone switchboard that was still open. He promptly called MacArthur's headquarters to tell the general about the catastrophe that had ensued, and then vacated the area himself.

Al soon hooked up with Maj. Everett Warner, a former provost marshal at Camp John Hay, whom Al liked because he still wanted to fight the enemy. So wild and mountainous was that part of northern Luzon in 1941 that the Japanese took a long time to penetrate much of it. Thus, Al was able to sequester considerable stocks of medicine, canned goods, other food, and ammunition that would be of great value to the guerrilla groups already beginning to take shape in the area. Several small engagements with wandering Japanese patrols ensued, in the course of which Al must have comported himself well, since MacArthur's headquarters, then still on Corregidor, authorized Warner to commission him a second lieutenant April 25, 1942, and a captain soon after. It was one of the first such commissions granted to freelance operators in the Philippines.

Not long afterward Al came down with malaria. Luck-

ily, there was a capable Filipino doctor in the vicinity with
an American wife who was a nurse. They stayed by him
faithfully for about a month and provided him with good
food, medicine, and care, lacking which he would have
died. After he recovered, Warner asked him to round up
some Igorot *cargadores* (porters) and transport all the gasoline they had accumulated, some one hundred gallons,
south into the lowlands. Igorots are a mountain people
who dislike the low country and are normally reluctant to
go far into it or to stay there long. These *cargadores* were
typical: they took the gasoline only part of the way and
then went home, leaving Al alone in an area by now teem-
ing with Japanese patrols. Several patrols got wind of him,
and he exchanged gunfire with three of them before he
finally fled up a river into a jungle with which he was
totally unacquainted. Here he lay in the brush for many
hours until the enemy eventually stopped looking for him.
When he finally dared to arise and move around, he was
hopelessly lost. For at least two weeks, perhaps longer, he
wandered aimlessly in the jungle, barely subsisting on such
fruits and berries as he could find. Eventually some Filipino woodcutters found him, so nearly starved to death
that they thought him an apparition. They carried him to
a hut in a jungle clearing and tried to feed him, but his
stomach was so shrunken that he vomited immediately.
Then they carried him off to a barrio where other Filipinos
fed him more gradually and gave him native remedies for
his dysentery. Gradually he recovered sufficiently to think
of resuming his original trip into the lowlands.

His Filipino benefactors then expedited his journey in a
fashion he said he would never forget. He was put on a
raft, along with two exceptionally big, husky young Filipinos. The raft was then pushed out into a wild river that
coursed out of the mountains. The frail craft twisted, spun,
submerged, momentarily, then sprang back to the surface
of the water that roared down a rock-walled canyon. Man-
ning long, strong hardwood poles expertly, the Filipino
boatmen maneuvered the raft past boulders as big as
houses, narrowly averted head-on collisions with sheer

rock walls, threaded their way through the deeper passages in whitewater rapids, and skirted murderous eddies with saw-toothed rocks lurking just beneath their surfaces. Every hundred yards Al was sure he had breathed his last. At length, after perhaps five miles of such memorable navigation, the water slackened and they went ashore. Here his companions hid him for a time and moved him about periodically to avoid the numerous Japanese patrols.

At length the patrols became so frequent that the Filipinos were too frightened to help Al any longer, so he decided to head back northward on the chance that he might be able to resume some former contacts there. He made his way through the jungle by nights and eventually got back to Lusod, a village that had been a lumbering center in the north before the war. Here, in August or September 1942, he met Volckmann and Blackburn, who were on their way back north after escaping from Bataan and spending many weeks at the Fassoth camp. The three of them and a few others managed to secure some supplies that the Japanese had not yet found. Nonetheless, by now great numbers of Japanese were pouring into even this wild, remote area. Volckmann, who quickly assumed command locally, asked Al to go back southward once more to try to find out what was happening. Before he could leave, the whole area was raided by a Japanese patrol. In the ensuing pandemonium Blackburn, Volckmann, and Al all escaped but became separated. Al hid out in the jungle for nine days. On the last day he fell about fifteen feet near a waterfall and knocked himself cold. Once more he surely would have died had he not been found by some Filipinos. They carried him into a cave and fed him for some days. Luckily he had not broken any bones, so he soon recovered.

Now he struck off southward again. Near San Nicolas in Pangasinan province, an area that would subsequently be my own headquarters, he met Bill Moule, a civilian he had once known in the north. The pair continued southward, dodging the everlasting Japanese patrols along the way, and eventually reached Bob Lapham's headquarters. By now Al had a recurrence of malaria. Lapham welcomed Hendrickson and gave him some precious quinine that Moule had managed to secure. Once more Al recovered his health. Lapham then made him commander of Tarlac province.

This appointment stabilized Al's life somewhat, but it was by no means the end of his gut-wrenching adventures. Early in March of 1943 Charles Cushing spent a night at Al's camp. He told Al he was tired of fleeing the Japanese and intended to surrender soon, which he did. Sometimes those who surrendered volunteered information to the enemy, sometimes they would provide information if threatened, sometimes the Japanese tortured it out of them. Whether Cushing ever gave any information to the enemy nobody knows for sure. Hendrickson always suspected that he might have, for a Nipponese patrol made its way near Al's headquarters a few days after Cushing's visit. The Japanese caught a sentry asleep and so were able to slip undetected up to the very house in which Al was staying. He became aware of their presence so late that he ran headlong right *through* the wall of his grass shack and into a bamboo thicket. The latter was so dense it stopped him in his tracks. Half-bouncing, half-backing out of it, he managed to get into a river unseen and run down it pell mell while the Japanese shot up the bamboo thicket he had just vacated.

After having lived so long with Filipinos I was overjoyed to meet an American, and Al and I became good friends at once. In fact, we celebrated by staging a dance near Victoria, Tarlac. The orchestra consisted of members of Al's private army. For one night we relaxed our guard, forgot the enemy, drank freely, and enjoyed life.

The enemy might have been forgettable, but the booze was not. There were many different liquids one could drink in the Philippines. They ranged from puzzling to lethal. In some places trucks and cars ran on coconut alcohol. This was drinkable if it passed through copper tubing; but there were instances of men drinking it after it had run through galvanized pipe, in which cases the thirsty topers went blind.[36] Another common drink was *tuba*, which was made from palm buds. I drank some of it on occasion and found it not too bad. What our local Filipinos had, though, was two different kinds of wine: *basi,* made from sugarcane, and *miding,* concocted from some portion of the nipa palm. The former destroyed one's stomach, the latter one's mind. We drank both and suffered fearsome hangovers next morning.

I can't claim that this was a lesson to me, but the longer the war lasted the less I drank of anything alcoholic. The reason was practical. If you drank a lot, you increased the chance that the enemy might capture you when you were incapacitated.[37]

Soon after I arrived, Al appointed me his executive officer and proclaimed me a captain. What followed indicated a good deal about the informality of our existence. Al asked Lapham's headquarters to confirm my status. Harry McKenzie, Lapham's executive officer, said he thought second lieutenant was a sufficiently high rank for such a newcomer. A brief dispute ensued, but eventually everything was settled in my favor on the ground that nobody concerned expected to survive the war anyway, and the higher promotion would enable my family to get more government money after the war. One of Al's boys carved a pair of bamboo captain's bars to embellish me suitably.

In our exuberance at having each other for company, we engaged in several skirmishes with Japanese patrols. Little damage was done, but the Japanese, with their unfailing talent for mangling the English language, responded by putting out circulars calling for the capture of an American named Allen Ray (Al and Ray). Spies soon straightened them out, and eventually Al had a price of $50,000 on his head and I one of $10,000 on mine. The offer stood for eight months before the American Lingayen Gulf landings in January 1945.

Al was a great talker, and we spent many hours exchanging accounts of our personal adventures. Some of the wilder of his I have already related. He told me of others, comparably spine-tingling, that had happened after he joined Lapham's organization but before he met me. A couple I remember still. Once Al, Little Joe (his body-guard), and four of his men were invited to dinner by a local mayor. On a dark night they set off in a *calesa* (buggy) down a gravelled road that crossed a railroad track. Another buggy was sent ahead, and scouts had been dispatched to reconnoiter the railroad. For some reason the latter didn't do their job. The first *calesa* crossed the track without incident, but when Al and his party came to it a Japanese patrol sprang out of the darkness. One Japanese grabbed the horse's reins, one tried to grab the legs of a man sitting at the back end of the buggy, and a third shoved a rifle into the buggy, perhaps merely for fun without realizing that the buggy contained several armed guer-rillas. Little Joe had the presence of mind to ward off the intruding rifle barrel with his own. The sudden clash of steel against steel so startled everyone concerned that those in the buggy were able to jump out and dash away in the darkness before anyone fired a shot.

The silence was short. Little Joe ran full tilt into a wire fence, bounced back into Hendrickson, who was close on his heels, and knocked both of them down. As soon as they recovered their wits, they crawled under the fence, jumped off a bank into a small river, wallowed their way across, and scrambled up the far bank. The accompanying noise and curses alerted every Japanese and every dog in the neigh-borhood. At once Japanese bullets whistled about in the darkness amid a cacophonous chorus of barks and yelps. Nonetheless, the luck of Al and Little Joe held. They made it safely to a heavily timbered hill some distance away.

Not long afterward Al suffered one of his recurring at-tacks of malaria. Little Joe, whose devotion to Al was absolute and unquestioning, feared he would die, so he told some Filipinos in a nearby barrio that he would kill them if they did not carry Al into one of their houses and treat him. Despite their fright, for they knew the Japanese would kill anyone caught harboring an American, the ci-vilians took Al in, got him a doctor and some quinine, and persuaded a local girl to be his nurse. Recovery was slow, and before it was completed one of Al's men impregnated his nurse. After Al left, the Lothario declined to marry the maiden he had wronged, whereupon she fled to Al's camp in the mountains and asked *him* to marry her, presumably because he should regard her as a friend. Al was not ungrateful for her past medical services, but he had no desire to embrace matrimony in such circumstances, so he sent her back to her home village. The complexities of war are not all on the battlefield.

There were several memorable characters in Al's immediate entourage. One of them was his girlfriend Lee, a beautiful Filipina who could shoot a .45 better than most men. More important, she was intelligent, and she knew many people in the towns and villages where we operated. Thus, she was invaluable in supplying us with information. At one time Al wanted to marry her, and he continued to write to her after the war, but she died young of tuberculosis in 1946.

Another nonpareil was Little Joe, whose worth I soon came to appreciate. Good-humored, almost totally uneducated, and innocuous looking, Little Joe was hardly five feet tall and might have weighed ninety pounds with a rifle on his back and his pockets full of ammunition. As a presumed bodyguard for the husky Hendrickson he appeared ludicrous. Nonetheless, he knew his business thoroughly, and in dangerous situations he invariably proved to be resourceful and fearless. He could handle weapons skillfully, and he controlled and drilled recruits with the panache of a Prussian sergeant.

The outcome of one of his drills was both pathetic and funny. In our travels we often picked up volunteers. One memorable one we did not want. He was a Filipino boy named Norberto Sula, maybe thirteen years old, but small for that age and with a slightly deformed foot. One day he simply showed up and attached himself to us. Nobody knew where he had come from or who his family was. In such cases it was not uncommon to execute an intruder on suspicion that he might be a Japanese spy, but we contented ourselves with trying to shoo the boy away. He would not be dissuaded. No matter how many times he was chased off, he always turned up at the next stop, saying he wanted to become a guerrilla. One day Al lost patience and told Little Joe to give the kid a rifle and drill him. Little Joe set to the task enthusiastically. He slammed a rifle into the boy's hands and marched him unmercifully in the heat and dust. Every time "Norby," as we had come to call him, made a mistake, Little Joe would deluge him with loud shouts and insults that would have impressed an old-time marine sergeant. Despite the harshness of it all, Al and I couldn't help doubling up with laughter at the spectacle, especially when Little Joe would shout periodically, "Do you want to go home now?" only to receive the same dogged "No" from the boy, after which Little Joe would step up the tempo of the drill. Finally Al had enough. He called the boy over and asked him if he truly wanted to become a guerrilla. Despite all the dirt and heat and punishment, the boy immediately replied, "Yes, sir." Al then told him to raise his right hand, and swore him into our ranks. Norby never had much of a childhood, but he became a valuable member of our outfit. Boundlessly loyal, he regarded Al with a respect approaching adoration. More significant, like Lee and Little Joe, Norby had a good head to go along with a brave heart. Since he looked like a mere child, it was easy to send him into towns to gather information, find food, and let local inhabitants know that their future prospects would be brighter if they cooperated with us. After the American army landed in north Luzon in 1945, Norby finally got a suitable reward: he was made a sergeant of artillery in the Philippine army.

Of course, we did not try to train most guerrillas the way Little Joe "trained" Norby. In fact, training them at all was difficult since most were civilians who knew nothing about military regularity. Consequently, they relished some kinds of training, hated others, and tended to ignore what they disliked. What most of them enjoyed most was competitive drill and repeatedly cleaning their weapons. They especially delighted in contests to see who could most rapidly take apart and then correctly assemble weapons when blindfolded. The weapons themselves were often in a terrible state. Many had been buried in the grass roofs of houses, others in the ground. I was surprised to discover that those buried directly in the dirt were usually in a less deplorable condition than those that had been wrapped in cloth before burial. In either case, many rifles had rotten, worm-eaten stocks that had to be replaced. Many of those that had been wrapped had "sweated" until their bolts and firing pins had been fused by rust and their firing chambers pitted.

Some of our rifles and other equipment were secured by ambushing the enemy, though the utility of material so acquired was limited severely by the ambivalent attitude of the Filipinos toward it. For instance, it was convenient to wear uniforms taken off dead Japanese, yet because Filipinos and Japanese are about the same size physically this made it hard to tell friend from foe. The best way, if one was close, was to look at the feet. Filipinos often liked to go barefooted, but the Japanese had some superstition about it and never did. Japanese boots the Filipinos disliked because their hobnailed soles made impressions in the dirt that scared people. Nipponese rifles were objectionable because they had a sound that a trained ear could easily distinguish from that of American weapons. Thus, in nighttime operations no guerrilla wanted to fire a Japanese rifle lest he be mistaken for the enemy and fired on by his comrades.

Whatever the origins of rifles, or their condition, we could not give our men much training firing them, both because we were habitually short of ammunition and because we were usually close to Japanese garrisons whose inmates might hear the noise. To some degree we got around the latter by digging pits in the ground and covering them with grass to muffle the sound of the rifle shots, or by practicing during thunderstorms when thunder would mask the reports of the rifle.

What it came down to eventually was that every squad leader trained his own men as he thought best. The excellent performance of the guerrillas after the American landings late in 1944 is the clearest evidence that sometimes ad hoc arrangements are better than adhering rigorously to some "system."

Donald Blackburn wrote that one of the most onerous features of guerrilla life was boredom: that much of the time about all there was to do was keep out of sight, check impulses, control tempers, and wait.[38] For me personally that was not true. Blackburn spent much of his time well up in the mountains of north Luzon at considerable distance from the enemy, while I lived in the lowlands with the enemy all around me and thus found greater safety in moving about regularly than in just sitting. Blackburn was right about most Filipino guerrillas, though. They got bored easily unless there was some action.

Organizationally, we did what we could. We tried to construct our units according to the U.S. Army Table of Organization, and discipline them, when possible or appropriate, with the Manual of Courts Martial as a guide. We designated company leaders and bestowed commissions on them, assigned areas of responsibility, and outlined missions to be performed and objectives to be attained. We tried to add seriousness to the guerrilla profession and to reinforce a spirit of regularity by requiring each inductee to swear to the following oath of enlistment:

The Undersigned, being of legal age, do hereby enlist in the Guerrilla forces of Luzon. In doing so, I pledge allegiance to the Commonwealth of the Philippines and to the United States of America. I agree to protect said governments against all enemies, foreign or domestic. I further agree to respect and obey all orders from my superiors and to remain under the control of said organization, until released by proper authority. I swear that my enlistment is voluntary, of my own free will and without mental reservation or purpose of evasion, So Help Me God.

WITNESSED _____ DATE _____

One principle I took special pains to impress upon recruits was that unlike our rivals, the Huks, we were not going to coerce the civilian population. If the civilians would not support us voluntarily, we would simply disband. Anyone who used weapons for personal gain, to commit crimes, or to bully civilians would be punished, and since we had neither jails nor jailers there could be only one punishment. To be sure, we did lean on the Japanese-appointed leaders in areas we intended to organize. Such dignitaries as a governor of a province, mayors of towns, or village chiefs and elders were warned that we expected their cooperation. Most complied readily, either because they feared us more than they did the Japanese or because, in most cases, they were secretly friendly to us anyway. Civilians en masse proved to be no problem at all. They helped us wholeheartedly. Farmers contributed much rice and livestock, and sold so much in return for what amounted to U.S. government IOUs that in some areas guerrillas ate better than civilians. Sometimes the Japanese would try to deny food to guerrillas by moving all the people out of a given area so they could not produce food, but this proved self-defeating since the longer the war lasted the more the Japanese themselves became dependent on Philippine food.[39]

The problem of whether to pay for food and supplies, and if so how much, to whom, and in what kind of currency, was a tangled one. Much of the support our outfit got came from people who did not expect to be reimbursed. Contrarily, many wealthy landowners and city people donated money to guerrillas but wanted receipts showing that they had contributed prewar Philippine pesos that had been worth about 50¢ in U.S. money. The problem here was that the Japanese had replaced such prewar money with their own military scrip, printed on cheap paper and not even numbered. Filipinos disdainfully named this money *gurami* after a small, worthless Philippine fish, but the conquerors required everyone to accept it at face value. I once received a ten-thousand-peso contribution in *gurami*, for which the donor wanted a receipt specifying postwar payment in prewar Philippine currency. I had to turn him down. Blackburn says he and Volckmann gave out IOUs worth some 10 million pesos for food, clothing, and supplies, all of which the U.S. government redeemed after the war.[40] If so, the recipients lived far more grandly than anyone in Al's outfit, or my own later. I never signed for more than a tiny fraction of that amount.

A reader might suppose that we would have sought the most inaccessible mountain fastnesses of Luzon to establish our base of operations. A few individual American escapees tried to do this and then just wait for the end of the war; and in the far north Volckmann's guerrilla headquarters was well up in the mountains, though he controlled large areas of lowland in the Cagayan Valley too. Where I was, however, first in Tarlac province and then in Pangasinan, this was simply not practical. It was hard to find much food in the mountains, difficult to keep in contact with the civilians on whose support we depended, and miserable trying to move about on mountainsides that might look inviting from a distance but which were often covered with sawgrass ten to fifteen feet high that ripped clothing and flesh impartially, not to speak of obscuring numberless rocks, ravines, and chasms. Moreover, if we holed up in the mountains we would draw the Japanese there after us, and they would then oppress the mountain people atrociously. In the lowlands enemy cruelty toward civilians was at least tempered by the consideration that food was produced there. Since the Japanese grew increasingly dependent on it, there was a practical limit to how beastly they could behave toward the Filipinos who produced it. Thus, we stayed out of the mountains and moved about almost constantly across the ricefields of central Luzon.

Our strength varied enormously, and it is difficult even to estimate it with any accuracy since every guerrilla outfit consisted of a small core of permanent semi-professional soldiers; a much larger force of occasional warriors; and a vastly more numerous retinue of supporters, sympathizers, and periodic helpers of varying stripes and degrees. If one counts only those whose regular activities were gathering information, fighting, training, and making plans to fight, then all guerrilla forces were small. If one counts all the peripheral people too, then they appear large. Bob Lapham eventually "controlled" some 15,000 men, and by the end of 1944 I could have mustered 3,400 for a given occasion, though it would have stretched the truth to call all of them soldiers. Most of the time we, and other irregular groups as well, had far fewer, and we always travelled with far fewer since a small force could move faster and was harder to detect. I tried to maintain a small headquarters contingent of ten to twenty men, but often roamed the countryside with as few as four. Most of our troops, after all, were rice farmers who joined us actively only on occasions when some specific need existed.

Travel was highly varied. We rode on handcars on the railroad, in horse-drawn buggies on lightly travelled roads, on horses or carabao through fields when we could, and walked the rest of the time. It was not uncommon for us to move thirty miles in a night across fields that had no trails and rivers that had no bridges, all without lights.

We never could have made it without help from the "puppet" leaders, whose loyalty to their Japanese masters was only nominal, and the Neighborhood Guards. The latter were civilian groups organized to prevent stealing. They became our best friends. They kept us supplied with up-to-date information about the enemy and provided the guides who were invaluable on our numerous moves. But we used guides with all possible caution: in relays and for short distances only. We gave each one different, and false, information about our destination just in case one of them might be pro-Japanese or might be captured. At night we put out a double circle of civilian guards at every trail the Japanese might take, and then inside these a third ring of our own guerrilla guards. We were comparably careful about our personal security. Though individual habits varied, I always slept fully clothed, my rifle at my side, and my .45 in its holster with a bullet in the chamber and the hammer at half-cock position.

The most difficult obstacles to our nocturnal travels were

ricefields during the rainy season, after the ground had been broken and planted. Then we had to follow a zigzag course atop the dikes that surrounded the fields. The dikes themselves varied greatly in height, width, and strength. All of us took many a header into a sodden rice paddy whose retaining walls proved weaker than they looked. Of course, this was disagreeable for the victim of the moment, but for onlookers it provided some occasions for laughter in circumstances where humor was sorely needed.

If a person didn't get soaked from falling into rice paddies, he usually did from the awesome rainstorms that descended periodically, turning every gully into a raging torrent and virtually drowning any person caught outdoors. Still, the rain was warm and did not discommode us unduly.

What I hated and feared more than rain or mud was light. Most American troops in the Pacific heartily disliked night operations, but not I. I always felt far more secure in the dark, and whenever I could I moved my men in the dark. Moonlit nights, though beautiful aesthetically, were especially dreaded because they enabled enemy patrols to move about easily without lights, thus increasing the danger that they might slip up on us. Normally the Japanese used lights on dark nights and so could be detected from long distances. By contrast, we had become accustomed to moving in the dark without lights and so had an advantage on moonless nights. Moonlight seemed to cause dogs to bark more than usual too, and I have never forgotten the fear that invariably gripped me when dogs began to bark or howl at night.

Thus, guerrilla existence was hard, dangerous, unpredictable, and psychologically wearing. Still, as Margaret Utinsky, a valiant Red Cross nurse, once put it, it was better than being a prisoner of war, for a guerrilla was still a free man, a volunteer. She should have known, for she was both prisoner and guerrilla during the war, and as a prisoner she had been tortured shamefully by her Japanese captors. She also made another sagacious observation: she said that she would never have survived the war had she been able to see into the future; that people can do impossible things *if they don't know what is coming*, if they don't know that they will be called on to do the seemingly impossible.[41] I agree totally. In war you must live from day to day, even minute to minute. Highstrung or unduly thoughtful people crack up in war. You need to be stolid, to put your imagination on the shelf for the duration; otherwise you simply cannot bear to witness the gory demise of friends and associates, or their sudden disappearance, and yet go on about your business knowing the next may be yourself.

As I related earlier, when I first began to form a guerrilla band I had not expected to fight pitched battles with regular Japanese troops but to ambush small detachments of them, particularly to pick off the Kempeitai. From memories of the Death March and the sight of what the enemy had done to Filipino civilians, I thought less of a Japanese life than of that of an animal. One of the reasons we moved around so much, sometimes toward Japanese garrisons, sometimes away from them, was that we were often looking for opportunities to set an ambush.

Chick Parsons, who was in contact with guerrillas throughout the Philippines during the last two years of the war, described one of the commonest ruses employed by them. It went something like this. Since the Japanese always wanted to lure guerrillas into the open to fight pitched battles, they would set an ambush and try to entice guerrillas to fall into it. The irregulars would pretend to take the bait, and would pepper the enemy a bit with rifle fire from concealed positions just to pin him down long enough for Filipino civilians to flee out of harm's way. Then the guerrillas would withdraw into the bush and try to induce the Japanese to follow them to places where they had set ambushes of their own. Thus, they acted defensively against initial Japanese harassment, then offensively if the enemy tried to penetrate the mountains or jungle that protected them.[42] Sometimes we tried stratagems of this general character, but most of our strikes were simple hit-and-run operations, after which my men would scatter, hide their weapons, go back to their homes, and appear to the world to be ordinary rice farmers.

On one of these occasions I learned a valuable lesson in the inherent limitations of planning and regulation. I assigned a Filipino lieutenant to undertake a particular ambush and prepared an elaborate plan for him. After explaining each portion of it to him I would stop and ask him if he understood. He invariably answered, "Yes, sir." I gradually became suspicious that he did *not* understand, so when I had finished I asked him to repeat the entire order to me. All he could explain was what it was he was to attack. At first I was enraged, but after simmering down I reflected that he was an utterly loyal man of respectable ability who could probably do a better job in his own way. Since our problem was usually to restrain Filipinos rather than encourage them, since they had their own hatred and priorities, since our control over them was only tenuous anyway, since language barriers frequently blurred understanding, and since we did not dare write out specific battle orders, it simply worked better to pick a Filipino subordinate whom you trusted, tell him in general what you wanted done, and then leave him alone. Perhaps needless to add, circumstances like these do not make it easier, after a war has ended, to determine who was and who was not a "war criminal."

Historically, wars have been waged by men, but long before the advent of Women's Liberation it was a rare conflict in which women did not figure significantly in some capacity. So it was in our theater. I have already noted Al Hendrickson's girlfriend, Lee, who travelled about with him frequently. Soon I had one too, Herminia (Minang) Dizon, a schoolteacher before the war and one of the most remarkable individuals I have ever had anything to do with. If I was allowed only one word to describe her, it would be "fierce." Long before I knew Minang, she had developed a liking for American men. She had taken up with Maj. Claude Thorpe before the fall of Bataan, she had accompanied him on his escape with

Lapham and other Americans and Filipinos, and she had been captured with Thorpe. The Japanese had beheaded Thorpe, but they were content to compel Minang to tour central Luzon in the company of Japanese guards and deliver speeches in which she praised her conquerors and denounced guerrillas. While a few Japanese knew an occasional Filipino dialect, most of them knew none, whereas Minang had an excellent command of English and knew several Philippine dialects as well. Soon her guards were asking her why her audiences seemed to laugh at unexpected times during her speeches, which were given in Pampangano. It never seemed to occur to them that she would dare to sabotage them verbally. On the contrary, some of her captors were quite taken with her. One high ranking Japanese officer even offered to take her with him when his countrymen conquered Australia. Others showed her a map, given to them by a Filipino collaborator, that had led them to the hideaway of Thorpe and herself. To her horror, she recognized it as having been drawn by her uncle, a man whom she had trusted implicity.

One day Minang got a chance to escape and did so, but her life was precarious in the extreme because she was pursued not only by the Japanese but by the communist guerrillas (Huks), who hated her, and by her uncle who wanted her killed because she was, at least for a time, the only person who knew that he was the collaborator who had been responsible for the capture and execution of Thorpe.

Minang was a tough and resourceful woman. She was not especially pretty, though she did have flashing eyes, but she was intelligent, well organized, and articulate. She was also ambitious and told me that she would never marry a Filipino, only an American or a mestizo. Oddly, I cannot recall the first time I saw this extraordinary female. It must have been at least six months after Al had enlisted her as one of his first guerrillas at Pura, in Tarlac, in January 1943. Whenever it was, I soon became smitten with her and she with me.

Perhaps because we now had regular girlfriends, Al and

I shaved regularly. This was not the least of our sacrifices during the war. Most Filipino men have scanty beards, and often pull out their few whiskers with bamboo tweezers rather than shave. Initially I thought this an odd practice, but after gaining some experience with Filipino barbers I came to understand it better. Nobody knows why, but virtually every Filipino, male or female, aspires to be a barber. This would be of little consquence in itself were they not unanimously convinced that a few dabs of cold water constitute an excellent preparation for scraping a victim's face with a dull straight razor. One's skin does toughen when repeatedly subjected to this regimen, save only on the upper lip. When one of these self-taught barbers worked over this area, tears would roll down my cheeks no matter how tightly I shut my eyes. Minang was an accomplished woman in many ways, but as a barber she was only run-of-the-mill.

There would be no point in devoting so much attention to Minang in this narrative had she been only my ladylove. In fact, she soon became a vital figure in our organization. Though she was just a little slip of a girl who weighed no more than ninety pounds and could stand under my outstretched arm, no lion ever had a stouter heart. When we approached a strange town or village, she and Lee would go on ahead, meet the local authorities, tell them what we expected of them, reassure them that we would treat them well if they were cooperative, and make arrangements with them to conceal us from our enemies. Though she knew there was a price on her head, she would go boldly into town markets in daylight to purchase food, medicine, clothing, and often bolts of cloth from which she would personally make garments for us.

A casual reader might wonder how it was possible for us to go into unfamiliar villages at all, Minang's courage or no, when the Japanese controlled the Philippine government. We could do so simply because the great majority of ordinary Filipinos sympathized with us, and most of the rest were sufficiently afraid of us to make no trouble.

Despite her several masculine qualities, one side of Minang's complex makeup was totally feminine. She nursed me when I was sick, anticipated my every need, and devoted herself to me unreservedly. She was also scheming and quickwitted in feminine ways, as I eventually discovered. Months after it had happened, Little Joe, Al's bodyguard, told me one day that Chinang de Leon had tried to come to see me but had been intercepted by Minang. The latter had a .38 on her hip and, apparently, determination in her voice, for my erstwhile fiancée had turned her buggy around and gone home. Little Joe was still disgusted by the whole episode because, as he put it, "She had a whole *calesa* load of candies and other gifts." On my part, as I grew increasingly enamored of Minang I gradually forgot Chinang, the girl I had once planned to marry. Doubtless it was for the best. Chinang was a fine and brave girl but not at all suited for the rough, precarious existence of a guerrilla in the field. Minang was "man enough" for anything.

Another of Minang's maneuvers I discovered rather late in the day, too. Al and I had noticed that whenever we moved into a new village there never seemed to be any young girls around. Minang told us that the village leaders moved them out in case trouble should develop. Later Gregorio Agaton, who eventually replaced José Balekow as my Filipino bodyguard, told me the truth of it. When Minang preceded us into a village, she would tell the elders that it was my order that all young girls should leave the barrio before we arrived. Thus did she eliminate potential competition. Though I was furious with her when I learned what she had done, I must admit, forty years later, that her instinct was sound. When I was young, I had a roving eye.

7

Hukbalahaps and Constabulary

OUR OPERATIONS IN CENTRAL LUZON WERE COMPLICATED immensely by the presence of a rival and bitterly hostile guerrilla organization, the Hukbalahaps. Generations before the war Spanish entrepreneurs had gained control of much of the good farmland in the Philippines and turned it into great estates for the commercial production of various commodities, notably sugar. Gradually, and particularly in the twentieth century, many Filipinos had also become large landowners. Actual work on the estates was done by sharecroppers and hired laborers. Like similar people at other times and places, they scratched out a bare living for themselves, and slowly fell hopelessly into debt to their increasingly wealthy landlords.[1] Because of this long-standing condition there was much peasant unrest in the Philippines on the eve of the war. It was most intense in central Luzon, particularly in Pampanga province.

Several protest movements had developed in response to this situation, only two of which concern us here. One was the Communist Party. Its Philippine branch was organized in 1930, and outlawed by the Commonwealth government in 1931. Throughout the 1930s the communists tried to exploit peasant grievances, to polarize Philippine politics by gaining control of movements that were anti-American or anti-Commonwealth, and to pose as doughty fighters against whatever they chose to call "fascism." By the time the war began, the party was dominated by the Lavas, a wealthy family of intellectual Marxists from Manila, whose most famous member, Vincente Lava, was a chemist with a doctorate from Columbia University and an international reputation.[2]

The other movement that championed peasants against landlords was Christian socialist, founded by Pedro Abad Santos but led by a young peasant named Luis Taruc. At heart Taruc was a religious man who never entirely abandoned his Christian principles during his several political metamorphoses, and who eventually returned to them entirely long after World War II. In 1942 he was convinced that since the majority of Filipinos were Christians they would never turn communist; therefore there was no danger in forming a common front with communists to try to bring about a redistribution of lands and to resist the Japanese conquerors. To further these objectives various "progressives" and "peasant leaders" held a series of meetings early in 1942. From them came a merger of Taruc's socialists with the communists under a new name, Hukbo ng Bayan Labon sa Hapon (People's Army to Fight the Japanese), or Hukbalahap for short. The twenty-nine-year-old Taruc was made its leader. Though it took Taruc some time to realize it, what happened to him was what often happens to people who attempt to form a common front with communists. The latter, who have clear, fixed objectives permanently in mind, who have had much experience in intrigue and plotting, and who are unhampered by scruples, quickly reduce their gullible allies to mere tools, use them as long as it is expedient, and then cast them aside. In this case, all the two factions had in common, ultimately, was hostility to the Japanese.[3]

In the first half of 1942 efforts were made to coordinate the activities of the Huks with resistance being planned by USAFFE officers. These culminated in a meeting on

July 7, 1942, between several members of Thorpe's staff and Taruc and some of his associates. Each side had something of value to offer. The Huks were already well organized and had a considerable following in the villages and barrios of Pampanga province. They had carried out a number of small raids against the Japanese that had gained them credit in the eyes of local Filipinos. And they knew the countryside well. Thorpe and his associates could provide training and professional military skills that the Huks lacked at that time. The Huks offered to amalgamate and make the Americans colonels in the Huk army. What they hoped to get in return, seemingly, was official U.S. Army recognition and eventually pay from the American government for their work as guerrillas. A tentative agreement was reached to collaborate on everything relating to plans and the disposition of military supplies, but nothing came of it. The reason seems to have been that neither party was willing to subordinate itself to the other. Thorpe thought guerrillas would be effective only if they were a strictly military organization with their eyes on a single objective: military victory. This would mean that the Huks would have to abandon their political goals. Understandably, they declined.[4]

"Progressive" writers have clothed the Huks in regal splendor: they were warm-hearted agricultural reformers, heroic freedom fighters, and crusaders against American imperialists who worked hand-in-glove with fascist oppressors. Everywhere the Huks were friends of the peasants and beloved by them in turn. They were also the best organized and most effective of all the guerrilla bands. Alas! Their yeoman services and sacrifices went unappreciated and unrewarded at the end of the war because a sinister coalition of Filipino collaborators, jealous USAFFE officers, and American big business interests put them down, returned to power the old masters of the peasants, and fixed elections, all in order to continue their prewar exploitation of the Filipino people.[5]

There is no question that the Huks were shrewd and ruthless, and that they tried to maintain a tight organization. They made the forgery of ID cards a local industry. They also had a clever system for raising troops. A recruiter would work an area where he knew the local population and they knew him. Thus, he could get loyal recruits and keep out Japanese spies. Once a man was recruited, he was required to give a sworn statement that he was anti-Japanese. At any hint of subsequent insubordination his superiors could allow this statement to "fall into the hands" of the enemy. Thus, one who enlisted in the Huks generally *stayed* enlisted.[6]

My personal experiences with the Huks were always unpleasant, and my impressions of them were entirely unfavorable. Those I knew "were much better assassins than soldiers."[7] Tightly disciplined and led by fanatics, they murdered some landlords and drove others off to the comparative safety of Manila. They were not above plundering and torturing ordinary Filipinos to get the food and supplies they needed; and they were implacable and treacherous enemies of all other guerrillas. Like their communist partisan counterparts in Europe, they were in the process of developing a new kind of conflict: war and revolution at the same time, the erosion of the power and authority of a foreign invader while simultaneously wearing down and discrediting traditional groups and institutions in their own country. Whether in a dozen European countries or in the Philippines, this translated into a policy of quarrelling with, sometimes fighting with, and always attempting to subvert non-communist guerrillas, while keeping one's attention fixed on the main objective: to turn their country communist at the end of the war, by *any* means.[8]

Admittedly, there was much difference between many of the rank and file Huks and their leaders. The vast majority of Filipino peasants knew nothing about Marxism and simply wanted redress of long-standing grievances and some liberalization of the old landlord system. In the Huk army most ordinary guerrillas, at least early in the war, wanted mostly either to escape the Japanese or to fight the Japanese, or else they thought life inside the organization was better than that outside. Not so their leaders. Most of these men were cold, urban intellectual types who cared nothing for peasant discontents save as vehicles for advancing faster along the Highway of History that must end in the earthly kingdom of Universal Marxism.[9]

The Huks were convinced that Americans would be more impressed by their power than by their principles, so they tried to secure as many weapons as they could and then use them to weaken other guerrilla units. All attempts to cooperate with them failed, and we eventually waged war against the Huks quite as much as against the Japanese. In fact, up in Nueva Ecija province a situation developed that in less serious circumstances would have been a subject for comic opera. During the occupation the Japanese reorganized the old Philippine Constabulary in an effort to use it against guerrillas. Unknown to them, most members of the Constabulary were themselves secret guerrillas, or so afraid of guerrillas that they might as well have been. Moreover, the governor of Nueva Ecija, though appointed by the Japanese, had a secret understanding with the partisans. He supplied them with Philippine Constabulary uniforms and insignia, and they often travelled about with regular Japanese troops seeking out the Huks and fighting pitched battles with them. Eventually these ill-assorted allies drove all the Huks out of the province.[10]

On a day-to-day basis the Huks had a lot of the same problems we did: they had attracted too many bandits, adventurers, self-seekers, corruptionists, and assorted crazies who undermined their peasant support by such follies as stealing carabao, and destroyed much of their public credit by gratuitous assassinations. Once such incident stands out. A fierce woman, Felipa Culala, whom her followers called Dayang-Dayang, organized an irregular unit of her own, fought against the Japanese, and cooperated with the Huks. Unfortunately for her, she also spoke frankly about her intention to get rich from plunder in the process. Even though she was widely regarded as a heroine, Huk general headquarters had her executed.[11]

Estimates of Huk strength and effectiveness vary widely.

U.S. Army Intelligence in Australia during the war figured Huk strength at 10,000 men and 3,000 rifles.[12] Other estimates run higher or lower, depending mostly on how "reserves" are defined and counted. There is similar uncertainty about how many casualties they inflicted on the Japanese.[13] But whether the Huks killed 30,000 Japanese or only 5,000, the state of our relations with them is indicated by their common designation of us as "USAFFE robbers," and by various incidents. A typical one occurred once when Bob Lapham decided to make an earnest attempt to effect some kind of working agreement with the Huks against the common enemy. He sent his executive officer, Maj. Harry McKenzie, and his adjutant, Lt. Jeremías Serafica, to arrange a meeting with the Huk leaders. Memories vary about whether Harry rashly charged some Huks, or the Huks set an ambush. Whichever happened, McKenzie was shot in the chest. As he lay on the ground with blood spurting from his wound with each heartbeat, the boy who had shot him moved his rifle to finish him off, then lowered it slowly and remarked, "I'm sorry, sir. I fought on Bataan just as you did," and walked away.

McKenzie was triply lucky. The bullet did not hit a vital organ, he happened to get medical attention quickly, and the wound did not become infected. So he lived, but he never forgot or forgave. From that time forward open war blazed between the Huks and Lapham's guerrillas. Whether meetings with Huks were accidental or were arranged with Huk prisoners, they commonly ended in gunfire. Afterward stories circulated that whenever McKenzie engaged captured Huks, or suspected Huks, in conversation, he did so seated at a table with a loaded and cocked .45 in his hand, the barrel resting on the table top in front of him and pointed at the person being addressed. It usually went off before the interrogation was completed. Like so many colorful wartime tales, though, the accuracy of this one is highly questionable. Bob Lapham, who was in virtual daily contact with McKenzie, says he cannot recall any Huk ever getting close to McKenzie again.[14]

With Huks and USAFFE guerrillas perpetually at swords' points the Japanese never tried to interfere in disputes between us. Why should they? Every bullet we fired at each other was one fewer fired at them.

Another organization that complicated our lives to some degree was the Philippine Constabulary, though our relations with its members were always far more amicable than with the Huks. In fact, we were eventually able to effect an informal working alliance with the Constabulary after all efforts to cooperate with the Huks had failed. This development was due to our increasing ability to vex the Japanese, and their increasing frustration at being unable to do much about it.

Of course, it was always possible for the Japanese to raise as many as a thousand troops and chase us back into the mountains and jungle, but by the end of 1943 we had become too numerous and well organized to be routed by small enemy patrols, and it was simply not practical for our foes to employ great numbers of men to perpetually comb the countryside in pursuit of isolated handfuls of guerrillas, most of whom, if they could get out of sight for a brief time, would make their next public appearances in fields behind plows and carabao, indistinguishable from several million other Filipino peasants. From a Japanese standpoint, attempting to deal with guerrillas was always frustrating, rather like a cow switching her tail to drive off flies.

In an effort to deal with us guerrillas, who were passing from nuisance to menace, the Japanese organized a new Philippine Constabulary. This body should not be confused with the old prewar Constabulary which, along with the Philippine army and Philippine Scouts, had been closely linked to the American army. The new Constabulary was composed, in part, of civilian volunteers and of men who simply needed jobs to feed their families. The core of it, though, consisted of Filipino prisoners taken after the fall of Bataan and Corregidor. These men were gradually released by the Japanese with the proviso that they join the new Constabulary. Nominally, they were then to perform ordinary police duties. Actually, the Japanese planned to train them to become a new army to help defend the Philippines against a possible future American attack. In this role they would absorb some casualties that would otherwise be Japanese; and their presence would enable the Japanese to pose more convincingly as friendly neighbors helping allies defend their homeland against attack. The commander of the new Constabulary was Gen. Guillermo Francisco, a Filipino officer who had served on Bataan and whom the Japanese put through a de-Americanization program before his "promotion."[15]

Though the new Philippine Constabulary eventually came to comprise thirty thousand men, the Japanese never knew quite what to do with their creation. If the Constabulary was to be effective, its members had to be well armed, fed, and paid. Yet the Japanese knew that, at bottom, neither these Filipino "volunteers" nor their commanding officer were trustworthy, so they were loath to arm them effectively.

The result was a series of sad compromises, as compromises so often are. Constabulary morale was always low because the men had been humiliated and oppressed by their conquerors, who now watched them closely in the bargain. To Filipino civilians they looked like puppets at best and traitors at worst. Their masters gave them rifles of all types captured from U.S. forces, and special clothing. Thus armed and supervised, they were supposed to maintain domestic peace and order. Some of them were rough on civilians—abusing people, profiteering, and extorting bribes. With some who acted thus the reason was probably low salary, with others a natural response to the tough training they had received from the Japanese, with still others the common phenomenon of power going easily to one's head. Whenever Constabularymen did anything unpopular, they excused themselves on the ground that they had no choice but to follow Japanese orders.[16] A majority of them, though, just went through the motions of performing their duties, especially when looking for guerrillas. They seldom discovered any of the latter; and if they did, usually managed to do little about it. In many sectors there were tacit understandings that the Constabulary would go easy on Filipino civilians and would not take patrols into areas dominated by guerrillas, in return for which guerrillas would not ambush Constabulary troops. If operations against irregulars did take place in the mountains, the Constabulary forces invariably returned severely depleted, from casualties incurred during guerrilla ambushes, their leaders said, but in truth from extensive defections to the guerrillas. On our side, we had no desire to destroy the Constabulary and see them replaced by regular Japanese troops. On their side, as Chick Parsons predicted in a formal report to General Willoughby as early as June 1943,[17] and as the actions of the Constabularymen in the last months of the war proved, about three-quarters of them were just biding their time until the day it would become safe to desert either to guerrillas or to an invading American army. Throughout the war some of the best American intelligence operatives were camouflaged as Constabularymen.

Once it became apparent to us that the Huks would be implacable enemies, we decided to try cooperation with the Constabulary instead, specifically to see if they would allow us to slip some guerrillas into their ranks in order to combat the Huks more effectively. Contact was made with the commander of the Constabulary for Tarlac province, and a secret rendezvous was arranged. Some of our men brought the commander and one of his lieutenants to the prearranged side by a circuitous route designed to avoid detection by the Japanese. The conference was held in an ordinary Philippine house on stilts. Though this *bahay* was bigger than most, the room was packed with guerrilla observers. Those of us who were to be directly involved in the negotiations were jammed together around a table like the proverbial sardines.

In substance, the conference proved uneventful. After some discussion an agreement was reached with the Constabulary representatives, we shook hands all around, and the Constabularymen were led away first so the direction of our departure would remain unknown to them.

The fallout from the meeting was another matter, one that causes me to chuckle to this day. Before the conference began, some inspired and generous soul had managed to find some good American whiskey and had passed it around. Most of us had taken a couple of drinks, which may or may not have caused Al and me to get into a sufficiently loud argument that Filipinos grabbed both of us to prevent what they feared would be a fight. A short while later Al had to relieve himself. The house was so jammed he couldn't get downstairs, so he did the simplest thing: went to a back bedroom that had an open window. Unfortunately, he lost his balance and pitched head first out the window to the ground eight feet below, landing with a thump heard plainly by everyone inside.

Luckily, the fall only knocked the wind out of Al, so, soon after, he and I climbed into a wooden-wheeled cart for the return trip to our current hideaway. The cart was pulled by a carabao who had the misfortune also to be ridden by the biggest Filipino I have ever seen. Somebody had thrown an old mattress on the bed of the cart, and Hendrickson and I sat on it opposite each other. We had gone only a short distance when Al shouted at the driver, "Tigil!" (stop). Then he revived the argument with me that had almost brought us to blows at the conference, asking me if I didn't really think he had been right after all. I replied "Hell, no!" and told the driver to go on. We rode in silence for a few hundred yards; then Al shouted "Tigil!" again and took up the argument once more. After this had happened several times, I finally told him I would never agree with him and that if we didn't put an end to the stopping and starting we would get caught by daylight, which would be distinctly hazardous to our health.

The last part of the trip was on horseback. It proved as bizarre as the cart ride. A Philippine horse, called a *kabayo*, is small, a little larger than a Shetland pony. A tall man's feet will almost drag on the ground when he rides one. Al got aboard an unlucky little horse and promptly put it into a brisk gallop, his feet nearly trailing in the dirt. I almost fell off my own horse from laughing. When we arrived at our hideout, Al reined in his *kabayo* so sharply that the animal reared on its hind legs, causing him to slide off its back. For the second time that night he hit the ground with a resounding thud. I couldn't resist shouting, "Heigh Ho, Silver!" Al growled something unintelligible and stalked off. Now, forty years later, he says he cannot remember anything about the whole evening save arguing with me in the cart.

The moral must be that all of us have selective memories about past foibles, since I have no recollection of a comparable incident that Hendrickson swears happened. As he tells it, once I had tooth troubles and he took me to a dentist who turned out to be a good-looking young Filipina with a hand drill. While she ground away on my molars, I allegedly developed a more-than-professional interest in her. I can't even imagine my thoughts turning to romance with a dentist's drill in my mouth.

As for appearance, on the night of Al's memorable ride on the overloaded little horse I must have looked as ludicrous as he did, for I was then in the habit of wearing a .45 on my right hip, a .38 backwards on my left hip, and a Garand M-1 rifle slung across my back, an arrangement that permitted me to draw a gun from any possible position. This elaborate regalia was further embellished by two bandoliers crisscrossing my chest and fastened to a webbed belt, all of which together sometimes contained as many as 120 rounds of 30-caliber and 50 rounds of sidearm ammunition. The whole ensemble was topped by a hat fashioned from half a gourd. Any outsider who could have seen Al and me that night, not to speak of the towering Filipino on the carabao, would have sworn we were Mexican revolutionaries in some Hollywood movie.

Al eventually got even with me for laughing at him and quarrelling with him, though it was after the war and in circumstances that seem funny now. Once when he was in a tavern in my native St. Louis, Al got into a noisy argument about General MacArthur. Some officious soul called the police. When they arrived, Al persuaded them to let him go by telling them he was "Ray Hunt, a local war hero."

8

Guerrilla Life

A FEW AMERICANS WHO MANAGED TO MAKE IT BY BOAT from the Philippines to Australia in 1942 described Philippine guerrillas they had known as ragged, starved, almost defenseless, and reduced to something close to banditry just to stay alive.[1] Donald Blackburn paints a vivid picture of Robert Arnold, long missing and presumed dead, when he walked into Blackburn's headquarters in north Luzon in the spring of 1943. Arnold was covered with tropical ulcers, many of them infected and filled with pus. Embittered against all guerrilla organizations, even the Volckmann-Blackburn unit to which he had just come, because he thought them ineffectual, Arnold said he had lived for the past year on a diet of rats and corn, and that he knew other guerrillas who were cannibals as well as bandits. Blackburn adds that after a week or so of plentiful food, a good bed, and some medical treatment Arnold changed his mind, came to appreciate the abilities of his hosts, and even wanted to join their organization.[2] Yay Panlilio says that some men in Marking's guerrillas succumbed to a combination of tension and boredom and began to do such mad things as play Russian roulette, at which several shot themselves.[3] She adds that the combination of privation, danger, and quarrelling among leaders eroded morale seriously. Men grumbled sourly that they were wasting their lives, that the Japanese harmed the Filipino people far more than they (the guerrillas) were able to harm the Japanese, and that the Americans would never come back. Many simply could not endure it, she said; they despaired and went back to the towns.[4]

That such conditions existed in some other irregular outfits, I have no doubt, and we had our share of such problems, too, perhaps the worst being gut-wrenching decisions that had to be made about the disposition of prisoners, real or suspected spies, and disobedient subordinates—as will be related in bloody detail later in this narrative. Every one of us also knew that each day might be his last. Even so, neither Al Hendrickson and I together, nor either of us separately, ever had any morale problems of the magnitude described by others.

We moved around a lot, seldom staying in one place for more than a week. Contrary to what some might assume, though, these sojourns did not consist of marching up and down main roads seeking pitched battles with the Japanese. Most of our days were humdrum, spent in simple, obvious ways: hiding, sleeping, gathering and evaluating information, planning, nursing each other, rustling food, recruiting new followers, looking for opportunities to accumulate arms, and occasionally circulating propaganda or committing some act of sabotage.[5] Of such activities much the most important was collecting intelligence. Merely ambushing half a dozen Japanese now and then could not have much effect on the outcome of the war.

Still, as time passed it became increasingly evident that we were discommoding our foes. As early as March 19, 1943, Radio Tokyo had made reference to Philippine guerrilla activity, an indication that the Japanese already regarded it as a problem of some consequence. By the end of 1943 Japanese soldiers no longer wandered about alone. Now every Japanese outpost contained at least four men, and they dug trenches under the buildings in which they lived. One night we stopped close to a Nipponese outpost and listened to those inside praying to their emperor to bolster their spirits. Clearly life was a lot less agreeable for them than it had been.

Meanwhile the villagers who hid us went about their customary activities as their ancestors had done for generations. The women squatted on the banks of streams and beat the dirt out of family clothing with wooden paddles, in the process often chewing betel nut or indulging in the strange practice of smoking cigarettes with the lighted ends inside their mouths. Now and then they would take a break and undertake a collective assault on the head lice that are commonplace in the Philippines. They would sit in a line, one behind the other like a row of monkeys, and each would pick the lice and nits from the head of the woman in front of her. I never did figure out how the last one in line was accommodated. It seemed to me that a circle would have been a more logical configuration.

During the rainy season sudden fierce downpours were common, but nobody seemed to mind, or even notice it much. The men, usually barefooted, dressed in shorts and, armed with bolos in wooden scabbards attached to their belts, went about their business as usual. Women would pack whatever they had to sell and walk off to market quite as readily during a cloudburst as on a sunny day. Funerals were frequent, rain or shine, and were always joyous occasions; never sad. Wine and sweet foods would be shared, as at a party. When the deceased was being taken to his final resting place, his cortege was always preceded by a brass band if anyone could find or assemble one.

Still, we lived under constant strain because we never knew when the Japanese might spring a surprise attack and capture us. The danger seemed especially great at night. I never reached the point where I could take it all in stride, and I don't think Al Hendrickson did either. It seemed that every Filipino farmer had at least two dogs and that every one of them for miles around would bark at the slightest provocation. We all became light sleepers; and Al, who had exceptionally keen hearing, would awaken almost every night, nudge me, and ask me if I had heard "that"—whether "that" happened to be the millionth dog barking, the sound of a truck on a distant road, or something else. I would routinely remind him that we had three rings of guards all around us and tell him to go back to sleep; but I was so edgy that I seldom followed my own advice. Scores of times I got out of bed and made a nocturnal tour of the guards to make sure all of them were awake and alert.

Months later when I was in Pangasinan province, I established a simple and seemingly foolproof method of recognizing friends and foiling enemies in the dark. A guard, when challenging someone, would say, "Halt!" and then follow up with a number, such as "two." The person challenged would then reply with some other number, "three," "four," or whatever number comprised the code for that night. This safeguarded us against Japanese, who were adept at repeating English words flung at them as challenges but would have no way of knowing what different word or number was expected on a given occasion. Al preferred a different but comparably simple system: using words from Filipino dialects, which very few Japanese knew, as passwords.

Whatever the system, a person never felt entirely safe; never sure that something unforeseen would not happen. An episode with a particularly bloody ending has always stuck in my memory. It took place near San Nicolas in eastern Pangasinan. Here two Americans, one of them bearing the memorable name of Jewel French, were being protected, they supposed, by a Filipino bodyguard. One night he picked up an automatic rifle, riddled them as they slept, kicked their bodies into the Agno River, and went over to the Japanese. The guerrillas never captured the man, but they settled accounts with him nonetheless. A few weeks later he was with a small company of Japanese who fell into an ambush.[6]

Many of our persistent difficulties with our bands of irregulars were rooted in the elementary fact that our control over them was only tenuous. To be sure, all our men recognized Al and myself as their leaders and they would obey us when we were with them, but at any given time only a few of them would be armed and actually with us. Routine guerrilla operations, moreover, were usually carried out by underlings to whom we gave only general directions. Often subordinates would embark on enterprises of their own choosing without bothering to notify superiors. Likewise, the superiors did not always *want* to know everything their lieutenants were doing.

Many times, too, operations were undertaken not for any real military purpose but simply to avenge atrocities against civilians. Panlilio records that on one occasion Marking became so enraged at some particularly fiendish Japanese cruelty that he marched their whole outfit over the Sierra Madre Mountains to fight the Japanese, saying that he was determined to kill as many of the enemy as he could even if the whole Filipino nation perished in the process. Fortunately, his rage subsided before he was able to do anything suicidal.[7]

I have read that Filipinos, whether guerrillas or ordinary civilians, were often reluctant to fight. Maybe they were in some places or at some times, but my experience with them was quite the reverse. Many times individual Filipino civilians killed Japanese on their own, without reference to guerrillas at all. Many a Filipino, guerrilla or otherwise, came to me with tears in his eyes begging for a gun so he could kill a Japanese who had committed atrocities against his family. Much as I sympathized with such people, and great as my delight would have been to accommodate them, my problem was always to quiet them down and persuade them that it was essential to avoid trouble that would activate the enemy's military police, who might then catch me and inflict some hideous mass punishment on the helpless Filipino civilians who had harbored me. But sometimes we attacked Japanese patrols or small installations for no reason other than to keep up the morale of our men, to allow them to let off steam.[8]

Many a raid, too, was undertaken mostly to get supplies. The Japanese occupation forces and their creation, the new Philippine Costabulary, were outfitted heavily with what had been taken from Americans after the fall of Bataan and Corregidor. Guerrillas would then raid Japanese installations, kill the defenders, and take back the arms, ammunition, food, gas masks, shoes, money, and wrist watches sequestered earlier by their foes. Japanese corpses were even fished up from rivers to get such commodities. How precarious life often was for everyone in the wartime Philippines can be indicated by a number of disparate incidents, some funny, some grim, some both. One night Al Hendrickson and I were on the move when we came to a broad, deep ditch bridged by a single large bamboo pole with a frail hand rail attached. As mentioned earlier, Al had exceptional hearing. He tested the bamboo bridge and jumped back, asking me if I had heard it crack. I said I hadn't, and assured him that it was strong enough to bear an elephant. Al was still skeptical, but at my urging he started to cross it. He edged out cautiously to the middle when, with a crack like a pistol shot, the bamboo broke. Al plummeted into the water several feet below. Fortunately, the water wasn't deep, but the mud beneath it was both deep and stinking. As Al strugged to climb out of the mess, he let loose a torrent of profanity. Most of it was directed at me for having urged him on in the first place, and now for laughing at his predicament. He was doubly infuriated when I refused to walk close to him because of the stench of the mud.

Al was still simmering from this mishap when we came to an exceptionally large ricefield. Clomping around the near edge of the paddy was an old man carrying a lamp that consisted of a lighted wick in a Vaseline jar full of coconut oil. He said he was trying to catch frogs. Al, who knew the local dialect, directed him to lead us along the dikes to our destination across the field. Since the dikes in and around this ricefield went in every direction, it was hardly surprising that after much walking in complete darkness we found ourselves back at our starting place. Nevertheless, we were dismayed; and Al was still burning from having fallen into the stinking mud earlier. Now he

stormed at the old Filipino as though he would explode.
He drew his .45 and cursed the old man in English until
his vocabulary was exhausted. Then he repeated the cuss-
ing in Finnish, then in Spanish, then in the old man's
dialect, and finished by telling the frog hunter he was going to be shot because he was a Japanese spy. I'm sure the
poor fellow expected to be killed before Al cooled off and
we moved on.

As if we didn't have enough routine troubles, the Huks
began to undertake nuisance raids against us late in 1943.
In an effort to put an end to this, Hendrickson made arrangements for one more conference with Huk leaders,
this time in a small village near La Paz in Tarlac province.
Of course, I can see now, four decades later, that it was
always useless to try to make common cause with the Huks
about anything since we, quite as much as the Japanese,
were obstacles to their ultimate aims, but if we still tried
to deal fruitfully with communists periodically it can at
least be pleaded that we were no more gullible than Allied
governments who strove to treat amicably with the USSR
in the same years.

To get to the meeting place we first had to ride in a
calesa along a well-travelled road. Then we transferred to
a railroad handcar propelled by a long pole, and then to
horses. We finished the trip on foot. This was typical of
the precautions necessary when moving in no man's land
where everyone was suspect. We knew well enough the
risk we were taking in meeting the Huks on their home
ground, and when we finally arrived I was decidedly un-
easy. About Al's state of mind I am less certain. He told
me afterward that he knew that the Huk leader had stashed
a couple of his men in a shack behind us where they could
shoot us if they wished, adding that he had countered this
maneuver by posting a BAR (Browning Automatic Rifle)
man and a rifleman of ours behind *them*. Apparently he
found this setup reassuring since he spoke to the Huks
bluntly; though once, during a breather, he remarked to
me half-ruefully that he wondered if we would get out of
the place alive. Maybe the Huks did not mind Al's hard

words unduly or simply did not have orders to kill us; anyway, they let us depart unmolested. The effort itself was a waste of time, as we should have expected after they had shot Harry McKenzie.

Proverbially, we had escaped the frying pan only to fall into the fire. As soon as we got back to our area, we found that the Japanese army and military police had decided to combine and make an effort to capture as many guerrillas as possible, Al and me in particular. To this end they devised a new tactic: to send a handful of soldiers, for some reason called "snipers," to slip up to individual Filipino houses at night, where they would listen to conversations. On the basis of whatever information they gleaned, the Japanese would then undertake guerrilla-type countermeasures. This development produced panic not only among civilians but among some of our own men as well.

Since the new Japanese stratagem was reported to involve two thousand men, Al and I decided it was time to depart. We left Tarlac and moved off northward into Pangasinan province. Here we settled for a short time near the town of Bayambang on the Agno River in an area known locally as the "fishponds" because fish were raised there commercially. There was so much water everywhere that we had to move at night by boat, as though we were in Venice. One night we passed through a narrow canal where fish nets had to be removed so we could get by. In the process the fish became so excited they leaped out of the water in all directions, some of them into our boat. The boats themselves were distressingly primitive: mere hollowed logs so overloaded with men and equipment that when I gripped the sides of mine my fingers were in the water. Needless to say, nobody made any unnecessary movements. I was too scared even to ask the depth of the water.

One evening we stopped at a large hacienda. Here were beds with mattresses, a luxury we had not seen for two years. Unhappily, our anticipated joy in getting to sleep in a real bed proved illusory. After trying it a few hours we awoke with our bodies sore from the unaccustomed softness and spent the rest of the night on the floor.

Unquestionably, the best thing that happened to me at this stage of the war, the spring of 1944, was that I selected a new bodyguard, Gregorio S. Agaton. Greg was young, clean-cut, alert, fearless and absolutely loyal. He saved my life several times, the first time not long after he joined me. The occasion arose amid resolution of a persistent problem that has vexed genuine guerrillas for generations: how to deal with "armies" that profess to be guerrillas but are actually mere gangs of bandits.[9]

Shortly before we fled north into Pangasinan, reports began to come in from distressed people in western Tarlac that a certain Filipino freebooter there was trying to organize a "guerrilla" force of this sort and to exact contributions from civilians. Since nobody in his outfit was known to have fired a shot at a Japanese and since he had made no contact with our headquarters, it was hard to imagine anything constructive coming from his operations. So we sent out an arrest order for him. Three days later he was delivered to us. According to reports, he had made a number of statements highly critical of our organization, so we exercised utmost caution when he was called before us. Greg and Little Joe, Al's bodyguard, and several more of our men trailed the arrested man closely as he walked into our room. The fellow was wearing a native shirt that hung loosely outside his trousers. During our first verbal exchange he made a sudden motion with his right hand toward his right hip pocket. Al and I immediately drew our .45s. He returned his hand to the front. We then told him he was about to die.

Several of our own men at once interceded for the suspect, saying that he now realized how things stood and would not do anything contrary to our wishes. The suspect added his own profuse assurances that this was indeed the case. So, after a warning, we let him go. After he had departed, I noticed Greg and some of our boys grouped together examining something. I stepped closer to see what it was. It was a strange looking .38-caliber revolver. I asked Greg where it had come from. He said he had pulled it from the back of the belt of the man we had just released, precisely at the time when Al and I drew our .45s. Thus, we had not misinterpreted his intention at all, and had it not been for Greg's alertness one or both of us might have died right then.

The recurrence of episodes like this had much to do with the reluctance of guerrillas to take prisoners and to their general tendency to shoot first and ask questions afterward. They also intensified the constant tensions of guerrilla life. Vernon Fassoth recalls once being hidden in a gloomy, stinking jungle, famished, frightened, utterly spent, and enmeshed in clinging vines. Suddenly he could endure it no longer. Overwhelmed with rage and frustration, he seized his .45 and aimlessly defied fate by shooting wildly at the vines even though he knew the Japanese might hear the shots. Vernon also once saw a big, brawny man gradually sink into exhaustion from carrying a load too heavy for his smaller buddies. After hours of backbreaking toil the giant suddenly stopped and hurled the hated bundle into a rice paddy even though it contained food and other commodities sorely needed by his whole party.[10]

I sometimes responded to similar pressures by similar recklessness, though more often in a way that reflected elation or fatalism than frustration or depression. Al said he liked me because I was usually good-natured, talkative, and ready for anything, where many of the American guerrillas were grim and humorless. In fact, Filipinos who knew us looked upon both Al and me as something like playboys since we would sometimes go to dances in rural barrios and dance with the local girls. I would jitterbug, Al would dance an Irish jig, and his girlfriend Lee would sing, all to the delight of the local people. We knew the risks involved, but I, at least, simply did not care because I did not expect to live through the war anyway.

Once I did something that a psychiatrist would probably ascribe to temporary insanity. It was December 1943, and we appeared to be well settled in Eastern Pangasinan. December 11 was my twenty-fourth birthday. For the occasion we located a cameraman with good equipment and had him take some pictures of our headquarters staff. I really knew better than to do this, and if one of my subordinates had done it I would have punished him. Why I did it I cannot explain convincingly even to myself. Anyway, I did take the precaution of having only one print made of each picture, and had it delivered to me. The negatives were hidden by the photographer. It soon became evident that Murphy's Law applied in the Philippines just as it does everywhere else. We heard that the photographer had been picked up by the Japanese. We sweated blood. Everyone in the picture would be wanted immediately. Most of those concerned rushed into hiding. I ordered a search made at once for the negatives. Luckily they were found, hidden under the grass roof of a house.

Another instance involved defective judgment, too, but at least the blunder was less egregious. This time we were holed up in a village near Bayambang in southern Pangasinan in December 1943, when a Filipino from a neighboring barrio came to us one day and said he had a radio receiver powered by an automobile battery. He asked us if we wanted to hear a news broadcast. He assured us that he did not mean Tokyo Rose, the notorious Japanese propagandist, but an American broadcast. Since we hadn't heard a radio report in two years, we assented. Then came the bad news. The receiver was on the opposite side of a town occupied by the enemy. Probably we would have been discreet and stayed where we were, had our informant not added that the town contained an ice plant where we could get ice cream, something we had not enjoyed since the war started. That clinched it. We followed our man, crossed a river in a canoe, then climbed into a *calesa* for a ride around the outskirts of the town. As we rolled along, our guide informed us casually that we would soon have to pass a Japanese sentry. For a moment I was paralyzed with fear, and I would guess that Al was too, but neither of us wanted to lose face in front of the other so we rolled down the buggy's side curtains, pulled out our

.45s, and laid them across our laps. For insurance I prayed that we would not be challenged. If we were, the first thing that would happen would be that we would leave a dead Japanese soldier lying in the road, but of course the gunfire would be followed by an alarm and there was no obvious place for us to try to escape. Luckily for all concerned, we rolled serenely past the guard, who gave us a perfunctory wave.

The radio was hidden in a haystack near a large mango tree, which our guide climbed to secure the antenna. We sat down to listen to the news and music. I particularly recall hearing Bing Crosby sing, of all songs for our locale, "White Christmas." No doubt this would have buoyed up the spirits of many, but it had the opposite effect on Al and me. For me every Christmas since 1939 had seemed more depressing than the last. To hear this song brought back memories of my father, mother, sisters, and friends back home, whom I had trained myself for many months *not* to think about. I now thought of how good wheat bread and ice cream would taste; of what a pleasure it would be to smoke a Camel instead of uncured Philippine tobacco cut into strips and rolled into cigars so strong that for months I got a cheap drunk every time I smoked one. It was all a dismal reminder of how lonely, forlorn, and precarious our present existence was. Now, if there is one thing a guerrilla must battle constantly it is depression and despair.[11] This experience was not helpful.

Sometimes combatting depression took strange forms. I recall once when Hendrickson was feeling particularly down that I tried to cheer him up by telling him that I did not expect to survive the war either but that we ought to die fighting, shot in the front, not shot in the back while running away or beheaded by the Japanese in some prison. He never told me whether he found this rumination consoling. Be that as it may, after we had listened to the radio we rode back unmolested past the same guard. Though he never knew it, his inattention to duty saved his life.

Men and women who lived in Japanese prison camps have related much more about the depression attending

150

such an existence than I will ever know. Still, it was apparent to me how depressed many prisoners became during the war. For instance, some of the American prisoners at Cabanatuan, which was not far from where we operated, were assigned to drive trucks to nearby towns to secure vegetables and rice to feed those in the camp. Many times I had individual guerrillas approach these drivers and urge them to escape. They always got the same reply: "Not now, Joe, maybe later." It surely was not that they had no desire to escape, since all prison camp literature indicates that most prisoners think about escape a great deal. I eventually learned, too, that the prisoners in Cabanatuan knew guerrillas were active in the vicinity; indeed, that they sometimes heard gun battles between guerrillas and Japanese, and saw dead Japanese soldiers being hauled back to the camp in trucks. The truth seems to be that there is a vast gulf between thinking idly about escape, or even planning an escape, and actually trying to get away, especially when one is weak from disease and undernourishment, and when he knows that if he is captured not only will he be killed but that quite possibly as many as ten of his fellow prisoners will also be killed in reprisal. I have often wondered how many of the drivers whom our men tried unsuccessfully to lure away survived the war. Some died in the camps themselves; others were killed inadvertently by American bombs and submarine torpedoes when the Japanese tried to transfer them in unmarked ships to Japan; still others died in Japan itself.

Soon after our narrow escape when listening to the clandestine radio, Japanese activity in the area increased, so Al and I vacated the environs of Bayambang and headed off northeastward across Pangasinan. As we travelled, we met several heavily armed units belonging to Lapham's command. Each escorted us to the next one within the area. Along the way I traded my old M-1 rifle for another and got myself into a predicament which illustrates some of the constant problems we had with weapons. Whenever possible, we tested rifles before having to depend on them in combat. Greg took this new one into the usual underground covered pit and fired it. The ejector tore away part of the shell rim, leaving the shell casing in the chamber. I looked at the gun and discovered that the chamber was so badly pitted that I would have to use a ramrod every time I fired the piece in order to knock out the old casing. I didn't have a ramrod, and several hours of laborious filing to try to smooth the chamber proved fruitless.

Eventually the problem was solved in a way not prescribed in any manual. A few days later we met a Filipino Constabularyman who had been armed by the Japanese with an M-1. I proposed to him that we trade rifles, or parts of them. He said he couldn't because his Japanese masters would notice the different serial number. I wasn't worried about *his* problems, so I offered him an alternative: trade rifles or join our guerrillas on the spot. He traded.

One morning when we had proceeded some thirty or forty miles northeastward from Bayambang into the vicinity of San Manuel in eastern Pangasinan, we ran into a nest of Japanese. We sighted some to the north across a ricefield and so turned south to a village where we promptly encountered more. Runners told us there were still more to the west, so we did the only thing possible: we moved east until we reached the Agno River, a large stream that flows out of the central Luzon mountains southwestward across Pangasinan and then turns north and runs into Lingayen Gulf. Here our prospects looked dark indeed: surrounded on three sides by the enemy and with the far side of the river an unknown quantity. For all we knew, the Japanese might have set an ambush there. No matter. To cross was our only chance.

Many times before this Al and I had crossed streams by a means that will surely seem odd to Americans: we had been "bobbed" over by Filipinos. The method was simplicity itself. Though we were bigger than Filipinos, each of us would climb onto the back of one, the man would leap into the stream, hit bottom, leap upward, gulp in air when his head bobbed out of the water, spring off the bottom again, and so on. Each motion carried "bobber" and rider farther downstream, but both gradually got across.

This time no such luxurious mode of transit was available to us, for the rainy season had arrived and the Agno had become a raging torrent. Some Filipino civilians saved the day by bringing us some large gourds wrapped with vines. We put our sidearms and ammunition inside, tied our rifles across the top, grasped the vines with one hand, and paddled energetically with the other. Everyone got across satisfactorily save a Filipino spy whom we had unwisely kept with us. As soon as he got into the water, he swam downstream as fast as possible, returned to the same side where we had started, and took off across the countryside. We didn't dare shoot at him because the noise would alert the Japanese, who were too close to us already. Now he was free again; free, as we subsequently learned, to go back to his home, a place fortified with a stone wall topped with broken glass and surrounded by floodlights.

Luckily for us, the Japanese disliked big, fast streams, perhaps this one especially since on earlier occasions several of them had drowned in the Agno. Now they came up to the river, looked over the situation, and decided to camp on the shore opposite us. This gave us a sorely needed breather—and a chance to get ahead of them once more. The respite was brief. Soon they made their way across, picked up our trail, and pursued us relentlessly. For five days and nights Al and I and about fifty guerrillas moved steadily eastward across southern Pangasinan with the enemy never more than a village behind us and sometimes separated from us only by a ricefield.

Still, much as they hated guerrillas, and much as they would have exulted to use all of us for bayonet practice, the Japanese were a calculating lot. If they were in unfamiliar territory, or knew local irregulars had them outnumbered, they usually discovered compelling reasons to stay in their encampments. In our case, they did not dare to close with us, both because we were more numerous and because they would have had to advance toward us across open fields in daylight while we were protected by groves of trees around villages. So they spent their days torturing civilians and pondering what to try when night fell.

It has been observed many times that if habitually destitute people happen to get a little unexpected money, often they will not do the "sensible" thing and purchase necessities with it but will instead spend it "foolishly" on some luxury—at least in the opinion of people who are not destitute. Whatever quirk of human psychology is responsible for such conduct cropped up among us on the fifth day of our flight from our pursuers. We were in a village close to the mountains east of the town of Umingan, collecting provisions. Next day we were going up into the foothills. The Japanese were one village away, making their own preparations to follow us. In these circumstances, when one would suppose that every one of us would have been serious and vigilant in the highest degree, Al bet me that Lee could field-strip an M-1 as fast as I could. Like a hungry bass who has heard a frog jump into the water, I rose to the bait and bet she couldn't beat me even if I was blindfolded. Anyone could guess what happened next. Just as we got our rifles dismantled, the enemy began to advance toward us. Al shoved Lee aside, I tore off my blindfold, and he and I began feverishly to reassemble the rifles. Alas! One part became interchanged and neither gun would work! So we had to tear them apart and put them back together again since by now both of us had long since come to subscribe to what the infantryman had told me during the Battle of the Points, that a soldier must become wedded to his rifle.

A tense competition in self-control between ourselves and the Japanese followed. We moved out of the east side of the village and down a creek bed while the enemy poured into the village from the west side. Not a shot was fired; on the Japanese side, presumably, because they were not looking for a gun battle in which we would be hidden and they would be in the open; on our side because we did not want to give our foes an extra pretext to maltreat the village people who had helped us. Besides, we hoped next day to be in a place where we would have all the advantages in a battle and there would be no civilians about to complicate matters.

That night we slipped into a farmhouse where the natives from the last village had been preparing rice for us, but almost immediately had to move on when the enemy continued to advance. With the heartening bravery I witnessed so many times in the Philippines, the villagers, even with our common enemy in their midst, tried to deliver the food to us, in the dark, in our new location. Some Japanese snipers, uncharacteristically moving about after dark, jumped them and one villager was bayoneted. The others escaped, though without the food, and ran to our new hideout to warn us.

There followed a scramble that might have been lifted from an old Abbott and Costello movie. Both Al and I were asleep in a pitch-dark room. He ordinarily took off his pants when retiring, and had done so now. I habitually slept in my clothing but had unbuckled my sidearms and had leaned my rifle against the wall. When we got the alarm, both Al and I immediately appreciated the urgency of the situation, but we were still half-asleep when we sprang into action. I rushed to the wall to get my rifle but couldn't find it because I had gone to the wrong wall. I whispered, "Where is my rifle?" then finally found it, and only afterward remembered that I also had to find my sidearms and put them on. Al, equally confused, stormed around in the dark shouting, "Where the hell are my pants?"

We half-climbed, half-fell out of the house down a bamboo ladder, exchanged quick whispers with the men who had alerted us, and prepared to move out when Al complained that his pants, which he had finally located, didn't feel right. There was a good reason: he had put them on backwards. Despite our hazardous circumstances, I couldn't help laughing, adding that now the Japs would shoot him in the back for sure. Al responded profanely, but we got out of there so fast he didn't bother to change his reversed trousers.

We spent the rest of the night up in the foothills, but after surveying the countryside with binoculars the next morning we decided to move back down into the flatlands. At once we ran headlong into the enemy. All day long we skirmished with the Japanese but could gain no advantage. By evening we had to decide what to do next.

During the American Revolution, 165 years before, Francis Marion, the "Swamp Fox," would have his men scatter in every direction after an engagement, thereby making enemy pursuit impossible, following which they would eventually meet at some prearranged place.[12] Though I knew nothing about Marion's tactics at that time, we had long used a similar stratagem. When we were in some danger and felt compelled to break up, we would select three possible meeting places, number them in order of their attractiveness, and then try to meet at one of them. Nearly always at least one place would be available and reasonably safe. This time the Japanese probably expected us to go back into the foothills again after dark, but instead we slipped through their lines back into the central rice plains from whence we had come.

We did this for three reasons. The most basic was that we thought the Japanese would not expect it. We were also short of food, and there would be little back in the mountains. Finally, we were worn down physically, and traversing Philippine mountain trails is particularly difficult for Westerners. In most parts of the world mountain roads or trails follow terrain that offers the least resistance; they usually angle upward along mountainsides, frequently by means of switchbacks. Not so in the Philippines. The first time I saw little Igorot tribesmen shoulder heavy loads and lope, not walk, along paths that went straight up mountainsides, I was dumbfounded. Of course, the shortest distance between two points is a straight line, but many Igorots develop enlarged hearts from heeding this axiom of geometry while we Occidentals could not travel rapidly in this way at all. Laboriously we trekked back across

156

Pangasinan, along the way we had come, and went back into Tarlac province. A major change in my fortunes took place soon after.

As noted earlier, most guerrilla existence was an amalgam of danger, privation, and occasional boredom, interspersed with life's ordinary problems and vexations. It also bore another aspect which has heretofore received only passing notice in this narrative. That side was grim, cruel, bloody, and degrading, but given the character and deeds of our enemies, unavoidable.

We Americans are notoriously poor judges of the psychology of other peoples and maladroit in our dealings with them. In the 1940s the Japanese were incomparably worse. Had they treated the Filipinos with kindness and generosity from the first day of the war, many of the latter would have accepted their fate, and many who remained loyal to America initially would have gradually gone over to the conquerors as months of Japanese occupation stretched into years. But the Japanese army was filled with hubris as a result of its quick and easy conquests, and Japanese field commanders usually acted harshly in an effort to scare civilians into cooperation. Japanese military administration, by contrast, gradually began to urge leniency in an effort to win the sympathy of civilians. The latter might have worked had it been instituted in December 1941, but by 1943 there had been far too many crimes committed by Japanese against Filipinos for such a policy to have any chance of success. If military administration secured the release of some prisoners, few evidenced any gratitude. Most soon showed up with guerrillas, or worked with them secretly. As soon as guerrillas became strong enough to provide an alternative focus for the loyalty of Filipino civilians, they put pressure on local officials appointed by the Japanese and neutralized them as Japanese instruments. Moreover, the struggles of guerrillas against the Japanese soon passed into Filipino folklore and strengthened the Pro-American sentiments of most civilians. The Japanese were never able to counter this effectively. As the famous nineteenth-century German chancellor Bismarck used to say, it is the imponderables that are the most important factors in human affairs.[13]

By the time I became a guerrilla, it had been learned long before by hard experience that if the enemy secured rosters of guerrillas they would confiscate the property of these men, and then seize their families and torture them. It is impossible to conceive a more effective tool to use against Filipinos, whose primary allegiance has always been to their families rather than to the nation or state. The Japanese would also do such things as enter a village, herd everyone into the marketplace, then lead out an informer completely cloaked from head to foot save for slits for his eyes, and compel every person in the village to pass before him. When the informer lifted an arm, the individual then passing would be seized by the Japanese and put aside. When all had passed before the collaborator, and those who had aided guerrillas or otherwise shown themselves to be anti-Japanese had been pointed out, the hapless victims were marched to a field, made to dig a pit for their own burial, and then bayoneted to death.[14] Another ploy of the Japanese was to send out their own agents, who would say they were collecting money and supplies for the guerrillas. Those who contributed would then be seized and tortured or killed, or both.[15] If a guerrilla was captured, the Japanese would often torture him to death, stretching out the process over many days. The enemy would sometimes even behead the corpses of guerrillas.[16]

The techniques employed by the Japanese to extract information from prisoners and civilians, or to punish their enemies, were revolting, but some of them must be described if the reader is to comprehend the unbridled ferocity with which guerrillas often responded to such deeds. A favorite Japanese punishment was to "flood" a victim; that is, force water into his stomach until it was three times normal size, then pound the victim with their fists as if he were a punching bag, or jump on him, thus forcing liquids to squirt out all his body orifices.[17] Another favorite treatment of theirs was to tie a victim's thumbs behind his back, toss the rope over a beam, and pull him up until his feet were off the floor. In an effort to get information the Japanese once crucified a Filipino boy for three days and then killed him with a sabre.[18] At the war crimes trial of General Yamashita, a Filipina woman testified that two Japanese soldiers had held her while two others tried to cut out her husband's tongue because he would not give them information, which he did not have, about local authorities.[19]

Simply to punish persons who had crossed them in some way the Japanese did such things as pull out all the victim's teeth, toenails, and fingernails,[20] or chain him to a slab of galvanized iron in the hot sun, to be slowly fried alive.[21] Merely to terrorize civilians the Japanese would sometimes send out a patrol at dawn to gather underneath a Filipino house-on-stilts. Many Filipino families then slept all together on the floor. At a signal the Japanese soldiers would thrust their bayonets violently up through the thin bamboo flooring, impaling men, women, and children indiscriminately, until blood would drip down through the floor onto the assailants. They they would burn down the house.[22]

Ideally, guerrillas should have captured the Japanese responsible for such atrocities and executed them. In practice, this was impossible since the Japanese ordinarily fought to the death rather than surrender, even on those comparatively rare occasions when there was some chance to take prisoners. What was usually done as second best was to ferret out Japanese spies and collaborators among Filipino civilians, and punish *them*.

Now many writers have charged, after the event, that all guerrillas were unreasonably hard on anyone who collaborated with the Japanese.[23] Their point of view is understandable, but many times we had to take drastic action on not much more than suspicion, or simply disband. We had organized guerrilla units in the first place to make life difficult for the Japanese and to collect information for Allied headquarters in Australia. We could not do either one without consistent, widespread, predictable civilian support. We could not get that support unless we made it safe for civilians to cooperate with us. Thus, our foremost immediate problem was always to pursue informers relentlessly and exterminate them. This not only made life safer for civilians sympathetic to us; it also caused fence sitters to gravitate to our side. The way we dealt with spies and suspected spies does not make pleasant reading, nor does it give rise to happy memories even forty years later but, like so much in war, it was the result of excruciating quandaries that armchair moralists never have to face.

There is no question that some guerrillas, both Filipinos and American, exceeded all norms of reason and humanity in their relentless pursuit of informers and subsequent treatment of them. Most Filipinos are mild, peaceful people, but if aroused or enraged they can become vindictive and capable of frightful cruelties. Illif David Richardson relates an instance on Leyte that illustrates the point. Some Filipino guerrillas there caught some of their countrymen collaborating with the Japanese, so they minced their bodies and floated the pieces downstream into Filipino villages. The number of collaborators dropped off sharply.[24] An even more sickening case on the same island involved a luckless ten-year-old Filipino boy whom the Japanese had taught to become a sharpshooter for them. Some guerrillas of the criminal sort caught the poor youngster, smashed his face to a pulp, collected a cup of his blood and tried to force his twelve-year-old sister to drink it, a barbarity that immediately provoked a fight between the American commander of the units and the men involved.[25] I never *saw* atrocities at this depth of depravity and madness, but I saw enough that I don't doubt that such tales are true.

One such case I will never forget because it took place in my own outfit after Hendrickson and I separated. It was one of those many instances in which guerrilla underlings acted on their own and only afterward told their superiors what had taken place. In this instance a spy was bled to death, and each guerrilla in the band that had captured him drank his blood. His heart was then torn from his body and roasted over an open fire, after which each guerrilla ate a bit of it. The whole ghastly business was done in public to impress civilians. Afterwards I asked the officer in charge how it had affected him. He said it made him feel brave. I was sickened, but I could not resurrect the victim, and to have executed the whole guerrilla troop responsible would have demoralized all my men, so I did nothing.

Yay Panlilio, an intelligent woman and seemingly a humane one as well, says she did all she could to insure that Marking's guerrillas killed Japanese and traitors quickly and cleanly because she did not want their men to become sadists. But even she could be provoked beyond endurance. She acknowledges that once in an especially atrocious case she personally killed one of the victims who had murdered a friend of hers and had then violated the corpse.[26] In most guerrilla outfits collaborators were routinely executed, with or without benefit of a trial, usually by beheading, shooting, or being buried alive.[27]

No matter how callous it seems to say this, and since the Vietnam War no matter how unpopular, it comes down to this: we could not allow the Japanese to terrorize civilians with impunity or to employ spies among us without exacting a prompt and proportionate vengeance. Otherwise, no Filipino civilian would dare to aid us. We also had the new Philippine Constabulary to consider. A high proportion of men in it remained loyal to America in their hearts, but others became genuinely converted to the Japanese cause by persuasion, despair, or pay, or some combination of these; and there were many who fell somewhere in between. Those who were pro-American could not openly avow it lest their pro-Japanese colleagues betray them to the enemy. Of course, it was impossible for any outsider to sort them all out accurately, yet we could not disregard the Constabulary, for if the pro-Japanese elements in it were never opposed or molested they would dominate their fellows and make the Constabulary an effective force that would then allow the Japanese to release thousands of their own regular troops for duty elsewhere. As Russell Volckmann once put it, guerrilla life is no place for the tender-minded.[28]

The ideal way to deal with a suspected spy would have been to turn the person over to an ordinary civilian court for a formal trial under American or Philippine law. But there were no such civilian courts where we were, nor any regularly constituted court martial system either. After I became commander of Pangasinan province in the summer of 1944, I did the best I could: I organized a company of military police whose duty it was to apprehend anyone suspected of spying, or of committing murder, rape, robbery, or any other serious crime against a civilian. When a case existed against someone, he was arrested, brought before the officers of this military unit, and tried. It wasn't a trial that would have pleased the American Bar Association, since those who passed judgment were mostly simple men untrained in the law, but it was a step above a kangaroo court.

A worse difficulty has been noted earlier: there were no jails. Thus, no matter what the nature of any serious crime or the care we took to treat the accused as fairly as we could, the accused was either found innocent and released or found guilty and executed. Even if we had had jails, or guerrillas willing to become mere jailers, prisoners would then have had to be fed and clothed, when we sometimes had a hard time feeding and clothing ourselves. Moreover, if a prisoner escaped his only practical course would be to flee to the Japanese for protection. This would mean that the vengeance of the cruel conquerors would then descend on any Filipinos who had helped guerrillas, aided in the capture of the criminal, or guarded him. When weighing the lives of many friendly Filipinos—and their families as well, remember—against the life of one spy, collaborationist, or criminal, real or suspected, normally there could be only one decision. The Mexican revolutionary Pancho Villa once summed up the essence of the matter succinctly. When asked what to do with some prisoners when he lacked food for his own men, or any extra men to guard prisoners, he is supposed to have replied, "Let's shoot them for the time being."

Yay Panlilio acknowledges shooting prisoners before an impending battle, and also describes a grimly appropriate way in which Marking's guerrillas dealt with one of their own best fighters who had raped a woman who had given them much rice. They told the man they would fake his execution: shoot over his head. Then he should fall as if dead in order to satisfy the woman he had wronged. But the firing squad did not shoot *over* his head.[29]

Nobody will ever know how many innocent Filipinos lost their lives because they lacked proper identification, or were a long way from home for no clear reason, or because either guerrillas or Japanese considered that they could not take chances. For instance, a collegian from Manila joined the underground and fraternized with Japanese officers to get information about them. Some guerrillas observed this, did not realize what the boy was trying to do, and ambushed him. Another from the same school was guarding some machinery at a private estate when local guerrillas got the mistaken idea that the machinery was to be sold to the Japanese, so they murdered him.[30]

It is against this whole background that the reader should consider the disposition of two of the toughest spy cases I ever had to deal with. One day when we were fleeing from the Japanese, we crossed a river and holed up in a village where we hoped the enemy would not find us. Soon some men showed up who had not been with us when we crossed the river but who belonged to our organization. Acting on their own, they had dressed themselves in Philippine Constabulary uniforms, posed as members of the Constabulary, and questioned an old man whose clothing was made from gunnysacks. They told the man they were looking for Filipino and American guerrillas. Then they accused him of collaborating with guerrillas, which he indignantly denied. He insisted that, like themselves, he worked with Japanese. One of our phony Constabularymen then asked him how much the Japanese would give him if he led them to a Filipino or American guerrilla. He named a figure our men knew to be accurate, and added other information that indicated that he was indeed on familiar terms with the Japanese.

I first became aware of the affair when some of our men dragged the culprit into the house where I was staying. He had been beaten unmercifully, and it appeared that his back was broken. I then asked some of the village people if they had witnessed the affair. They said they had, adding that they had no doubt that the stranger was a Japanese spy. I then told the guerrilla lieutenant concerned to finish what he had started and bury the victim, but to make sure nobody fired a gun since that would reveal our position to the Japanese somewhere across the river. That done, I assumed that another messy incident with another spy was over. Alas! It was not.

Three days later a woman who was a stranger to the district, and about eight months pregnant in the bargain, entered the village in search of the recently deceased "spy." She said he was her husband. We arrested her and interrogated her about her alleged husband's connections with the Japanese. She denied repeatedly and tearfully that he was a spy at all, and did so with such conviction that to this day I wonder if our men did not make a tragic mistake. But what to do with her? She was bound to hate us for having killed her husband and the father of her unborn child. If we released her and she went to the Japanese, either because she too had been a spy all along, or because she wanted to avenge her husband, the enemy would burn the village to the ground and murder all the one hundred or so people who had already risked their lives to give us aid and shelter. We guerrillas could probably escape during such a Japanese attack, but civilians have to stay where they gain their livelihood, so ill-advised lenience on our part would condemn them rather than ourselves. Yet no civilized person wants to kill a woman eight months pregnant; doubly so when he fears that her jeopardy may be due to ghastly misjudgment by some of his own men.

Al called a meeting of himself, myself, Greg, a few of

the guerrillas, the village leader, and six villagers. We impressed upon the woman with the utmost seriousness, both in English and in her own Ilocano dialect, that she must never say a word to anyone about anything that had happened among us, and told her that if she did talk we would hunt her down and kill her. Then we took a desperate chance and let her go. She left with tears in her eyes, seemingly of gratitude, but who could ever know?

The second case was as excruciating as this one, and infuriating in the bargain. Professional soldiers, and most writers on military subjects too, like to believe that wars are won by brains and bravery. It seems much less heroic and inspiring to attribute victories to the efforts of spies, though good intelligence work has decided more wars than is generally admitted—or even known. A major reason is that spying is an equivocal business. Some spies are patriotic idealists, but many are victims of compulsion, and many more are scurvy characters motivated by nothing nobler than obscure private passions or the need for extra money. Those of the latter sort, if caught, can often be induced to change sides. The British were particularly successful "turning around" German spies in World War II. I have sometimes been asked if I ever "turned a spy around." I never tried: it always seemed too risky.

Like the Japanese though, we did employ a lot of spies, both male and female. Some have claimed that women make better spies than men because, allegedly, they do not become obsessed with their jobs; when not actually engaged in spying they think little about it and maintain their psychological balance better.[31] I am unconvinced. Some women unquestionably make excellent spies, but I don't think greater detachment or supposed superior psychological balance has anything to do with it. The most successful female spies we had were those who were at ease socially with Japanese officers in all kinds of situations. One of our best was a woman I shall call Dolores. The most charitable way to describe her prewar career would be to say that she was self-employed on the streets of Manila. Whatever her antecedents, she was energetic, thorough, smart, and brave. She made friends easily with Japanese officers, slept with a lot of them, and got much useful information from them which she rolled up in her hair curlers.

One day we heard that she was dead. We assumed that she had been caught and executed by the Japanese. We were astonished to learn that she had been picked up on suspicion by a temperamental Filipino guerrilla lieutenant of ours who had accused her of being a spy for the enemy. He had then simply shot her without a trial, without even so much as consulting anyone of higher rank! I don't recall Al's reaction, but I was momentarily blinded with fury. Had the lieutenant been where I was, I probably would have given him just what he gave Dolores. Since he wasn't present, we assembled a company of men and went looking for him. By the time we found him, I had cooled off enough to recollect that he had always been an energetic and loyal officer. His demeanor, however, very nearly restored my original rage, for I had never talked to a Filipino who simply stared at me with unconcealed insolence and whose whole bearing breathed insubordination. We had him disarmed and then asked him why, on mere suspicion, he had killed probably our best secret agent? He said he hated the "Hapons" and lived to kill as many of them as he could. He had heard that the woman was a prostitute for the "Hapons." She had been unable to identify herself or explain why she was so far from home, so he had concluded that she was a Japanese spy and shot her.

Rage surged back through me. How could this insolent, surly bonehead have taken it upon himself to kill out of hand a brave and valuable woman? But I will say for myself that at least I did not altogether stop thinking. We picked at random some twenty of the lieutenant's men and questioned each one separately about what he thought of his leader. All replied much the same: the lieutenant was tough as nails but basically fair and honest, and he hated the Japanese obsessively. Then Al and I talked again to the lieutenant himself. Finally we concluded that, however wretched his judgment had been he had probably acted from sincere conviction. Enough damage had been done already, and we did not want to lose anyone who wanted so badly to fight the enemy, so he was reprimanded as thoroughly as American vocabularies permitted and given back his guns. A few weeks later he was killed doing what he liked best, fighting the "Hapons."

The famous aviator Charles A. Lindbergh, who toured the Pacific during the war, came away convinced that American treatment of enemy prisoners and suspected spies was not much better than that of the Japanese, even though we professed to be fighting for civilization. Of course, it is generally wise in war to treat prisoners kindly since this gives enemy soldiers an incentive to surrender and save their lives. Moreover, once they are prisoners skilled interrogators can usually get useful information from them. But the Japanese were always exceptional: they simply did not play by rules of any kind. When an occasional one was captured, he could never be trusted, just as we guerrillas could not trust or take chances with real or suspected Japanese agents. Colonel Lindbergh, flying around in an airplane and penning memoirs afterward, simply never had to deal with the sickening quandaries that cropped up so often in the relentless ground war. Trying to distinguish "moral" from "immoral" conduct during struggles to the death with remorseless enemies has always seemed fruitless to me.

9

The Plight of the Filipinos

THE LOT OF SMALL NATIONS AND PEOPLES CAUGHT UP IN the struggles of great powers is never enviable. One has only to think of the Poles, trapped for a thousand years between Germans and Russians, and with Turks on their southern flank for five hundred of those years; or of Balkan peasants of many nationalities enmeshed for centuries in the wars between the Turks and the Holy Roman Empire. The Filipinos were similarly caught between America and Japan from 1941 to 1945.

The whole position of the Filipinos in the modern world has long been ambiguous. By geography and skin color they belong to the Orient: by religion and by four centuries of history and social experience, they belong to the Western world. The latter does not indicate merely a desire to appear "white," as some Caucasians have assumed. The Philippines never had a well-developed indigenous civilization like those of ancient China, India, and Japan. Thus, when the islands were conquered by Spain in the sixteenth century the victors did not have to displace a deeply rooted alien culture; they had only to impose their own. Spanish civilization and religion colored the Philippines heavily for more than three centuries, and was then succeeded by American civilization for forty years preceding World War II. In 1940 Filipinos were brown-skinned Asians, but their recent ancestors had spoken Spanish, the educated among them now spoke English rather than Tagalog, and their government was modelled on that of America. They were not typical Orientals but half-westernized east Asians who occupied a major outpost of the half-Christian, half-secular Occident.

Another factor that contributed to the Philippine identity problem was the special character of American imperialism. Americans positively encouraged the growth of Philippine nationalism, whereas the Dutch in Indonesia and the French in Indochina tried to discourage the growth of native nationalist sentiment, while the British in India and Burma were neutral toward it at best. As a consequence, movements to collaborate with the Japanese during the war were far stronger in Dutch, French, and British colonies than in the Philippines. The Filipinos were the only Asian colonial people who refused to capitulate to the Japanese without a fight; the only ones who remained loyal to and friendly with their former rulers; the only ones who called the eventual Allied victory "liberation" rather than "reoccupation." It was this loyalty that made possible the long stand on Bataan, and that led millions of Filipinos to risk their lives afterward either as guerrillas or to aid guerrillas who would fight the Japanese enemy.

There is no doubt that the character, personality, and deeds of Douglas MacArthur had contributed significantly to the pro-Americanism of most Filipinos, since they idolized the famous general. Sentimental attachment to America and principled admiration for democracy among the educated were also important. Most basic, despite all sorts of errors and injustices, American rule in the Philippines had been more enlightened than that of other imperial powers in eastern Asia. After the war of 1898 and the subsequent "pacification" of the Philippines had passed, there were no more massacres and no more pillage, and no unfairness toward Filipinos in courts. As the years passed, there were successive American concessions that pointed toward eventual Philippine self-government.

The Filipinos were grateful. An eloquent testimonial to the latter, and to the devotion of some of them to democracy, was penned by Tomas Confesor, a prewar governor of Iloilo who refused all Japanese offers to collaborate, took to the hills, organized a Free Philippines movement on Panay, and headed it during the Japanese occupation. He addressed himself thus to a Filipino collaborator:

There is a total war in which the issues between the warring parties are less concerned with territorial questions but more with forms of government, ways of life, and those that affect even the very thoughts, feelings and sentiments of every man. In other words, the question at stake with respect to the Philippines is not whether Japan or the United States should possess it but more fundamentally it is: what system of government would stand here and what ways of life, system of social organization and code of morals should govern our existence. . . .

You may not agree with me but the truth is that the present war is a blessing in disguise to our people and that the burden it imposes and the hardships it has brought upon us are a test of our character to determine the sincerity of our convictions and the integrity of our souls. In other words, this war has placed us in the crucible to assay the metal in our beings. For as a people, we have been living during the last forty years under a regime of justice and liberty regulated only by universally accepted principles of constitutional governments. We have come to enjoy personal privileges and civil liberties without much struggle, without undergoing any pain to attain them. They were practically a gift from a generous and magnanimous people—the people of the United States of America. Now that Japan is attempting to destroy those liberties, should we not exert every effort to defend them? Should we not be willing to suffer for their defense? If our people are undergoing hardships now, we are doing it gladly, it is because we are willing to pay the price for those constitutional liberties and privileges. You cannot become wealthy by honest means without sweating heavily. You know very well that the principles of democracy and democratic institutions were brought to life through bloodshed and fire. If we sincerely believe in those principles and institutions, as we who are resisting Japan do, we should contribute to the utmost of our capacity to the cost of its maintenance to save them from destruction and annihilation and such contribution should be in terms of painful sacrifices, the same currency that other peoples paid for those principles.[1]

The Japanese had no particular animosity toward Filipinos when the war began. They had attacked the Philippines only because American bases were there. But they always underestimated the desire of the Filipinos for freedom, and they were incredibly inept psychologists. When they stressed the common oriental heritage of Japanese and Filipinos and went out of their way to humiliate white people, this might have cut some ice with Filipinos who remembered ''white only'' golf clubs, ''Christian'' schools from which Filipinos were barred, and other subtler forms of American condescension. But the same ''fellow Orientals'' then killed them, tortured them, raped their women, stole their food, slapped their faces in public, and required them to bow to Japanese privates. For Japanese propaganda to extol the spartan life and decry American materialism was not impressive when Filipinos in any sizable town could see Japanese officers and civilian officials commandeer the country clubs and yacht clubs, move into the finest homes and hotels, and drive around in Cadillacs and Packards. The Greater East Asia Co-Prosperity Sphere would have seemed more attractive to Filipinos if its inventors had not closed Philippine schools and businesses, shut off public utilities, halted transport, banned theaters and then radios, stripped the country of so much food that Filipinos starved, tried to make everyone learn Japanese, and manipulated the currency in ways that amounted to ill-disguised plunder.Nothing made ordinary Filipinos so pro-American as the Japanese occupation.[2]

Filipino loyalty to the United States brought complications in its train that have not worked themselves out yet forty years after World War II. An important element in Filipino psychology is that when one accepts unsolicited favors or gifts from another he thereby incurs an obligation. Because Americans had done so much to promote democracy, public health, and education in the Philippines, Filipinos felt that they were obligated to help the United States resist the Japanese—who had, of course, invaded *their* homeland too. But then the Filipinos also assumed that their loyalty would be reciprocated; and they could never understand why the United States was lax in its military preparations before 1941, made its major wartime effort in Europe rather than in the Pacific, and did not compel the Japanese to pay war reparations to the Philippines afterward.[3]

Many thorny questions faced Filipinos in World War II. Was *any* kind of collaboration with the Japanese dishonorable at best, treasonous at worst? If not, how much or what kind *was* allowable? Did it make any difference if the collaborator was highly placed, or if he was coerced by the conquerors? coerced how much, and in what ways? Should distinctions be made between the avowed intentions of collaborators and their visible deeds? If so, who should make them? Above all, what should be done about it all when the war was over?

Before the French Revolution (1789-99), in most western countries treason was easily recognized: it was personal disloyalty to a ruler to whom one owed loyalty or homage. In the two centuries since then matters have grown more complex. The French Revolution did more than any other event in modern history to promote the idea that the interests of the "nation" or "people" should take precedence over all other values, though it is often exceedingly difficult to know just what those interest truly are. In totalitarian states anytime, and in democratic states as well in wartime, it does not even require specific acts for one to be regarded as a traitor; mere words, even attitudes or states of mind, suffice, at least for authorities and zealots. Mere lack of enthusiasm for an official ideology is regarded as something close to treason in totalitarian states like Nazi Germany and Soviet Russia. Often it is extremely difficult for a conscientious person to know where his primary loyalty *should* lie in the modern world: to his nation state, to its leaders-of-the-moment, to the nation itself though perhaps not to its present form of government, to his religious beliefs, to his family? If he is in the armed forces, to his military superiors? It is much easier to ask such questions than to answer them.

The questions are not hypothetical, either. One of the many reasons France fell so swiftly to the Wehrmacht in 1940 was that while many high-ranking French soldiers and politicians, of whom Marshal Pétain and Pierre Laval are perhaps the best examples, hated Germany, they also hated their own Third Republic and wanted to see it destroyed. In Yugoslavia, a land of many nationalities, most of whom dislike most of the others, Draja Mikhailovich, the leader of the Chetnik guerrillas, accepted British and American aid and at times used it to fight the German and Italian conquerors of his country, but what he wanted most of all was to insure that when the war was over Yugoslavia should not be communist, so he fought the partisan guerrillas of the communist Tito more enthusiastically than he did the fascist states, and many times he did not fight the latter at all since to do so would bring terrible reprisals down onto the Yugoslav people. Marshal Tito's Partisans also took Allied aid. They fought the Germans and Italians too, but with little concern for what happened to civilians of any sort. Their main objective was to communize the country, so they ambushed Chetniks and tried to destroy their credibility with the Allies. How could an ordinary citizen of Yugoslavia know where his duty lay in such circumstances, especially when one or both guerrilla groups had leaders or espoused policies inimical to the interests of people of his own nationality or religion? Or consider one individual citizen of that state, Milovan Djilas, who survived World War II and wrote much afterward. His father was shot by an Albanian nationalist, one of his brothers was killed by a Montenegrin militiaman serving under the Italians, another was tortured and killed by a Serb policeman working with the German Gestapo, and a pregnant sister was murdered by the Chetniks. To whom, or to what, should Djilas have been loyal? The whole question of whether one is morally obligated to obey military and political superiors when their orders are perceived to be either immoral or apt to lead the nation to ruin, was especially acute in Nazi Germany in World War II and led directly to the Nuremberg War Crimes Trials (1946). Their utility and wisdom have been debated ever since.

It might be objected that questions of this sort worry only intellectuals and thus were irrelevant to my concerns as a leader of Filipino guerrillas, nearly all of whom were simple, untutored people. Not so. Uneducated people are not necessarily stupid or incapable of understanding abstractions; nor are they less concerned than the educated to act honorably. Most Filipinos regarded their president, Manuel Quezon, as a national hero. He spent most of the war, until his death, in the United States, from where he exhorted his countrymen to remain loyal to America. Meantime other prominent Filipino politicians collaborated with the Japanese and, at least in public, urged their countrymen to do likewise. Still others tried to steer a middle course. Ordinary Filipinos, like most Asians, thought that in a crisis loyalty to one's own people should supersede loyalty to a particular political philosophy. In the world of deeds ordinary Filipino civilians were in a truly hopeless position, even worse than that of Europeans caught in the maelstrom of Nazis, Soviet communists, British, Americans, and their own divided resistance groups. The Filipinos were trapped, first of all, between the Japanese-sponsored Vargas or Laurel government in their homeland and the Quezon-Osmeña government-in-exile in the United States, each backed by a foreign army and each demanding their total allegiance. If they cooperated with the guerrillas, the Japanese killed them. If they worked with the Japanese, the guerrillas killed them. If they supported the Huks, they incurred the displeasure of all non-communist guerrillas. If they helped us USAFFE irregulars against the Huks, their lives were at once in danger from the communists. Much of the time from 1942 to 1945 large sections of Luzon resembled the State of Nature as envisioned by the seventeenth-century English philosopher Thomas Hobbes: a grim locale where there existed a perpetual war of all against all, and where life was, in consequence, "solitary, poor, nasty, brutish, and short."

An all-too-typical illustration of this melancholy state of affairs once took place in Tayabas province. Guerrillas entered a town, assembled all the people in the village church, read off the names of those deemed pro-Japanese, and shot them. The Japanese soon heard of what had happened, assembled the survivors, and shot all those they considered pro-American. The surviving corporal's guard fled to the hills.[4]

Another increasingly difficult problem in the twentieth century has been the credibility of oaths. Most are couched, as they have been for centuries, in religious phraseology. Would religious people regard them as binding if they were not so phrased? But to non-religious people such terminology means little. Indeed, is there any cause that should convince a secular humanist that an oath ought to bind him unconditionally? Worse, in practice, how about oaths taken half-willingly and half under duress, as was the case in Germany when all army officers had to swear a personal oath of loyalty to Adolf Hitler, following which many of them became convinced that he was leading their nation to ruin?

Many Filipinos, religious or not, were trapped in this morass. Consider the plight of a conscientious Filipino who had taken an oath of loyalty to the Philippine Commonwealth and to the United States before the war, perhaps on the occasion of joining the armed forces of either; after which he was induced to repudiate it and accept the Filipino-led collaborationist regime during the war; then required by the Japanese to swear fealty to Nippon; then compelled to cooperate with the Huks under threat of the torture and execution of his family; after which he escaped and joined an American guerrilla outfit in which he had to subscribe to American and Philippine Commonwealth oaths once more? What could he think of *any* solemn affirmation of loyalty when so many had been pressured out of him, when he did not know who would eventually win the war, and when he had no idea how his incompatible oaths and changes of front would be regarded by the eventual victors? The lot of ordinary Filipinos from 1941 to 1945 was not enviable.

Historically, the usual response of the Philippine ruling elite to conquest has been to come to terms with the invader in order to retain their own influence and to spare the islands and their peoples. So it had been with the Spaniards before 1898 and with the Americans afterward. In 1941 most Filipinos did not regard the Japanese as a friendly people, or trust them, but they did regard them with respect. The traditional Filipino elite doubtless would have responded to Japanese conquest and occupation as their forefathers had done to Spaniards and Americans if only Japanese propaganda had been less crude and unconvincing, and Japanese conduct less beastly.

Philippine President Manuel Quezon was a complex and "difficult" man. Intelligent, intensely ambitious, egotistical, mercurial, dictatorial, talkative, and flashy, he was a politician of consummate skill though hardly the great statesman he thought himself to be. Before the war he had been publicly loyal to the United States and had taken American aid to build a Philippine army, but he had also anticipated many a Third World government of the postwar era by taking out some "insurance policies." He accepted Japanese help in developing the Philippine economy, and he conducted secret talks with Tokyo that were discovered only after the war when American counterintelligence people went through Japanese foreign office files.[5] When Quezon was with the beleaguered Filamerican forces on Corregidor in January 1942 and began to realize that the policy of the Roosevelt administration was to give priority to the European war, he flew into a rage and proposed that both America and Japan withdraw all their armed forces and bases from the Philippines and jointly guarantee Philippine neutrality, in return for which he would disband the Philippine army. He was gradually talked out of this by his own vice president Sergio Osmeña, and by General MacArthur, supported by many assurances from President Roosevelt. Quezon then wrote a letter to MacArthur, clearly intended for the eyes of Roosevelt as well, asserting that he had instructed several prominent Filipino politicians to stay behind and do whatever circumstances required of them to spare the Filipino people as much as they could in what would certainly be tough times ahead. Then Quezon and Osmeña went into exile in America, where Quezon broadcast to his people back home, "Do not despair, for your liberation is certain. . . . Keep faith with America, which has kept faith with every nation and especially with us"—a statement quite as embellished with "terminological inexactitudes"—as were many of Roosevelt's pronouncements in the same era.[6]

Of course, not all Filipinos were either pro-American or simply inclined to bend with the winds of fortune. In 1941 Emilio Aguinaldo and Artemio Ricarte were still alive. Aguinaldo had led Philippine resistance to the United States after 1898, and Ricarte had been the only Filipino officer involved in that insurrection who had refused to lay down his arms and swear allegiance to the United States. In World War II both acted in ways displeasing to America but not innately shameful. Aguinaldo, who had seemed to have made his peace with the United States, at once became pro-Japanese and helped his new friends keep the Philippines quiet but did so in an effort to secure better treatment for Filipinos under the occupation, a risky course that his countrymen could easily misunderstand and for which they might well consign him to a painful death if Japan lost the war.[7] Ricarte had always been pro-Japanese. He had lived much of his adult life in Japan and had been treated well there. He simply remained loyal to his benefactors. He collaborated with them when he came back to the Philippines early in the war, and tried to use his influence with them to make life a bit easier for his countrymen.[8]

More complex and important collaborators were the members of the Sakdal and Kalibapi movements. In the mid-1930s the Sakdalistas were merely an association of peasants in central Luzon who nourished the same grievances as those who supported the Hukbalahaps. They were led by Benigno Ramos, a frustrated Tagalog poet who hated Quezon, denounced governmental corruption, and demanded distribution of lands to peasants, the abolition of taxation, and immediate independence for the Philippines. The Sakdalistas were repressed harshly by the Philippine government. Ramos, an embittered man, fled to Japan. He returned with the Japanese conquerors and gave them Sakdal membership lists which enabled them to compel anyone whose name was on the list to collaborate whether he wished to or not. Thus, mere membership in the Sakdalistas did not prove that one *wanted* to be pro-Japanese, though the Sakdalistas and their offspring, the Makapili, at times gave us guerrillas nearly as much trouble as the Huks.

The Kalibapi (Association for Service to the New Philippines) was a political party organized by the Japanese in December 1942 to function in their puppet "Philippine Republic." Many of its members had been Sakdals before the war, but the Japanese wanted a more impressive leader than Benigno Ramos and so chose as its director general an important prewar Commonwealth official noted for his fiery pro-Japanese speeches, Benigno Aquino. On the local level, the Kalibapi was a Japanese Neighborhood Association, the leaders of which divided every town into ten districts, each district into ten sections, and the sections into units of ten houses or families. The leader of each group was responsible for the conduct of everyone in that group. It was an effort, after the common totalitarian fashion of our century, to turn everyone into spies for the government.

None of these groups collaborated enthusiastically enough to please the Japanese, so late in 1944 they organized the Makapili (League of Patriotic Filipinos). Nominally, it was headed by Ramos, Ricarte, and Pio Duran, an anti-Western Filipino intellectual, but it was actually answerable directly to the Japanese army. Though the numbers of the Makapili were never significant, the organization was dreaded because the Japanese used hooded individual members publicly to point out suspected guerrillas or Filipino civilians friendly to guerrillas.[9]

There were also some collaborators who were mere profiteers, amoral self-seekers of the sort who proliferate in any time of political upheaval.

Finally, there was a considerable group of educated Filipinos who were essentially fence sitters. They were not uncritical admirers of Japanese civilization, but they were respectful and envious of the accomplishments of modern Japan. They observed how a Nipponese ruling elite had managed to Westernize that nation and make it powerful without either succumbing to Western imperialism or losing their own domestic preeminence. This was impressive to those Filipinos who regarded people like themselves as the only possible rulers of their own country.

Those Filipinos who eventually collaborated with their conquerors, either willingly or unwillingly, from whatever mixture of motives, have by now been praised, excused, denounced, and dissected in print so many times and in such detail that I cannot presume to add anything significant to the controversies that swirled about them for years. I did know two of them personally, though, Manuel Roxas and Ferdinand Marcos, and I can indicate how their actions and those of their colleagues appeared to me at the time and appear now, long afterward.

Early in the war Tokyo began to search eagerly for a front man to run the Philippines during Japanese occupation of the islands. Ideally, this would be someone with sufficient brains and public credit to win his people away from their loyalty to the exiled Quezon, and to make it

appear to the outside world that most Filipinos welcomed
their new Japanese masters. They hoped their man would
be Manuel Roxas, the highly intelligent prewar speaker of
the Philippine House of Representatives, but Roxas proved
sly and slippery and for a long time managed to evade the
Nipponese embrace.

As second best they settled on a distinguished ex-Su-
preme Court justice, José Laurel, whom some guerrillas
had tried to assassinate in June 1943. Probably because of
this the Japanese assumed that Laurel was both more important and more pro-Japanese than was really the case.

Estimates of Laurel vary widely. Partisans of the Left
insist that Laurel was one of the worst of the collaborationists: a man who studied Bushido, expressed admiration
for Japan before the war, and sent his sons to Nipponese
schools; a hater of democracy who repressed guerrillas,
recruited laborers to produce food for Japan, and freely
employed the Sakadalistas and Makapili at the behest of
his Japanese masters.[10]

A more moderate version of the same basic view holds
that, had he been a European, Laurel would have been
called a fascist. He was a Filipino nationalist who hated
colonialism. He was also anti-democratic: convinced that
only a few people of superior character and acumen truly
understand popular needs and are capable of ruling wisely.
What he admired about the Japanese was much like what
the Italian dictator Mussolini admired in the Germans:
their efficiency, decisiveness, and authoritarian government; and in the Japanese case, their use of the emperor
as a tool of social cohesion. Laurel thought his fellow
Filipinos should work harder and accept discipline, regi-
mentation, sacrifice, and service to the state. He overrated
the efficiency of totalitarian countries, and assumed
wrongly, or at least prematurely, that democracy is destined historically to be superseded by authoritarian governments everywhere. He regarded guerrilla resistance to
Japan as harmful to the nation and did not believe it would
have any effect on the outcome of the war. He regarded
peace, order, and compliance with directives from above

as essential to preserve Philippine society during foreign occupation.[11]

Others, some admirers of Laurel, some merely neutral toward him, have seen him mostly as a victim of circumstances. In their view, to have refused to become president of the "Philippine Republic" would only have insured that someone else more pliable would have taken his place. If he had studied Japanese civilization and culture extensively, that did not necessarily mean that he was an admirer of Japan. He had studied Western philosophy, religion, and government, too. He admired Western technology but preferred Oriental virtues; he feared that American culture and foreign policy would ruin the Philippines; and he overestimated the good will of the Japanese toward Filipinos. He thought that America would eventually win the war but that this would take from five to ten years, and that soon after the war Japan would be strong again. Meantime, *someone* must protect the Filipino people as much as possible. To this end he implored both Premier Tojo and General Homma to treat Filipinos kindly and used his influence in various ways to save the lives of such prominent Filipinos as Manuel Roxas, Gen. Guillermo Francisco, chief of the Philippine Constabulary, and Gen. Vincente Lim, commander of the Forty-first Philippine Division on Bataan. (To be sure, Lim was eventually executed by the Japanese, but Laurel's intervention saved him for a time.)

Laurel wrote into the new Philippine constitution provisions that made it difficult for any Philippine government to declare war, and then when the Japanese did at last compel him to declare war against the United States he managed to evade conscripting any soldiers to fight it. He never lived in the Presidential palace. He shared food with his underlings, tried to hunt down bandits and looters, and managed to maintain covert contact with guerrillas. He was a hero, not a traitor.[12]

Such was the man whom the Japanese in October 1943 made the first and only president of their personal political creation, the "Philippine Republic."

Whatever the worth of Laurel's political ideas, whatever his motivation, a combination of misjudgments and bad luck made his task hopeless. Perhaps the fundamental difficulty was that most Filipinos did not share his cool, detached, rational assessment of the overall course of history, or of the Japanese occupation of the moment. Most Filipinos, and all guerrillas, even the Huks, wanted to fight the Japanese and throw them out of the islands forever. Laurel was simply out of touch with the people he sought to reform and protect. Moreover, he always wore around his neck the albatross of collaboration. When the Japanese undertook an extensive campaign of "pacification" against guerrillas in the fall of 1943, and Laurel dutifully urged us all to lay down our arms, some complied. Others complied formally, after which they went right back to the mountains, a solution that pleased everyone save the Japanese. The majority simply redoubled their determination to resist the invaders. Laurel also overestimated the credibility of his own regime in the world at large. The "Philippine Republic" was recognized only by Japan, Nazi Germany, Franco's Spain, and the Japanese puppet state of Manchukuo.

Finally, Laurel overrated the strength and abilities of the Japanese. Tokyo professed to be in the process of establishing an interdependent economic sphere in east Asia and the western Pacific, but such an enterprise could be held together only by a huge merchant fleet. By the end of 1944 the Allies had sunk over 80 percent of the prewar Japanese merchant marine. As their ships disappeared, Japanese troops in the Philippines had to get more and more of their food from the islands themselves. This ruined any chance that Laurel's regime might have had to become popular, since he was no more able to deal successfully with the consequent food shortages among Filipinos than he had been to prevent the Japanese from taxing Filipinos to support the Nipponese war effort. Nowhere in Japan's new empire were there enough capable technicians, managers, engineers, teachers, even propagandists, to meet the suddenly expanded needs.[13] When this limitation was combined with the abominable behavior of so many Japanese troops, the popularity of Japan and any pro-Japanese regime inevitably plummeted.

One episode that illustrates several of these considerations was centered where I happened to be, in central Luzon. The Japanese developed a scheme to grow cotton in the Philippines, and created a Philippine Cotton Association to coordinate plans. When it came to the doing, however, necessary machinery, high yield seeds, and measures to control pests were all lacking. In addition, because of extensive fighting many fields had been burned and work animals killed. Various guerrilla bands, including mine, then gave the whole scheme the coup de grace by appealing to the Filipinos not to cooperate.

Of those prominent Filipinos who collaborated with the Japanese, some seemed to do so with enthusiasm, others with reluctance. All soon discovered that it was easier to begin collaboration than to stop. At the end of the war American Secretary of the Interior Harold Ickes, the American Left, the Huks in the Philippines, and an assortment of American and Filipino political writers denounced all Filipinos who had collaborated with their conquerors and clamored to have them tried for treason. It was alleged that most wealthy Filipinos were fascists, or at least reactionaries; that since Quezon was now dead they could safely pretend that he had asked them to stay behind and defend their countrymen; that they had not, in fact, defended those countrymen but their own financial interest; that they had simultaneously fooled the Americans, the Japanese, and their own people. Now, in 1945, so many of them were claiming that they had always been patriots and resisters that it appeared that "even the Japs in Tokyo are now pro-American."[14]

Recriminations about such questions have been endless because the wartime careers of many prominent Filipinos can only be called equivocal. That of José Laurel has already been considered. Laurel seemingly feared American judgment, since he fled to Formosa April 21, 1945, and then to Japan, where he was eventually arrested by the

Americans and indicted for treason. He always maintained, however, that the Japanese had coerced him,[15] and when he was flown back to the Philippines to face trial, crowds at the Manila airport cheered him when he got off the plane.[16] He was to have been tried by a Philippine court but was, in fact, never brought to trial. In 1948 Roxas, by then president of the newly independent Philippine Republic, included Laurel in a general amnesty of all alleged collaborators save common criminals. The Filipino people must have approved the gesture, since they voted Laurel into the national Senate two years later and have since honored him along with other Philippine presidents.

Jorge Vargas, another prominent prewar Filipino politician, who was once Quezon's secretary, headed a provisional Philippine government set up by the Japanese in January 1942, and appeared to collaborate willingly with his masters as long as they seemed to be winning the war. He even wanted to campaign against Laurel to become the first president of the puppet "Philippine Republic," and he once urged guerrilla leaders on Panay to surrender on the grounds that the Japanese fleet could always prevent the Americans from landing anything in the Philippines. One of the guerrillas sent him back four Delicious apples, a variety that does not grow in Japan or in the Philippines![17] One of Vargas's motives seems to have been a desire to shake off American domination of the Philippines. He never opposed the conquerors on any critical issue, while Laurel, by contrast, successfully evaded Japanese pressure to raise a Philippine army to fight the Americans. Vargas eventually tied himself so closely to the Japanese that he could not break connections with them even when it became clear that they would lose the war.[18]

Even so, fate was kind to Vargas. He returned to the Philippines and in 1947 was indicted on 115 counts of collaboration with the enemy. His trial dragged on for months. It appeared that he would eventually be acquitted on procedural grounds when President Roxas and the Philippine Congress rendered his case moot by amnestying (January-February 1948) all who had not actually borne arms against the Allies or acted as spies or informers for the Japanese.[19]

One case of alleged collaboration that I happened to know something about personally was that of Manuel Roxas. It was obvious from the actions of General MacArthur at the end of the war that some sort of unrecorded understanding involving himself, President Quezon, Roxas, and probably several other highly placed Philippine political figures had been reached early in the war, most likely when Quezon was still on Corregidor. This was in no way unusual, for in other Southeast Asian lands prominent political figures are known to have made unwritten agreements that some of them would be pro-British, or pro-Dutch, or pro-French, and some pro-Japanese, in order to spare their people as much as possible during the war and to make sure that they had a few spokesmen who would be in the good graces of whichever side eventually won. It was understood that those who had chosen the winning side would forgive those who had thrown in their lot with the losers. In the case of Roxas, for two years he evaded damaging legal entanglement with the Japanese, usually on the plea that his health was poor. This was an excuse, to be sure, and there were rumors that Roxas raised his temperature and made his "illnesses" appear more convincing by putting a piece of garlic in his anus. Even if he did this, his ill health was probably not wholly faked, since he died a few years after the war when he was still a comparatively young man. Supposedly fearing execution, Roxas eventually capitulated to the Japanese and became president of the Senate in the "Philippine Republic." There agreement about his actions and motives stops.

Writers whose sympathies are predominantly Left say Roxas was a slicker who cultivated MacArthur before the war and both Laurel and the Japanese during it. They say he flattered them all and took them all in. They say that he pretended to have contacts with guerrillas, but that his only true loyalties were to himself and to the wealthy Filipino collaborators with whom he habitually associated.[20] It should be added that Al Hendrickson, an observant man who was active with the Luzon guerrillas throughout the war and whose philosophical and political sympathies were not Left then or at any other time, was likewise convinced that Roxas was a shifty rascal and a consummate self-seeker. One of MacArthur's abler biographers sums up the anti-Roxas case by asserting that no guerrilla ever attested to any noteworthy anti-Japanese deed of Roxas.[21]

The last is untrue. I had several contacts with Roxas and know he did aid guerrillas. In fact, near the end of the war MacArthur told Roxas that to receive public approval he must secure a statement, signed by American guerrilla leaders, attesting to his pro-American sentiments and actions. I was one of those who signed it, and I did so gladly. Marking's guerrillas thought enough of Roxas that they offered to hide him in the mountains, and to supply and feed him. Their chronicler and co-leader adds that Roxas told her that he and Laurel kept in close contact, that they disagreed in public just enough so that the Japanese would take Laurel's advice rather than his own, that Laurel was a master at stalling, and that he (Roxas) regularly kept Laurel informed of much that the Japanese never told him. She added that she had no trouble believing him because she had played the same game with Vargas, Quezon's secretary, in February 1942 when she had been a broadcaster for station KZRH in Manila.[22]

When Quezon was preparing to leave Corregidor, he issued an executive order naming Roxas as his successor should he and Osmeña be killed. A few days later he added detailed instructions to Roxas about how to deal with every branch of the administration, including organizing, directing, and coordinating resistance to the Japanese.[23] In July 1943 Quezon sent his personal physician, Dr. Emgidio Cruz, on a secret mission to the Philippines to see how things were going generally, and specifically to see Roxas. The two held daily conversations about which public figures had been forced to bow to the will of the Japanese, and to what degree, who were true collaborators and who were merely shamming, and who could be counted on to rally the people to anti-Japanese action when the time came for a final military and political showdown. Cruz made a lengthy report of his odyssey to General Willoughby, MacArthur's chief of intelligence, which Willoughby subsequently published in his book, along with much other evidence that Roxas was essentially a mole in the Laurel regime who collected valuable information for USAFFE headquarters and gave much aid to guerrillas.[24]

At the end of the war, though MacArthur ordered the arrest of some other top Filipino leaders, he promoted Roxas to brigadier general and put him on inactive status. He explained that he knew Roxas was of good character, that he was innocent of collaboration, and that he had done much to aid guerrillas. Most of the Filipino people must have agreed, since they elected Roxas the first president of the independent Philippine Republic on April 23, 1946. Once in office, Roxas granted amnesty to all guerrillas who had fought against the Japanese during the war, and to the great bulk of those accused of collaboration with the Japanese. His enemies have always interpreted these actions as an endeavor to cover his own tracks, but there is a plausible alternative explanation. Just as the first Bourbon king of France, Henry IV, welcomed to his standard those of all political and religious persuasions in an effort to bind up the wounds of a long generation of savage civil wars (1559-98), and just as a later ruler of the same country, Napoleon Bonaparte, pursued a similar policy in an effort to weld France together again after the nation had been fragmented during the French Revolution, so any statesman of intelligence and good will would have tried to reunite the shattered Filipino people in the aftermath of World War II. In the case of amnestying guerrillas, moreover, a legal point needed settlement. Any Filipino who had taken arms in violation of the orders of the Japanese-sponsored "Philippine Republic" was, after all, formally a criminal since international law prescribes that citizens of an occupied country have a duty to cooperate with the occupying forces.

At the end of the war, mostly because of American pressure, 5,603 accusations of collaboration with the Japanese were legally filed. Only a few hundred of the accused were ever tried, only 156 convictions were secured, and only one of them was of a prominent person, Teofilo Sison, a prewar governor of Pangasinan province. All the other cases were dismissed or concluded with an amnesty.[25]

One of those put on trial was Claro M. Recto, a former member of the Philippine Senate and for a time foreign minister in the Laurel regime. Recto was a remarkably intelligent, far-sighted man. Long before the war he had perceived Japanese and Russian intentions in the Orient, had come to believe that domination of the smaller Asian peoples by other Asians would be worse than Western domination, and had urged that the Philippines must become strong militarily because the United States would never regard it as more than an expendable military outpost.[26]

During his trial Recto delivered an eloquent speech on his own behalf that summed up the general position of the collaborators. Those who, like himself, now stood accused, he said, had not fled to ease overseas where they could safely preach "defense of freedom" to their countrymen languishing under Japanese despotism. Only those who had stayed behind and tried to defend the lives and interests of the Filipino people could know what those people had faced, and how much temporizing and evasion they had been compelled to practice in order to live. No Americans were ever treated the way the Filipinos had been. No American cities were smashed either by barbarous conquerors or by the planes and bombs of "liberators." The American countryside was not laid waste; no American civilians were insulted, tortured, or bayoneted by a cruel enemy. How many Americans, he asked, would have collaborated if the Japanese had followed up Pearl Harbor with landings in California? How would they now be regarded?

Whatever the war might cost the Philippine people, Recto said, was only incidental to Americans, for the American objective was *overall* victory; but no civilized

Filipino public official could consider the matter with such objectivity. Philippine political leaders, even in the Laurel government, had turned a blind eye to much aid that had gone to guerrillas, had protested to Japanese authorities about atrocities against Filipinos, and had refused to raise an army to aid the Japanese even when pressed hard to do so. He added that the American government had known that it was pathetically unprepared to defend the Philippines, yet the Filipinos had remained loyal to America. And what of America's own "collaborators"? Washington had not merely excused Wainwright, Sharp, Cushing, Hilsman, Baker, and others who had surrendered to the enemy or had been compelled to make pro-Japanese statements, but had positively honored them on the ground that they had been victims of circumstances, casualties of American unpreparedness.[27] Was not exactly the same true of those Filipino leaders now accused of collaboration?

Recto then cited such political figures as Sukarno in Indonesia, Ba Maw in Burma, and Scavenius in Denmark, all of whom had collaborated with Japanese or German occupation forces but had been taken back into the good graces of the democratic nations as if nothing had happened. He concluded by insisting that in any case the spirit of democracy and self-government which infused the American constitution required that Filipinos, not Americans, should try their own accused collaborators.

It has always seemed to me that Recto's position is unassailable. War imposes hard necessities. Just as we guerrillas could not tolerate Japanese agents in our midst and survive, so the Filipino people as a whole could not have survived had not many of them cooperated at least passively with their conquerors. We Americans are in many ways the spoiled children of history. Though the Northern occupation of the Old Confederacy, 1864-76, was bitterly resented by Southerners, we have never had to endure the experience of being overrun and occupied by cruel foreign enemies and to make the compromises that necessarily follow such an experience. It was all very well for Franklin Roosevelt, Harold Ickes, and others ten thousand miles

away to talk bravely and to denigrate Filipino officials who
had to struggle and live with enemies who gradually killed
hundreds of thousands of their countrymen. So-called collaborators had little choice. On May 7, 1942, the Japanese
executed Philippine Chief Justice José Abad Santos for
refusing to serve under them. After that few Filipino leaders declined to take office. Once they were in office, their
conquerors did not scruple to take the sons of some of
them and send them to Japan to insure the good behavior
of their fathers.[28] What good purpose would have been
served had all of them emulated Abad Santos? They would
have been killed and replaced either by *real* pro-Japanese
like Benigno Ramos, Benigno Aquino (father of the Philippine opposition leader assassinated in 1983), Pio Duran,
and General Ricarte, or by amoral self-seekers. Would
ordinary Filipinos have been better off then? Or would the
United States, for that matter? Prudence is often the better
part of valor. Heroism is not only fighting and dying.
Death ends man's problems: staying alive increases them.
Those who stayed behind and tried to make the best of a
terrible situation served their people quite as much as did
Quezon and Osmeña in far off Washington.

Perhaps the best indication of how tepid and unwilling
so many collaborators were is that the Japanese never fully
trusted them, and with good reason. Thousands of lower
level "collaborators" were merely people who happened
to hold some public office at the time of the Japanese conquest and had to keep their jobs to support their families.
Few were seriously touched by Japanese indoctrination.
Whether their true motives were a noble desire to serve
their people or mere fear of reprisals, some aided the guer-
illas when they could; some sabotaged their conquerors in
small ways when they thought it safe; most simply waited
and hoped for better days. President Sergio Osmeña understood this, as he indicated in a speech made from Leyte
a few days after the American landing there on November
23, 1944. He took note of the compromises that had been
made under pressure, and promised to deal with accusa-

tions of collaboration justly and with dignity, on an individual basis.[29]

We Americans should be lenient in judging the Filipinos for other reasons too. Fundamentally, what was the correct policy for a Philippine government to follow in the war when its people had been promised independence by a colonial power that had brought war down upon them, then proved too weak to protect them, and might never return? Yet those victimized people had suffered and died alongside our own soldiers, and their civilians had risked the lives of themselves and their families to help Americans on innumerable occasions afterward. That many sat on the fence waiting to see who would win the war is true: it is also likely that Quezon, Osmeña, and Romulo would have done the same had they stayed in the Philippines instead of going to the United States. But what does this prove? We welcomed those Filipinos who accepted American hegemony after 1898. No stigma of "collaboration" was ever attached to them or to the Japanese who passively accepted American victory and domination after 1945. After the American Revolution most of the Tories were eventually absorbed into the new United States of America, as were the rebellious Confederates after the Civil War.

Finally we need to think of what the situation in the Philippines would have been like in 1945 had not some politicians tried to cushion the impact of the Japanese occupation on the Filipino people. Philippine politics would have been polarized between pro-Japanese Filipinos backed by the Japanese army, and the Huks and their sympathizers. Extremists on both sides wanted this. Had they gotten their wish and had the United States pushed the collaborationist issue hard in 1945-46, it is quite possible that the Huks would have ridden to power and the Philippines would have become another Soviet republic.[30]

The whole issue of collaboration, which seemed so explosive and fraught with menace near the end of the war, evaporated rapidly afterward. President Roosevelt died in the spring of 1945. Those American politicians most interested in Philippine affairs, men like Secretary of the

Interior Harold Ickes and Senators Millard Tydings and Paul McNutt, were either in disagreement or distracted by other problems. The new president, Harry Truman, was less avid to pursue collaborators than Roosevelt had been. By 1946, too, it was growing evident that the menace of the future would be Soviet Russia. This at once made the Huks, with their cries for vengeance against "the elite traitors of Manila," less attractive, and made it seem more important to check communist global expansion than to pursue old feuds from World War II. Thus, the whole issue faded away, and those who had dominated the Philippine Commonwealth before 1942 soon dominated the Philippine Republic that was established in 1946.

As noted earlier, one of the by-products of guerrilla life was that I became aquainted with several Filipino politicians who were either well known in the 1940s or rose to prominence after World War II. One of the latter, whom I happened to meet in 1944, was Ferdinand Marcos, later to become a famous and embattled president of the Philippines. One day he showed up at my headquarters barefooted and unarmed, accompanied by a Filipino writer, F.M. Verano, who sometimes assumed the alias "Lieutenant Winters" and acted as a liaison man between Manuel Roxas and my organization. Marcos was then a twenty-seven-year-old lawyer who already had an interesting past. Years before the war a political adversary of his father had once put a dummy in a coffin and draped it with a sign indicating that it ought to be Marcos's father. Outraged at the insult, the son hired the family chauffeur to shoot the offender. At the last moment the chauffeur could not go through with the act, so young Marcos grabbed a rifle and shot his father's foe himself. He was then tried for murder and convicted, but the case was appealed to a higher court. While it was still pending, young Marcos was admitted to the bar. A second trial was ordered, and in it he defended himself so skillfully that he was acquitted.

Shortly before the Philippine presidential election of 1965 a "campaign biography" of Marcos appeared in which it was claimed that Marcos had performed with exceptional valor during the defense of Bataan, that he was nearly tortured to death by the Japanese in Fort Santiago, that after his release he devoted months to an unsuccessful effort to band together all the guerrillas on all the Philippine islands, that he formed his own northern Luzon guerrilla band, the Maharlika (Free Men or Noble Ones), that late in the war he helped Volckmann clear all the bandit irregulars out of north Luzon, and that he played a key role in the reestablishment of civil government on Luzon in May 1945. For these heroic deeds Marcos came out of the war the most decorated man in Philippine history.[31]

For a long time I assumed offhand that most of this was true, maybe all of it. The principal reason was that I had little occasion to think about Marcos at all. To me, he would have been no more than one more barefoot Filipino had not Verano told me that he had once killed a foe of his father. Then, incongruously, twenty years later this man had become president of the Philippines. In fact, when the latter event took place I had to do some research to assure myself that the new ruler of the islands was the same Marcos I had once met during the war.

When Marcos eventually became the center of furious controversies at home and abroad, books and articles began to appear claiming that his wartime heroism had been grossly exaggerated and that many, perhaps most, of his medals had been manufactured after the war to commemorate exploits that had never taken place.[32] This evolution came to a climax shortly before the Philippine election of February 7, 1986, when many accounts appeared alleging that most of Marcos's war record was fraudulent. The stories were based on hundreds of pages of documents found in the U.S. National Archives by an American scholar, Dr. Alfred McCoy.[33]

I was drawn into this whole controversy because two of the documents bore my signature. They called for the arrest of all unauthorized guerrilla organizers in Pangasinan, and one of them mentioned Marcos specifically. Within a few days newspaper and television journalists descended on me from all points of the compass. I was interviewed repeatedly and my responses circulated broadly. It soon became evident that, for whatever reason, perhaps mere unaccustomed excitement, I had not chosen my words with sufficient care. I was widely quoted as having said that Marcos had never led any guerrilla organization of significance, and that I had either arrested him or had ordered his arrest for unauthorized solicitation of funds and for efforts to recruit guerrillas.

The best I can do now, after the event, is try to sort out the truths from the half-truths, and both from the falsities. At the risk of boring readers I must emphasize that the events in question took place more than forty years ago, that they did not then seem to be of much importance, and that it was a time of great stress and tumult. Consequently, my memory of the precise details is inexact. I do not recall that either Verano or Manuel Roxas, both of whom I knew fairly well, ever said anything to me about Marcos being a guerrilla. I know he did not command an *armed* guerrilla organization in *Pangasinan province*, but it is possible that he did organize guerrillas elsewhere. I do not recall ever ordering his arrest, and I believe the document purporting to show this is a forgery.[34] Of course, it is conceivable that some of my subordinates might have arrested him for a brief time without telling me about it, or that I might have been so informed but forgot about it merely because I attached little importance to it and had other matters on my mind.[35] To repeat yet again: in 1944 Ferdinand Marcos was not a famous man, and we had had so much trouble with so many would-be guerrillas that one more of the species was not likely to linger in my memory.

To be sure, General Willoughby attests that Marcos did command his own guerrilla unit and that it numbered over 8,000 men, 3,800 of whom were supposedly in Pangasinan.[36] Perhaps so, but it was and is always difficult to say with any precision how many people there are in any irregular outfit or resistance movement. If one counts only those who are actively engaged on a full-time basis, the number is almost always small. If one counts those who normally follow some civilian pursuit but regularly provide aid, information, and support, the number is considerably larger. If one counts all those who are basically sympathetic and who occasionally perform some service useful to the movement, the number is much larger. With "paper guerrillas" estimates are the merest guesses; and my own surmise (not unimpeachable knowledge) is that most of Marcos's followers were "paper guerrillas," particularly in Pangasinan.[37] In 1944-45 a "paper guerrilla" was a person who possessed a piece of paper identifying him as a member of a guerrilla organization, even though he did not have a gun. Some such people really wanted to be guerrillas. Others were former collaborators with the Japanese who wanted to cover their tracks. Others were fence-sitters who now judged that the Allies were going to win the war. Still others were out for personal gain of some kind. It did take some courage to become even a "paper guerrilla," and a bit more to organize a unit of such people, since anyone whose name was on such a list was likely to get short shrift if he was ever captured by the Japanese, though in 1944-45 this was a steadily diminishing risk. Whatever their intentions, and whatever the risks involved, "paper guerrillas" did little good and much harm. Sometimes they collected intelligence of some value, but this was vastly overbalanced by their interference with the recruiting efforts of genuine guerrillas, and by the disrepute they, as conspicuous johnny-come-latelys, brought down on the heads of genuine guerrillas whom they outnumbered by at least two to one near the war's end.

Wherever the truth lies between the claims of Marcos's admirers and adversaries, I tried to reestablish contact with him in 1982 when he paid a visit to the United States. I wrote him a letter reminding him of the circumstances under which he and I first met. He did not reply. In January 1986, Bob Lapham visited the Philippines. In the course of his stay he had a ninety-minute conversation with President Marcos. He told me afterward that Marcos had inquired about me.[38] Interestingly, prior to his meeting with Marcos in the Malacanang Palace, Bob was told by a close associate of Marcos that "bad blood" existed between Marcos and myself. No such feeling ever existed on my part; if it did (or does) on Marcos's side, the only reason I can imagine is that perhaps back in 1944 one of my men really did arrest the future president of the Philippines.

10

I Get My
Own Command

After the Japanese had driven us up to the mountains in extreme eastern Pangasinan and we had then slipped through their lines, we moved steadily back southwestward into Tarlac province once more, a sojourn typical of our harried, nomadic life. Minang had not shared our adventures around Umingan because, earlier, she had gone off northward to look for Maj. Bob Lapham. Now, as we made our way back into Tarlac in June 1944, she rejoined us, bringing with her some splendid news and some that was equivocal. The good news was tangible: .45-caliber ammunition with 1943 dates on the casings, American magazines, boxes of matches, and Camel and Chesterfield cigarettes, all decorated with American and Philippine flags and with the signature of General MacArthur beneath the pledge "I shall return."

Even better was the story behind it. Robert V. Ball, an enlisted man on Mindoro when Corregidor fell, had, like so many, refused to surrender and taken to the bush. He had fallen under the jurisdiction of Col. Wendell Fertig, who had appreciated his talents and commissioned him a captain. In May 1944 he had been dispatched northward from the island of Samar in a small sailboat carrying one radio transmitter. After many tribulations he had managed to land south of Baler Bay on the east coast of Luzon, unannounced and practically under the noses of the Japanese.

My spirits bounded upward. Here at last was the linkup we had needed so badly for so long. Soon we would have a transmitter of our own to pass on to general headquarters in Australia everything we knew about the enemy.

The jubilation was tempered by some other news. Lapham had decided to reorganize his whole command and had sent along with Minang a written directive for me to assume command of Pangasinan province, leaving Tarlac to Hendrickson. I cannot deny that I was pleased to receive what was clearly a promotion. It was recognition of past services and an expression of confidence in me personally, but at the same time it meant leaving Al, whom I had come to regard as a fast friend despite our arguments and misadventures. Al took the news in stride and told me I could take anyone I liked with me as a bodyguard save his own Little Joe. I asked to keep Gregorio Agaton, and Al released him to me promptly. I then mounted a Philippine pony and set off back north once more into the Japanese-infested province we had just fled. I might be the newly minted commander of an entire province, but my retinue could hardly have been more modest: only Greg and Minang, each also on a pony. It was June 21, 1944, twenty-six months after I had tumbled off the road into a ditch on the Bataan Death March.

Much had happened at USAFFE headquarters in Australia during those two years. General MacArthur had never lost faith in the potential of guerrilla operations all over the Philippines. When his initial radio contacts with Praeger and others gave out or appeared about ready to do so, he began to undertake imaginative remedial measures. On December 27, 1942, he sent the Filipino air ace, Capt. Jesus Villamor, by submarine to the Visayan Islands north of Mindanao. Beginning February 18, 1943, Lt. Cmdr. Charles (Chick) Parsons and Capt. Charles Smith were posted to Mindanao. All were charged to contact prominent local people of assured loyalty and to set up regular chains of communication, preferably by radio, with Australia.

Parsons was a particularly inspired choice for a mission of this sort. Sufficiently short and dark to look somewhat like a Filipino, energetic and imaginative, he had lived in the islands for years before the war and had prospered. Early in the war he had been caught by the Japanese and tortured in Fort Santiago, but unlike most who had undergone such an experience he had been freed and had eventually made his way to Australia, where he had volunteered for special duty. No irregular operation can survive on love of freedom alone. It is also essential to have an overall plan, outside encouragement, leadership, discipline, arms, ammunition, supplies, and synchronization of communications. All this Parsons was to supply, by submarine, for the last two years of the war.[1]

Villamor, Smith, and Parsons were all told to give specific orders to local guerrillas to gather and communicate information, and to forswear military action that would call Japanese attention to them and bring down reprisals on the heads of civilians who aided them, all before American forces could be in a position to afford them any protection. Anyone who has gotten this far in the present narrative is aware of how casually guerrillas everywhere heeded directives like this one. Finally, Dr. Emgidio Cruz, President Quezon's personal physician in far-off Washington, was brought back to Australia. In July 1943 he was smuggled into the Philippines to find out just what was going on, in high places and low. He secured valuable information and made it safely back to Australia.[2]

Meanwhile a major organizational shakeup was taking place in Australia. Col. Allison Ind's Philippine Subsection of the Allied Intelligence Bureau, which had tried for ten months to oversee Philippine guerrilla activity, was replaced in May 1943 by a much larger Philippine Regional Section, which reported directly to general MacArthur and was run by Gen. Courtney Whitney, one of his personal confidants. Whitney had been a regular army officer in the Philippines in the 1920s. He had resigned his commission and pursued a civilian career for years, but volunteered his services to the air corps when the war began.

Few men have been so variously estimated as this prominent prewar Manila lawyer and businessman. Many have agreed with one of MacArthur's biographers, William Manchester,who calls Whitney a consummate flatterer and an odious reactionary who was a disaster as coordinator of guerrilla operations because he was condescending to all Filipinos save those who, like himself, had big investments in the islands. Some of Manchester's antipathy may have derived from Whitney's refusal to allow dissemination of propaganda pamphlets composed by Robert Sherwood that reflected conventional American liberal views circa 1943-45.[3] Other American writers, some of whom worked closely with Whitney, describe him as a "splendid gentleman" who was keen, perceptive, energetic, rugged, aggressive, fearless, a natural leader, a masterful interrogator,and a fine judge of men who got on well with others.[4]

Filipino writers have also offered varied assessments both of Whitney and of the broader question of guerrilla operations themselves. Uldarico Baclagon, for instance, acknowledges that MacArthur appreciated the utility of guerrilla activity, but thinks he did not value it enough. He maintains that if irregular operations had been undertaken on a scale comparable to that of the Russians in Europe—i.e., enlisting the whole civilian population—the Japanese would have had to either abandon the archipelago entirely or tie up the bulk of their forces just to secure communications with their operations farther south. Yet Baclagon seems to have doubts about his own analysis, for he notes how many different Filipino peoples live on Luzon, how numerous were the jealousies and rivalries among the many guerrilla bands,and how little overall direction and planning existed throughout the first half of the war.[5] It seems to me that he also fails to consider the truly horrible reprisals the Japanese would have visited on all Filipinos had a policy of wholesale resistance been undertaken at a time when American forces in Australia were still unable to offer partisan groups much more than sympathy.

Villamor, the Filipino aviator, thinks the supreme commander would have done more had he not been systematically misled by Whitney and others near him. Villamor claims that the Filipino contribution to irregular activity was always more important than that of Americans but that this has never been properly recognized. One reason was that many Filipinos seemed to think Americans were more intelligent than themselves and so felt more comfortable if Americans were in charge. More important, he says, many around USAFFE headquarters, and Whitney most of all, were unabashed racists who regarded Filipinos as natural inferiors, treated them patronizingly, failed to give them proper support, and then hogged all the credit for Americans. He even asserts that Whitney sabotaged his own (Villamor's) messages to MacArthur.[6]

I never knew Whitney, so I cannot pass judgment on his character or alleged lack of egalitarian spirit. Likewise, since I was never at MacArthur's headquarters in Australia, I cannot know for certain whether more could have been done to aid us or whether everything reasonable *was* done. I can judge only by the official record and by what happened where I was. On these bases, it is clear that Whitney got things going promptly. Even before settling into his new job on May 24, 1943, he managed to find some radio transmitters in England that could be carried on a man's back (when the best American transmitters weighed a ton), and began to order them by the dozens, then by the hundreds. He persuaded some five hundred men of Filipino extraction from U.S. military units on the west coast and in Hawaii to volunteer for special service, then brought them to Australia, gave them crash courses in such subjects as radio operation and maintenance, weather and plane observation, and sabotage, and sent them into the Philippines. Whitney and his aides devised codes for secret communication, flooded the Philippines with American newspapers and magazines, put the "I shall return" message onto millions of packages of cigarettes, gum, candy bars, matches, and toothpaste, and shipped these into the islands on submarines provided by the navy. Ball's landing near Baler Bay was the first of many such expeditions, though it was undertaken primarily to establish a communication linkage with Southwest Pacific Area command (SWPA) in Australia. It was also the only one made by sailboat. Guns, ammunition, clothing, other supplies, and the men trained for special services followed soon after by submarine.

At the sight of such commodities, and particularly the message they bore, guerrillas and Filipino civilians alike burst into tears of joy, for at last the aid so long hoped for and expected was coming.[7] Panlilio says she and others in Marking's guerrillas were devastated when they learned that Bernard Anderson, with whom they enjoyed good relations, had burned most of his U.S. magazines, newspapers, and other propaganda lest Filipinos caught with even a scrap of it be tortured and killed by the Japanese.[8] My people were overjoyed like the rest, but my troubles were different from those Anderson envisioned. Some of the papers and magazines we received fell into the hands of "paper" guerrillas, really bandits, who used them to recruit followers. A few who persisted after being warned had to be killed.

By the time of the Leyte landings in October 1944, a whole network of 134 clandestine radio stations and 23 weather observation posts had been established all over the Philippines. They supplied MacArthur's headquarters with detailed information about everything down to which barber shop cut the hair of which Japanese lieutenant.[9]

Eventually, in July 1944, I got one of these imported transmitters, in my case a set originally built in the Dutch East Indies. It was a strange piece of machinery. It got its power from being pedalled like a bicycle. One had to pump vigorously to receive a message on it, and to build his leg muscles up to Olympic standards if he wanted to transmit.

The contraption had other drawbacks as well. Unlike the new English models, this one was too heavy for a man to carry. It had to be hauled over rough roads and trails and across open fields either in carts or on the backs of carabao. In either case it was constantly jiggled and sometimes shaken off. It seemed to me that we spent half our time trying to repair it—usually without spare parts.[10] When the instrument did work, we immediately courted trouble of a different sort: we had to change our location after each transmission lest the Japanese locate us by triangulation. Even so, we used our Rube Goldberg transmitter to send much useful information to Australia. More important for us narrowly, though not for the prosecution of the war overall, we were now able to establish rendezvous points with U.S. submarines and thus get consignments of all sorts of sorely needed arms and supplies on a semi-regular basis.

The radio and submarines were the means whereby I soon made a couple of memorable political acquaintances. As soon as I learned that submarines would be landing along the Luzon coast with some regularity, I contacted Manuel Roxas and offered to help him get to a submarine and escape from Luzon. He refused on the ground that the Japanese might retaliate against his family, but he gave me all sorts of valuable information which I at once radioed to Australia. Among those many messages was one from the family of Gen. Carlos P. Romulo, then on Mac-Arthur's staff. Romulo personally thanked me when I met him for the first time in the Sir Francis Drake Hotel in San Francisco in June, 1945.

Bob Lapham's letter of June 21, 1944, authorized me to command in Pangasinan province, to enlist personnel there, and to appoint appropriate officers. That would seem to have been clear enough, but in fact trouble began almost immediately. Lt. Col. Russell W. Volckmann, a West Point career officer who had never surrendered on Bataan and who had assumed command of guerrilla forces in north Luzon following the deaths of Colonels Moses and Noble, now sent a runner to inform me that I should place myself and my men under his command. I replied by letter that this was impossible, since I was already under the command of Major Lapham, who had himself earlier resisted being absorbed into Volckmann's organization. I compared my position to that of a baserunner caught between bases, destined to be tagged out either way I went. Volckmann was not impressed by my baseball metaphor. He repeated his orders. I don't recall exactly how I phrased my reply this time, but it meant, unmistakably, "No." Volckmann did not give up easily. Not long afterward two Americans under his command came to see me. My response was typical of the mistrust that existed among so many irregulars. I suspected that their intention was to arrest me, so I told my men to be alert and, if necessary, to seize them, after which I would ship them back north. My fears proved unfounded. The pair had come only to talk. One of them needed glasses badly and I was able to get him some from Manila, so we parted amicably.

A few months later, though, Volckmann threatened to have me court martialled for desertion if I persisted in maintaining my independence from him. This time I consulted Lapham by runner and received a letter from him, October 31, 1944, in which he advised me simply to ignore Volckmann. The latter, he said, had no business giving me orders at all; nor did he have any authority to court martial me for desertion, disobedience, or anything else, since a guerrilla is a volunteer.

My real reason for spurning Volckmann was that I did not want to break connections with Lapham. I had joined his forces willingly, and he had treated me well. Though I had never met Bob at this time, I had already come to admire him as a reasonable man and a fighter. I knew he had not subordinated himself to Volckmann, and I thought my primary loyalty should be to him. Finally, both of us believed we had a better organization than Volckmann, many of whose troops were said to be armed only with bolos.[11]

To this day I am not sure what Volckmann's motive was

in these transactions. At the time I thought it was mere empire building. There are several other possibilities, though. Volckmann may have genuinely believed he could make better use of Lapham's men, or mine, than we could ourselves. From all written accounts his own guerrillas performed admirably after the American landings in north Luzon in 1945. Perhaps he wanted our units as sources of supply for his own? Most of his followers were holed up in the mountains of the far north while we operated in the heavily populated, fertile central plain of Luzon, where food was abundant.

It may also have been that both natural inclination and experience had convinced Volckmann that everyone should be fitted into a single disciplined organization, albeit with himself at the top. Unlike those of us farther south, Volckmann removed his guerrillas from their barrios, put them in company camps for training, and disciplined them strictly (even to ordering that anyone who surrendered or let himself be captured by the enemy would be shot on sight); after which he broke them into small units and let them attack the Japanese periodically to keep up their spirits.[12] These Prussian procedures would have been impossible where we were in the lowlands, but Blackburn, Volckmann's chief aide, says they were welcomed by guerrillas and civilians alike in the wild, remote north where there had been an urgent need for control and direction for many months. He adds that he and Volckmann received much willing cooperation from wise old Igorot chiefs who were themselves good organizers and who appreciated what was being attempted.[13] Villamor, who did not esteem most American guerrillas, calls Volckmann "tough" in an admiring way, and contrasts favorably Volckmann's centralization of authority with the "useless overlapping" of the many units in central Luzon.[14]

On the last point I must disagree with both Volckmann and Villamor. Much history is against them. Both in the Spanish resistance to Napoleon, and all over Europe in World War II, efforts to integrate different, competing, and often hostile guerrilla bands into one organization failed completely.

Not the least interesting aspect of the matter is the way Volckmann and Blackburn deal with it in their books. Blackburn barely mentions Lapham; and myself not at all. Volckmann's book, *We Remained*, is quite informative generally, and it is calm and measured in tone. Yet in it Volckmann says nothing at all about his efforts to absorb Bob's command earlier in the war or mine in 1944!

Looking back four decades later, I still cannot see how anything would have been gained by merging our units with Volckmann's. We would have merely passed under the command of someone from a different area who was accustomed to operating under different conditions, and at a time when none of us, individually or collectively, had enough guns or ammunition to undertake a major battle with Japanese. At the time my main regret about the whole affair was that during it Lapham asked me to give up my bicycle-powered radio transmitter to Maj. Parker Calvert, commander of Volckmann's First District. The reason was that Volckmann had not yet received his first supplies by submarine and so needed a radio to send his messages to Lapham, who then relayed them to Australia.

While I was fending off the unwelcome attentions of Volckmann, I was also trying to put my new domain in order. Majs. Edwin Ramsey and Charles Cushing had once tried to organize it, but it had since fallen apart. I now went around recruiting leaders and men, some ex-followers of theirs, some new men, and explaining to both what our major objectives should be.

Right off I had what I regarded as a stroke of luck. Many of those whom I recruited were Igorots, mountaineers who inhabit the cordillera of northern Luzon. The diverse peoples of the Philippines vary considerably in native capacity and attitude toward life; and no less diverse were the opinions of various Americans *about* them. Donald Blackburn, for instance, thought it was useless to try to make soldiers out of Ilocanos. They were hopeless, he said: undisciplined, indifferent, undependable, and brainlessly good natured, in every way inferior to the husky, bright, energetic little Igorots.[15] Al Hendrickson, by contrast, rated Ilocanos above Igorots for education, intelligence, and bravery. He disliked Igorots because they were unwilling to venture out of the mountains. Tom Chengay, he said, was the only one of them he ever knew who readily went down into the lowlands to fight. I don't agree entirely with either Blackburn or Al. I think Blackburn downgraded the Ilocanos unduly, but like him I did think Igorots were better fighters and more loyal than Ilocanos. They were also tough physically, amazingly agile, and strong. Religiously, most of them were pagans; and many, though not all, were still primitive.

Not the least interesting characteristic of Filipinos was their superstitions, those of the pagans being the most picturesque. Both Volckmann and Blackburn lived among Igorots and other pagan tribes, and they relate a number of interesting anecdotes about them. Once Igorot pagan priests sacrificed several chickens and studied their spleens to determine if it was safe for Blackburn and Volckmann to stay in their house. They decided that it was, and no harm befell them. Another time a pagan priest prayed and sacrificed chickens when Blackburn was sick. He got better at once. Still another time Volckmann was ill. An old native said it was due to a witch, and that the bewitchment could be undone only by another witch. An ancient one was procured. She decided she needed a consultant. The next day the two of them prayed until they were exhausted. Volckmann's condition improved promptly.[16] Volckmann himself records that he once wanted to leave an area in north Luzon because he had heard that a Japanese patrol was headed in that direction. The leader of a pagan tribe there, a man whom Volckmann trusted, insisted that pagan priests be consulted. Four of these dignitaries then cut open four chickens, their favorite vehicle for divination, studied the spleens, and directed that the legs of the chickens be buried on the trail leading to Volckmann's camp. They assured him that when the Japanese reached that spot they would grow lethargic and would not continue to look for him. Nothing Volckmann could say or do would move either the chief or the priests from their resolve. They buried the chicken legs. Soon the Japanese came to the burial spot. They stopped, then changed directions and went off down a river valley.[17] I'm not sure what the moral is; perhaps that not all the world's medical expertise is found in high priced American hospitals.

These tales have long reminded me of comparisons that have been made, partly tongue-in-cheek, between healers of different cultures in different historical epochs. The clerical exorcists of medieval and early modern Europe used to try to cure patients by praying over them and casting devils out of them. For centuries, perhaps millennia, African witch doctors, garbed in grotesque regalia, shaking bones and spouting incantations, have tried to do essentially the same thing. In the twentieth-century Western world, psychoanalysts put patients on couches and try to induce them to confront and transform their malign subconscious impulses. Among these varied practitioners, rates of cure appear to have been comparable, but the psychoanalysts are much the most expensive. (Of course, contemporary psychiatrists employ an array of recently discovered drugs to help a higher proportion of their patients than their predecessors could.)

None of my Igorots did anything as striking as Volckmann's and Blackburn's consultants, but the beliefs of some of them were intriguing. It had once been the custom among them that a prospective bridegroom should demonstrate his eligibility for matrimony by bringing in the head of a Christian before the wedding. They also had an equally memorable, and considerably more appealing, custom. A man sometimes selected a prospective wife and lived with her for several months. If she did not become pregnant, he returned her to her family and undertook the same experiment with another girl. This must have been a great locale for a young man who was infertile—or would have been for someone who had had a vasectomy.

These idle speculations aside, the most valuable of the Igorots I had was a highly intelligent, tough and absolutely fearless little fellow named Tomas Chengay. Tom had worked in the gold mines of the north before the war. Here he had become familiar with Americans and had grown to like them. Early in the war he had served under Volckmann, and he had been with Al Hendrickson when Al raided the Itogon mine in north Luzon in October 1942. When Tom and I met, he commanded a small detachment of his fellow Igorot guerrillas. He joined our forces readily and became one of my most trustworthy officers. He hated spies and collaborators passionately and did an excellent job of clearing them out wherever we went. He had a particularly mercurial temperament. If enraged at someone bigger than himself, he would leap straight up in the air and strike at the taller man. Because of his attitude toward enemies of any sort, he was sometimes called "No Retreat."

Two of our recruits, Joseph and William Henry, are worth mentioning by name because their cases illustrate why it was never hard to fill guerrilla ranks. Their father was an American, their mother a Filipina. Their father had died in 1942, and the Japanese had laughed when they viewed his body. For the brothers this was a deadly insult. They sought revenge, and so joined my guerrilla band. Many recruits had some personal motive like this; most often either they or some member of their family had been brutalized by the Japanese in some sickening way.

Before long a large part of Pangasinan was unified, at least on paper. I then divided the province into four sectors and placed a captain over each: Tom Chengay over the north district, Antonio Garcia over the west, Emilio Hernandez over the central, and his brother Antonio Hernandez over the east. For my headquarters staff I selected Maj. Severino M. Obaña of the Philippine army as my second in command; for supply officer, a former newspaperman and writer, Jimmy Galura; and for chief of intelligence, a college graduate named Juan Utleg, who proved to be an inspired choice. The whole organization, while impromptu, was patterned as closely on regular American army tables of organization as circumstances permitted. We had doctors and nurses of sorts, Protestant and Catholic chaplains, demolition experts, an elite fighting company composed exclusively of ex-Filipino Scouts, a special sabotage squadron, and a squadron of military police. One of the main duties of the last was to handle the complaints of civilians. So dominant had guerrillas become in the Philippine countryside by 1944 that if a peasant's carabao was stolen or some comparable crime was committed against him or his family, he would not ordinarily take his grievance to either the Japanese or some representative of their puppet Philippine Republic, but to the local guerrillas. In our unit the military police would then deal with the matter as best they could.

All our units had experienced leadership. The official army history (Robert Ross-Smith, *Triumph in the Philippines*) refers to several of our units combined as the Buena Vista Regiment, a body that gave an excellent account of itself fighting in tandem with the Thirty-second (Red Arrow) Division along the Villa Verde Trail in the northern mountains in the spring of 1945, where I myself spent my last days in the Philippines.

I tried to pay equivalent attention to the civilian and diplomatic sectors. I sought out Alfred Balingao, the governor of Pangasinan, explained our circumstances and problems to him, and offered him our cooperation in return for his loyalty. He agreed readily, and put no obstacles in the way of our recruitment. One of my particular objectives was to gather into our organization as many men as we could from the Constabulary. If we were successful, we could bleed the Constabulary white, and could add trained and armed recruits to our own forces. To this end, I took a professional printer, his family, and his equipment; hid them; took care of all their needs; and put him to work printing leaflets to circulate among civilians and to call on Constabularymen to come over to us. Undoubtedly, some of these missives fell into the hands of the Japanese, but we were feeling our oats by now, growing stronger every day, and simply did not care any longer. The effort itself, I must admit, was not much of a success.

We gained the sympathy and cooperation of many members of the Constabulary, but few of them actually joined our ranks.

Picking Captain Juan Utleg to head the intelligence section proved to be the best appointment I made, even though the man eventually forced upon me the most agonizing decision I have ever had to make about anything. Juan was a neat, personable Filipino with a college degree in forestry. When I first met him, I found that his beliefs and sympathies were close to my own. I talked to him many times and finally asked him to join our organization. He declined at first because he had a family, then abruptly volunteered. Juan proved to be an excellent organizer and showed uncommon practical sense in his job as well. He recruited all sorts of people and paid them to gather all sorts of information. Soon he designated specific assignments to specific persons who had demonstrated expertise at particular tasks. He worked their varied findings into intelligence briefs, and thereby produced reliable intelligence summaries for me. In short order he collected an impressive amount of information about Japanese installations, troop strength, movements, and plans. Later reports showed it to have been remarkably accurate.

The most significant of Utleg's accomplishments was to map Japanese installations at San Fernando, La Union, north of Lingayen Gulf on the west coast of Luzon. In the latter part of 1944 all signs pointed to American landings somewhere on Luzon before many more months. But where? The Japanese did not know, but it was clear that they regarded the coast around San Fernando as a likely locale, because they steadily moved heavy American guns from as far away as Corregidor and fixed them in strongly fortified tunnels dug into the hillside above Poro Point. Lingayen Gulf itself, a few miles south, was also a possible landing site but a risky one because of unfavorable tides. We discovered afterward that the information our operatives gathered about the Japanese gun emplacements was studied carefully by General Willoughby, MacArthur's G-2 in Australia. On the basis of it the original landing plans were changed and the uncertain tides and surf in the gulf were risked. As a consequence, the Japanese were surprised and not well situated to resist the landings save by kamikaze attacks, and untold hundreds of American lives were thereby saved. Overall, it was a clear vindication of the dictum of the British military strategist B.H. Liddell Hart that obstacles of nature should always be accepted and combatted in preference to undertaking a frontal assault against an enemy in a prepared position. For me personally, if I had never accomplished anything else in the whole war I would have regarded my time as having been spent profitably.

Juan Utleg's value as an intelligence officer eventually forced me into the most excruciating dilemma I have ever confronted, even worse than dealing with the killer of Dolores. As described above, Juan had learned all about Japanese defensive preparations near San Fernando. Moreover, his counterespionage people had enabled him to catch several Filipinos who were spying for the Japanese. Of course, it did not take the enemy long to learn who was responsible for this or to find out what his position was in my outfit. As an example of how fast such news got around, the governor of Pangasinan once told me that the local Japanese Kempeitai commander had asked him if he knew Capt. Ray Hunt. The governor replied that he had heard of me but did not know me. The Japanese then remarked that the governor must know I was in his area, and added with an understanding smile, "When you see him, tell him I said 'Hello,' and that some day we will get him." The governor relayed this message to me, adding that the Japanese knew my exact description, even to the color of my hair and eyes.

Juan knew the Kempeitai were looking for him too. One day when he was home he saw some Japanese troops approaching the house. He slipped out a rear window into a bamboo grove. The visitors then questioned his wife. She said Juan was not at home. The Japanese then took Mrs. Utleg and their young son, and left a message with villagers that the two would be retained as hostages and would be killed if Juan did not surrender.

Juan was a brave man as well as an able one, but, like most Filipinos, he treasured his family above all else. He came to me with tears in his eyes and begged me to let him surrender. I excused myself and went out to consult Greg. When I came back, I had the first of several long talks with Juan. Finally, I told him I absolutely could not let him go. He knew all the leading members of the guerrilla forces in Pangasinan, all our strengths and weaknesses, all our battle plans, all our spies, informers, and sympathizers, and everything about how we were now getting occasional reinforcements from submarines. He promised over and over that he would never reveal anything to the Japanese. I reminded him quite as often that the enemy was familiar with every means known to man of extracting information from even the bravest and strongest, and that they would stop at nothing when dealing with someone as valuable as himself. For this reason we simply could not let him go to them. All our plans to aid the returning American troops might be destroyed. Juan knew this, of course, but it simply reminded him afresh of what the Japanese might do to his wife and son if he did not surrender. He unfolded his whole life to me, told me how much he loved his family, and begged me to relent. I simply could not. Heartless though it must seem, I had to weigh the lives of Mrs. Utleg and her son against those of many hundreds of guerrillas and civilian supporters of ours. I had Juan placed under arrest, sedated, and guarded heavily. For several days I prayed with more fervor than I had ever done before—or have since. A few days later a light appeared in Juan's house again. His wife and child were home unharmed. Why, I don't know. Sometimes the Japanese simply acted in legendary "inscrutable" Oriental fashion. Whatever their reasons, and even though we still had to keep Juan in hiding, the way things turned out lifted from me the most terrible burden I have ever had to bear. What I would have done if Juan's wife and child had been killed I cannot imagine.

It has sometimes been asked rhetorically what kind of job requires the keenest intelligence and the highest level of general ability: research scientist, medical doctor, manager of a big business, president of a university or school system, political leader, army commander, or what have you? I cannot pretend to know the answer, and anyone in any prominent position has difficult decisions to make occasionally, but I don't believe anyone in any civilian occupation ever has to face dilemmas as cruel as some of those that crop up in wars. The case of Juan Utleg was Exhibit A in my experience.

Governor Balingao of Pangasinan, who had conveyed to me greetings from the local Kempeitai commander, also told me a story about a macabre incident of a different sort that he had witnessed. The Japanese had set to work to build a crude wooden bridge over a river near Umingan. When it was almost finished, the river flooded and the bridge was carried away. They rebuilt it, only to have another flood sweep it away again. Then they built it a third time. When they were finished, two Japanese soldiers sat down cross legged, one at each end of the bridge, and their companions piled wood about them. Then all the Japanese began a ceremonial prayer. In the midst of it the wood was lighted and the two soldiers were burned to death without making a movement or a sound. Such actions illustrate the impassable psychological barrier that separated Japanese from Westerners. It also availed them little: a few weeks later we burned the bridge to the water's edge.

Fortunately for our sanity, life was not always as sordid as a recital of these grim episodes might indicate. In fact, once I got things reasonably well organized in Pangasinan I began to think, for the first time since the war began, that I might survive it. We even had some good news of a conventional sort occasionally. Nine months after he had become my bodyguard, Greg Agaton surprised us all by revealing that he planned to get married. Of course, we were all pleased for him personally. We found a minister, I loaned him some clothing, and he and his bride, Petronia

M. Ruiz, were properly wed in our camp on September 15, 1944. My own feelings were mixed, since I had come to respect, trust, and rely on Greg a great deal. I assumed that once married he would quit the guerrillas and I would have to find a new aide. But he did not: instead he sent his new wife back to her home in San Nicolas, Pangasinan, near where we were now encamped, and continued as my number one man. The wedding did produce a break between us eventually, though. Before this I had promised Greg that if I lived through the war I would take him back to the United States with me, if he wanted to go. I extended the offer again after the war, but by then he and his wife were in the process of acquiring a family of five sons, and he felt that their collective future was in the Philippines. We did finally meet once more, but it was decades later, in Honolulu, in December 1984. The reunion was tearful.

In 1943 we had had a lot of trouble either getting information to Australia or securing supplies for our own troops. As indicated earlier, many of our arms were secured by capture from the enemy. Things improved in 1944 when submarines began to land periodically near Baler Bay in Tayabas province on the east coast of Luzon. The site was close to a Japanese naval base, but it had to be chosen since the water was too shallow for submarines anywhere else along that coast. Prior contact had been made with Bob Lapham, who had already established a system of coast watchers in the hope that they might spot a submarine. Both Bob and Al Hendrickson sent many of their guerrillas over the Sierra Madre Mountains to contact the submarines and haul away their cargo. Neither I nor any of my men ever unloaded a submarine, but beginning in June 1944, when Minang came back from her trip to see Lapham, bearing my promotion to commander of Pangasinan, we began to get supplies from submarines.

Because the whole operation was exceedingly risky, the guerrillas involved were not told where they were going or for what purpose until they actually arrived and were put to work building bamboo rafts to unload submarines. After dark there would be an exchange of coded light signals, following which the sub would slip into shallow water, where it would be temporarily helpless: unable to submerge quickly and escape in case of detection. For this reason the captain and crew of a submarine always wanted to unload their cargo as fast as possible. This made problems. The deck of a submarine loomed eight feet above the bamboo rafts. The natural bobbing of the rafts in the sea combined with the haste of those unloading sometimes caused crates of arms to go to the bottom of the bay. We discovered that many destined for us must have contained .50-caliber machine guns, since we got enough .50 ammunition to shoot at everything that moved for the next several months, but no equivalent number of machine guns. We did receive many small arms of various types: carbines, "grease guns," tommyguns, M-1 Garands, and sidearms. Also included were various medicines and surgical instruments, radio transmitters, propaganda materials, money, and the usual assortment of cigarettes and candy. Gradually the subs began to appear more often to augment these supplies and to drop off specially trained men of various sorts: Filipino radio operators and repairmen, teams of demolition experts, and weather observers. Some fifty tons of commodities were sent to Lapham's headquarters; more intended for him was landed with shipments for Anderson.[18] How much of it I got, I do not know exactly: quite a bit.

A story of some sort went with or soon became attached to most of these items. A case we got marked "Money" was interesting in the sense that on the first submarine it was not broken open. On subsequent trips, however, it was discovered that whiskey and pesos tended to disappear en route. Finally some imaginative soul had an inspiration and took to marking these containers "Military Rations." None was molested thereafter.[19]

The medicines proved invaluable. In preceding months Al Hendrickson and I had occasionally gotten hold of a few quinine tablets or other medicines that happened to be already in the Philippines. With these meager supplies we had tried to doctor tropical ulcers, malaria, and other native maladies, as well as an array of ordinary cuts and bruises, especially those of children. How badly medical care was needed is indicated by tales related by other guerrillas. Col. Robert Arnold describes how he had a terrible stomachache which a local pastor, in default of a doctor, diagnosed as appendicitis. With no doctor, no operation was possible, but some natives suggested an alternative. The lining of a chicken's gizzard contains juices that will dissolve anything less formidable than an anvil, so all the dried chicken gizzard linings that could be found were boiled to make an incredibly bitter broth which Arnold forced himself to swallow twice a day. Eventually he recovered.[20] Illif David Richardson, a guerrilla on Leyte, once faced an even more bizarre medical problem. There the Japanese had bayoneted a Filipino in the stomach, ripping such a gash that the man's intestines hung out. Incredibly, the victim managed to run three miles without pushing his intestines back inside his body cavity, or even trying to hold them close to his stomach. Richardson consulted a medical book and decided nothing in it was applicable to present circumstances, so he cut the wound larger, stuffed the poor man's intestines back in, gave him all the sulfa drugs he happened to have, and stitched up the wound with abaca fiber, the only thread available, only to have his hapless patient die after all. Of the whole disheartening experience he said, "It is only in the storybooks that hard work, effort, trying and trying again come out to have a happy ending. Working in the guerrilla has taught me that much."[21] Most likely Richardson was just momentarily, and understandably, disheartened. I don't think a congenital pessimist could have lasted out the war with irregulars. Though I long thought, as a betting proposition, that I would not survive the war, I never acted on that assumption on a day-to-day basis.

One useful by-product of the periodic submarine contacts was that Hendrickson was able to send off to Australia five Americans whom he had fed and doctored for weeks but who were obviously too sick or dispirited, or both, to be of any value in battle. They were Captain Lage, Lieutenants Kiery and Naylor, and Sergeants Jellison and Bolstead. As narrated in chapter 4, above, Kiery refused to hike through a jungle and over a mountain to reach the submarine, choosing instead to row a rubber boat around a point of land. It capsized and he was drowned. One of the others told Al flatly that he was "sick of the God-damned war" and only wanted to get away from it, though he stayed in the army after 1945 and eventually attained considerable rank.

Of course, it occurred to us that if submarines could bring in supplies and take away the sick, they could also take away men liberated from Japanese prison camps, not to speak of ourselves. The last temptation was hard to resist. We American guerrillas had all been in combat zones for three years, we all wanted to save our skins, and doubtless we would have been permitted to leave had we asked. Nonetheless, Lapham, Hendrickson, and I stayed on longer, for reasons that will be explained later.

The weapons brought to us by the submarines were most welcome, obviously, though not every guerrilla unit got a sample of every type. I was keenly aware of what my organization needed but did not get. There were no artillery pieces, mortars, rifle grenades, mines, or dynamite, all of which would have been extremely useful to us. Of course, there was no use complaining about this. A submarine can carry only so much, and it cannot carry artillery at all.

Dynamite would have been invaluable for demolition. Lacking it, we once tried to blow up a bridge by attaching thirty-second fuses to some 75-mm. shells we happened to have. All they did was blow holes in the reinforced concrete deck. In fact, more damage was done to two of our own men, Eusebio Membrado and Juan Leal, than to the bridge; and the medical "treatment" they got afterward was worse than their original injuries. It made me sick to watch our company doctor, Fidel Ramirez, probe around in their wounds without an anesthetic, looking for fragments of concrete. When I questioned him about his crude procedures, he said he was a pediatrician, not exactly the medical specialty we needed most just then.

Every gun we got presented problems of some kind. All those in the semi-automatic class had different recoil actions. For each a minimum time had to elapse after firing before the gun would settle back into its original position so it could be fired again with some accuracy. If insufficient time was allowed, each successive shot would hit higher than the preceding one. One had to aim low and fire in short bursts, otherwise most of the bullets would go high and be wasted. Low shots at least had a chance to ricochet into the target. For me, the worst such weapon was the Browning automatic rifle (BAR). When it worked properly, it was a devastating gun; but it was heavy, had large, bulky clips, and jammed easily. I tried firing it from a sling and from the hip, but I could never control it. I practiced by shooting at tree roots. Invariably, within a few seconds I was shooting out treetops.

I liked the semi-automatic M-1 Garand 30.06 better, though it was also heavy and jammed easily if its ammunition clips were dented or dirty. Its sights were also sensitive and could be knocked awry merely by passing through brush. One had to spend a lot of time cleaning and sighting a Garand, but if it was properly kept up it was a fine weapon. Though less accurate than a Springfield, it spat out bullets in a stream.

My sentimental favorite was the Springfield .03. It was an older (World War I) rifle than the Garand but much the most reliable gun we had. It was bolt action, carried five shells individually inserted plus one in the chamber, and had open iron sights that were not easily jimmied. You could drop it in a river and expect it to fire faithfully when it was fished out. Lighter than a Garand, it was easier to carry save in dense brush. Not least, it had a good feel in one's hand, like a certain cue does to a pool player or a favorite old glove to a baseball player. Under primitive conditions a simple, durable weapon is often the most practical, as the global popularity of the Russian Kalashnikov rifle has demonstrated since World War II.

We got a few tommyguns: heavy, clumsy, short-barrelled .45-caliber blasters that fired either twenty-shot clips or fifty-round drums of bullets, though they were most effective when fired in bursts of five shots. The FBI made tommyguns famous. I used mine sometimes to hunt wild pigs.

We also got three weapons that were brand new, at least to me. One was a carbine, a light, flimsy, tinny sounding thing that looked like it might have been made from a Prince Albert tobacco can. Though its sights were not reliable, it was a good weapon in the brush because it splattered bullets all over the place. The grease gun was another .45, so called because it looked like a grease gun and poured out a seemingly endless stream of bullets. It had a retractable iron stock, and was short, heavy, awkward to carry, and hard to handle. Finally, we got a case of bazookas. We did not know what they were, and no instructions came with them. Not surprisingly, we had a hard time figuring out how they worked or what could be done with them. Filipinos are fond of guns, and many of our men had repeatedly taken apart and reassembled the ancient relics we had been carrying about for many months. Because they had sometimes made mistakes, we had had lots of misfires. Now they had some new toys to tinker with. Before long a couple of adventuresome tyros managed to fire a round from a bazooka by accident, fortunately without killing anyone in the process. I had a couple of narrow escapes myself. Once one of my men reported that his BAR would not fire in the automatic position. I had had so little to do with BARs that I did not realize that the mere force of loading would cause the firing pin to strike the cartridge. Thus, when I took his gun and began to look at it the first thing I did was inadvertently fire a shot that creased the arm of a curious Filipino lieutenant nearby. Another time I was casual with a tommygun inside a house and thereby fired an unplanned burst. This occasion was especially embarrassing, since I had just dressed down my men for being careless about misfires and for shooting when the Japanese were near enough to hear them. In this case, luckily, the walls of the house prevented the racket from reaching enemy ears.

In the last months of 1944, especially after the Leyte landings in October made it evident that American landings on Luzon could not be far off, general headquarters directed us to save our new weapons so they would be a surprise to the enemy when we went into serious action. We had always had trouble restraining the more impetuous of the Filipinos. Now that the tempo of everything was picking up visibly, and they had new guns in the bargain, I could not always contain them. When the bazooka was fired accidentally, the destructive force of its shell made an indelible impression on everyone nearby. At once my men begged me to let them take it down into the lowlands, well away from where we happened to be just then, and try it out against a Kempeitai outpost. After an argument, I relented. They dashed off, jubilant as six-year-olds at a birthday party. The bazooka was a tremendous success: those in the Japanese outpost never knew what hit them. There were no known survivors.

The whole episode typified a problem that guerrilla leaders had with Filipinos everywhere. Ordinarily they would listen to reason and would not attack Japanese in their own locale because of the reprisals against civilians that would follow. But now and then they would burn to retaliate for some enemy atrocity, or they would just get "antsy" and want some action, so they would go some distance away and attack Japanese there, thus insuring that enemy vengeance would at least fall on civilians under the wing of some other guerrillas.

An unauthorized, and more private, venture by a Filipino lieutenant was comparably noisy but much less successful then the bazooka attack. One day, dressed as a member of the Constabulary and armed with one of our new carbines, he stopped three Japanese riding along a dusty road in a buggy. He asked them to dismount and accompany him, saying he would take them to a village where a party was to be given in their honor. His real intention was probably to shoot them, since we had by then a standing rule that no Japanese prisoners were to be taken. Before long the presumed honored guests noticed the lieutenant's carbine, a weapon they had never seen before. Soon they put two and two together and started to run off. The lieutenant promptly laid down a hail of lead with his new firearm. Though he killed one Japanese, he was such a bad shot that he missed the other two, who of course rushed back to their garrison to tell their compatriots about the new American weapon. I was disgusted. If our man had killed all the Japanese it would have been fine: instead, he had revealed to the enemy a weapon we had planned to conceal. Thus, instead of being commended or decorated for bravery he was reprimanded and disciplined for bad judgment. So fine the line between hero and goat. . . .

As the foregoing incidents indicate, and especially when it became clear that the Japanese anticipated American landings soon, guerrilla morale bounded upward. Fortunately, there were many ways to keep the men busy, most notably after we were told by SWPA headquarters in Australia to be ready to give all-out support to the invasion forces whenever we received pertinent directives, five days before the landings. We started twenty things at once. We mapped towns and buildings where the enemy had stored supplies so American planes would (hopefully) not do unnecessary damage when bombing. We made plans to cut enemy communications and supply lines, and to sabotage fuel dumps. We picked strategic spots along roads and trails where we could set last-minute road blocks and ambushes. We built storehouses in the mountains and foothills in northern and eastern Pangasinan, and stored rice in them. We made arrangements to rescue and hide downed American pilots; and assigned each company specific duties in all these spheres before the anticipated invasion and during it.[22] Morale problems developed in some U.S. units during the fighting in northern Luzon in 1945, but among the guerrillas late in 1944 our main problem was to keep our men cool.

As mentioned before, among my constant vexations was dealing with nuisances who posed as guerrillas, as well as adventurers and bandits who formed "paper" guerrilla organizations as covers for illicit operations of various types. This grew much worse in the last year of the war and in the immediate postwar period. In particular, all the collaborators rushed to join some irregular unit in order to expunge their guilt and appear to returning American forces as fellow warriors in the struggle for freedom.

Another common type was the ambitious opportunist who wanted to be able to claim guerrilla service in order to promote himself in postwar Philippine politics. Men of this sort were forever raising imaginary armies which they invariably "commanded." One particular rascal of the political type I ordered arrested. One of my men, in ordinary Filipino dress, apprehended the man in broad daylight in a village full of Japanese troops, and told him "Captain Hunt wants to see you." The aspiring politician tried to offer some excuse to depart, but the guerrilla replied that he had orders to deliver the man alive or leave him dead in the dust. This information clarified the troublemaker's understanding marvellously, and he walked briskly in the direction of my current hideaway with the guard right behind him. Quite likely his thoughts were on an incident he had recently witnessed in his home village. There a guerrilla, like the present one tailing him, had simply opened a hollow gourd, pulled out a gun, and shot two Japanese at point blank range.

When the pair reached my abode, I let the prisoner wait a considerable time. When I came to see him at last, his forehead was covered with beads of perspiration. Probably he thought this day was going to be his last. I spoke to him quietly, asking him only about his recruiting efforts and whether he was in contact with American forces outside the Philippines. To the latter he replied eagerly that he did indeed have such contacts and that only a few days before he had received some smuggled American magazines which he now planned to distribute. I listened to this for a time, then asked Greg to bring me a new .45 grease gun. I pointed it out the window and shot some bark off a nearby tree. The man's eyes widened. Then I asked him if he knew what kind of gun it was? All he could answer was that it was new. I then asked him which he thought would do more harm to our common enemy, the magazines he proposed to distribute or the gun? He assured me profusely that he understood my meaning and that he would never do anything that would in any way interfere with the activities of true guerrillas. So I let him go. Similar pests got similar warnings, or else they were invited to take guns and become guerrillas on the spot. With most, that ended the conversation and we had no trouble from them afterward.

One day late in 1944 I was standing outdoors when I heard a long, low rumble. As I strained my eyes southward I saw something I had dreamed about for two and a half years; columns of smoke climbing into the sky, in this case from the direction of Clark Field in Pampanga. It indicated that American planes had bombed an enemy stronghold. All of us burst out with cries of joy and pummelled each other on the back with wild abandon. Every guerrilla on Luzon must have responded just as we did. Clay Conner called the bombing "the most beautiful sight imaginable." Frank Gyovai said it was the grandest sight he ever saw. Yay Panlilio wrote that even Marking's dog succumbed to the hysteria: whining, barking, and quivering with excitement as their guerrillas whooped and hollered and cried.[23]

A few days later we actually saw some American planes of a new type; P-38s, as it turned out. Then we saw occasional dogfights. Unlike those in the early days of the war, these invariably ended with the P-38s downing or chasing off their Japanese opponents. Soon navy planes began to fly over regularly. I thought of their pilots who would sleep between white sheets that night, with no fear of the Japanese. This, in turn, brought back thoughts of home, of seeing my parents and younger sisters again, of sleeping in a soft bed without either the company or the buzzing of insects, and of ice cream, cake, cheese, a cold bottle of beer, white bread, white women, merely the companionship of ordinary Americans again.

Those last three months of 1944, blurred in my memory now after the passage of four decades, were a strange mixture of matters of the utmost gravity, some bizarre personal adventures, and some mere frivolity. The serious part was that I knew time was growing short, and I worried about the accuracy of the intelligence we had gathered and whether I had drawn the proper conclusions from it.

Other concerns were less vital. One day on my way to our regular headquarters near San Quintin, I received an invitation to visit the home of a Spanish mestizo named Juan Bautista. Juan owned 7,500 acres of fine rice land, and from the standpoint of our guerrillas was an admirable fellow since he had once given us ten thousand pesos. To be sure, he had given it in Japanese scrip and now wanted a receipt indicating that he should be repaid one day in sound Philippine or American money. While I had to turn him down politely on that score, he must not have expected anything else, since he treated me royally to drinks and a feast of barbecued pig, followed by a siesta, and then a dance to a string band. The whole performance stretched over many hours in a beautiful house and was seasoned with pleasant conversation on a variety of topics.

The only puzzling aspect of the whole splendid evening was that at various times during it Juan introduced me to five fine looking young Filipinas, each one of whom he identified as his wife. Eventually curiosity got the better of good manners, and I asked him how he could possibly have five wives in a Christian country where divorce was illegal. He said it was really quite simple: they were all common-law wives, the daughters of various of his tenants, all of whom acquiesced in the arrangement since it made possible a better life for the girls and also for their families. Still curious, I asked him if the women ever became jealous. He said this was rare, since he treated them all equally, setting aside one night per week for each one; but if one became dissatisfied or made trouble she was simply returned to her parents and the arrangement with her was cancelled. He added that he also owned a fishing fleet and that on weekends he often fished. He probably did so in self-defense, from need of rest. I also noticed that despite the five wives there were no children on the premises. Juan admitted ruefully that he had none. Perhaps his exceptional romantic exertions had rendered him infertile. To top off the evening, Juan suggested that I stay in the Philippines after the war. He said he would give me some land to cultivate, build me a house, and help me collect five wives just as he had. For a young man it was a hard offer to turn down.

Some guerrillas have written that many of their people were hungry and sick much of the time, especially in 1944-45 when the Japanese began to strip the islands of much of their food to maintain their own troops. As my visit to Juan Bautista indicates, that forlorn condition was not universal. Where I was during the last half of the war, we had about the normal amount of sickness, malaria primarily; and we were always handicapped by lack of medicines and medical supplies and by a scarcity of trained doctors; but we were never seriously short of food. This was made evident to me again on December 11, 1944, one of the happiest days of my life. This was not merely because it was my twenty-fifth birthday, nor because it would be my last birthday in the Philippines (something I could not know); but because five hundred guerrillas and the poor farmers of the village of Pantabangan, near San José, gave me a tremendous party. There was much food and even a children's string band that delighted me by playing a lot of American numbers I hadn't heard since the war began. Everybody ate and drank and danced, and for a night forgot the war. It indicates how self-confident, not to say reckless, we had become by now, that the whole soirée took place with a Japanese garrison only three miles away. I remember the day distinctly for another reason as well. For the first time in three years, when Filipinos asked me when the Americans would return, I no longer had to put them off with "six months." Now I could honestly say it would be a good deal sooner.

It was about this time, too, that I had my last confrontation of the tempestuous sort with Minang. An outsider would doubtless say that this one, like some of our earlier squabbles, was my fault. In general, Filipinas make good wives. Most of them are used to work and hardship, and they ordinarily remain faithful to one man. Of course, Minang and I were not married, but she had been for some time my common-law wife. My attention span was somewhat short in those days, though, and one day when she was gone I was having a private tête-à-tête with a pretty young Filipina when Minang returned unexpectedly. Greg tried to intercept her, but she was suspicious, and when she came into the room her eyes were blazing. My new friend fled at once, and Minang proceeded to deluge me with a torrent of unladylike language. I have seen signs in taverns to the effect that one might as well have another drink since his wife can get only *so* mad, but in Minang's case this was not true. She still berated me that night after we had gone to bed, and everything she said seemed to intensify her outrage. For some time I closed my eyes and tried to tune her out. Then I became dimly aware that she was moving beside me. Next I heard the creak of leather. I sprang awake at once and grabbed in the dark for Minang. I caught her by the hand just as she was pulling my .45 from its holster. For the rest of that night I kept track of all the guns—and did not sleep much. I have often wondered since whether Minang intended to shoot me, herself, or both of us. Whatever the case, it would have been a helluva way to get a Purple Heart—or a funeral.

In retrospect, I believe I was attracted to Minang more because of her fiery, indomitable spirit than by romantic considerations of the usual sort. On one occasion—when we were not quarrelling—she had told me quietly and deliberately that if I left her and went back to the United States when the war was over she would be sad but would understand; but that if I ever left her for another Filipina she would kill the other woman. She added that if I was killed by the Japanese she would personally kill the Japanese commander responsible if she had to sacrifice her own life in the effort. It was hard not to take a woman like that seriously.

In truth, I owed Minang a lot, as did all our guerrillas. Near the end of the war I was able to get her commissioned a lieutenant in recognition of her wartime services. It was a position that secured for her some much needed money but, more important, she deserved it, and it pleased me greatly to get it for her.

11

The Americans Return

WHILE THE STRUGGLE FOR LEYTE RAGED DURING THE last two months of 1944, farther north both the Japanese and ourselves were laying plans. For the enemy, Gen. Tomoyuki Yamashita, whom the Japanese called "The Tiger of Malaya," had about 100,000 men on Luzon. With that irreverence which never seems to desert Americans even in the most dire adversity, GIs later renamed Yamashita variously as the "Badger of Baguio" or the "Gopher of Luzon," but Tiger, Badger, or Gopher, by now Yamashita had no illusions about his prospects. He did not control either the Japanese navy in Manila or the Fourth Japanese Air Force. He knew there would be no reinforcements from Japan, and that food shortages would eventually become his most pressing problem. Long before, he had urged his troops to behave with dignity toward civilians and prisoners of war, but by now he knew that they had done neither and that they were, consequently, hated whole-heartedly by nearly all Filipinos. The roads and railways of Luzon, once the best in the Orient after those of Japan itself, had fallen into ruin from a combination of Japanese neglect and sabotage by guerrillas. Munitions

229

were in short supply, and there was so little gasoline that distilled pine root oil was being used as a substitute.

Yamashita knew that defeat in Luzon was inevitable. All he would be able to do would be to defend the island for as long as possible, weaken the American invaders as much as he could, and thereby give his government the maximum time to prepare the Japanese home islands for the titanic battles that would decide the war. In short, Yamashita's predicament was not unlike that of Douglas MacArthur three years earlier. Where MacArthur had made his last stand on Bataan and Corregidor, Yamashita decided to try to hold the two-hundred-mile-long Cagayan Valley in north Luzon until he could strip it of stored food and harvest the rice crop there. He would hold down the civilians by terror, and then retreat into the northern mountains to wage a protracted, suicidal war against the Americans and Filipinos.[1]

Of course, I was not privy to all of General Yamashita's plans, but I had learned enough to be filled with foreboding. Our intelligence indicated that thousands of Japanese troops were streaming into Luzon, massing in towns and along beaches, determined to fight to the death. Some eight thousand of them were in Pangasinan alone.[2] The fact that they paid little attention to us guerrillas now was in itself ominous. Even if many of the worst battles of the war might now be behind for the American army as a whole, it was virtually certain that my fiercest battles lay in the near future. I thought of all the faithful Filipinos who were certain to lose their lives, or their property, or both. What could be left for survivors after the showdown? I thought every day about our growing conviction that, because of the strength of the enemy fortifications at San Fernando, the Americans should land in Lingayen Gulf. It was imperative that this be judged correctly since we had been forwarding our opinions about it to Australia and we planned to send runners in advance of the landings to convey our final information and advice. If we were right, many American lives would be saved. If we were wrong, our own men might never get ashore. Every day more

U.S. bombers and fighter planes crisscrossed the skies. Tension mounted apace.

The first break came January 4, 1945. Our camp was then situated in the mountains east of San Quintin along the eastern border of Pangasinan province. That morning I came upon one of our guards peering intently at a narrow pathway that snaked upward from rice fields into the foothills far below us. Slowly my man slipped his submachine gun off his shoulder, flipped the safety catch, and edged into a firing position. He was absorbed in some sort of movement down the trail. My immediate thought was that enemy troops must be approaching. I asked the guard what he had seen. He said someone was on the trail, coming our way. I called at once to Greg to bring me one of our prized possessions, a set of captured Japanese artillery binoculars, heavy and clumsy but extremely useful because they were powerful and graduated with range markings.

I focused in on the trail. A rider was coming toward us as fast as he could urge his sweat-lathered horse up the precipitous path. Several of us grabbed rifles and dashed down the trail to our lower level outpost. Just as we arrived, the winded pony stumbled forward, struggling to hold its footing on the steep ground. The rider hit the ground running and thrust a message toward me. I hastily tore open the envelope. It was from Major Lapham. The first line hit me like a stunning physical blow. I read it and reread it, but was so overcome with emotion that I could not read further. It said, "Begin operations immediately herewith in accordance with Operations Plan 12." It meant that the American invasion was coming in five days.

It has been observed many times that discontented intellectuals of a certain type agitate for revolution and plan carefully for it for many years, but when a revolutionary situation actually develops they become as bewildered and helpless as lost children. That was about my state. For what purpose had I strained every fiber to stay alive for the past three years? Why had I raised and trained a troop of guerrillas at all? Why had I tried so hard to collect information about the Japanese and send it to Australia if it was not in anticipation that some day my countrymen would return to begin a new war for the liberation of all of us? Now the time had come at last, and I couldn't believe it. I read the message still another time. At last it began to sink in. I composed myself enough to read it to those around me. They responded much as I had, dumbly at first. Then we all burst into tears. Whether I ever cried earlier in the war I can no longer remember, but this time the tears flowed in torrents. No doubt the nerves of all of us had become somewhat like a rubber band that has been stretched—and stretched—until it suddenly snaps.

As soon as we calmed down, I ordered the news dispatched to all company commanders in the province, as well as specific instructions about what each was to do in the immediate future. I took special care to make each message transparently clear since, for some reason, I happened to recall a story someone had once told me about Napoleon. Bonaparte had occasion to promote several of his officers, and he included on the list a member of his staff renowned chiefly for the slowness of his mental processes. One of the emperor's subordinates complained that this particular promotion should have been given to someone more talented. Napoleon replied that the dullard was especially valuable since it was his job to read all orders before they went to field commanders. If he understood an order, anyone else surely would!

No sooner had the orders been dispatched, than somebody in our headquarters detachment, perhaps Greg, suggested excitedly that we attack the Japanese garrison in nearby San Quintin that very night. One look at the faces of the others told me that enthusiasm for the idea was universal. I was in a quandary. The garrison was supposed to be attacked in due course by another company of ours. If we butted in now, we would upset long established plans. Worse, it was conceivable that in the darkness we might get into a battle with our own men. I began to remonstrate with the others in this vein but soon gave up.

Every half-perceptive football coach has known times when his team was so eager to get at the opponents of the hour that the best thing he could do was simply to name the starting lineup and get out of the way.

That night we set off single file down the trail. It was after dark when we reached the outskirts of San Quintin. Here we seized the first civilian we met and told him to take us to the mayor. That dignitary and other village leaders were overjoyed to hear that American liberation forces were due to land somewhere on Luzon in five days, but they were much less enthusiastic about our proposed attack on the Japanese garrison in their town. Only when we told them that we intended to shoot up the garrison whether they helped us or not, did they swallow their quite reasonable fears and agree to cooperate. Soon they drew us a map of the enemy compound. Inside a protective wire fence were two large rice warehouses, side by side. At the north end of them, like the cross on a *T,* was a third large building, a barracks that housed perhaps a hundred Japanese troops. The Japanese had only one guard. He was stationed outside the middle door of the barracks, facing a corridor between the two warehouses. We decided to attack from the south side of the stockade.

Somebody once said that confusion is the first flower that grows on a battlefield. He was dead right. We had hardly started off to get into position to attack when noise arose in a crescendo all about us. Dogs barked, pigs squealed, horses neighed, and frightened civilians dashed back and forth through the town loading *calesas* and carts and trying to get themselves, their families, and their possessions out of the area. One could hardly blame them, but I was sure the racket would alert every Japanese in the vicinity—which it did. Nonetheless, we made our way without incident up to the fence that surrounded the encampment. This we would have to climb. Immediately we stopped and sent two men, stripped down to their sidearms and dark-colored shorts, over the fence first. They were to slip down between the two rice warehouses, surprise the sentry and, hopefully, kill him without making any noise.

Then the rest of us, armed with light machine guns and automatic rifles, would follow close behind, burst through the barracks door, turn back to back and blast all the Japanese in their beds.

Everything went wrong. No sooner did our two advance men get over the fence, than two suspicious Japanese, alerted by the unusual noises in the town, stepped out of the eastern warehouse and shouted "Kuri" in Japanese and "Halto" in English and Spanish. Immediately Joseph Henry, one of my best men, forgot all about my order not to fire until I gave the command, and opened up with a tommygun. Then another lad, only a step behind me, began to blaze away. For an instant I thought the bullets were coming at me. I stepped backward in disgust. No matter; all hope for surprise had vanished. We did the only thing left: individually clamber over the fence as fast as we could. I raced for the side of the building where the two Japanese had appeared, shouting commands in English as I went. Henry had mowed down the pair, but one of them twitched his leg spasmodically just as I came to him. Already angry and excited, and long since conditioned by hard experience to take no chances with Japanese, I instinctively opened fire on him with my tommygun, at point blank range. Even in the dark I could see the man's face fly off in chunks. "What a hell of a way to die," I thought momentarily. I grabbed for what looked like a rifle lying across his body, but it turned out to be his sword, partly drawn from its scabbard. I have no idea why, but I yanked it free and handed it to Greg. All at once a machine gun our Filipino cartographer had forgotten to put on his map opened fire. We had to fall behind the building for protection.

Meantime a few of our men had been sent around to the opposite side of the garrison to attack a small native hut on stilts that contained a few Japanese. They were supposed to wait until they heard our fire, then when the Japanese in the hut awakened and came outside our men were to mow them down. Once more somebody got buck fever. One awakened a Japanese, who started to jump out a window but was shot immediately. He fell back into the house and thus alerted all his companions, who began to race about madly inside. One of our guerrillas, Virgilio Blando, then dashed under the *bahay,* whose floor was above his head, and began to fire up through the bamboo flooring. Afterward he told me excitedly that he was sure he must have killed many Japanese since streams of blood had poured down through the floor. The truth was more prosaic: he had shot up a big jar of water.

While this Marx Brothers battle (though waged with real weapons) was going on inside the stockade, things went better outside. Our men there burned a wooden bridge and cut the telephone wires on both sides of town. Those of us still inside fired a few parting shots into the rice warehouses and melted away in the dark without a casualty. The Japanese in the main barracks, who hardly knew what had happened all around them, then began to fire mortars in all directions without having any idea where we were. As we made our way back to our camp, we could hear much more firing coming from Umingan to the south where a battalion of our guerrillas was attacking another Japanese garrison. There the battle went on most of the night.

Next morning the enemy troops in San Quintin slipped out of town. A Filipino told us afterward that when they had heard commands given in English and found spent cartridges dated 1942 and 1943 they had concluded that they had been attacked by American paratroopers.

After I was informed on January 4 that an American landing was imminent, I trusted that it would come in Lingayen Gulf, about seventy miles west of our camp. On January 7 I sent runners off in that direction to seek contact with American forces. For three days they walked through ricefields full of Japanese troops, eventually making contact with Gen. Walter Krueger's Sixth Army on January 10, the day after the landings had begun. They were able to give him much information about enemy dispositions and our own situation. I would have been immensely relieved had I known that the actual Lingayen Gulf landings had been unexpectedly easy because U.S. carrier strikes around Manila had led the Japanese to expect landings there. The chief menace that had faced the Allies in Lingayen Gulf had proved to be kamikaze attacks.

Several days later the runners were back with abundant news of their own plus a pencilled order from Colonel Lassetter, the G-2 of First Corps headquarters. It was dated January 12, 1945. Paragraph five read, "You and your unit could be of best service by remaining in your areas and supplying us with required information at such time as our troops can reach you." Paragraph six added, "Congratulations on your good work."

Of course, I was pleased to be commended, but the rest of the message was a heavy blow because my men and I, after three years as nomads or guerrillas, were chafing to join the American forces. I was fully aware of what would follow if I stayed where I was. As U.S. regular troops advanced, they would push droves of the enemy eastward right into my lap. As the days passed, reports poured in from every side. I rushed them immediately to General Krueger, when I could, but communicating by runners was maddeningly slow: usually three days each way. Once civilians in San Quintin reported to me that their town contained a large concentration of enemy troops and tanks, commanded by two Japanese generals. How I wished for artillery, or even a decent radio so I could report it to our air force at once. Next morning the enemy had departed. I cursed my helplessness.

No doubt, I would have been less discontented had I known that my ex-sidekick Al Hendrickson was quite as isolated as myself, and in more pressing circumstances. Al and his men never really linked up with American forces at all. Instead, they fought alone near Tarlac City until January 16 when they finally took the town from a much larger Japanese force. Next day a single company of the U.S. Thirty-seventh Division finally managed to break through and establish contact with them.

All I learned for sure in these days was that Bob Lapham and Harry McKenzie had made their way through miles of territory held by the enemy to join the regular American forces. Meantime the retreating Japanese poured eastward and then split shortly before they would have reached our position. Some of them veered off northeast toward San Nicolas onto the Villa Verde Trail, a mountain pathway too narrow for either trucks or armored vehicles. Other Japanese passed virtually over our feet on their way south, where they would pick up the Santa Fe Trail which eventually turned northeast, intercepting the Villa Verde Trail and entering the Cagayan Valley. Fierce fighting took place in both sectors. The Japanese on the Villa Verde Trail were soon forced into a last stand on high ground that would be named Yamashita Ridge. Those farther south had their tanks run out of gasoline or break down. When this happened, they pushed their stranded tanks into hillside dugouts and used them as artillery against their oncoming foes. When they ran out of shells, they set fire to their tanks and burned them. As our own artillerymen blasted them out one by one, they could not forbear a grudging respect for the Japanese tank men who stayed to the death by their iron steeds quite as faithfully as beleaguered cavalrymen of legend had stayed by their horses. As for myself, there I sat with all this action taking place all about me, periodically devouring some new message like the one that came from Bob Lapham on January 15: "Remain where you are." I felt like the last inmate of an orphanage when the building was burning down.

On January 22 I finally received the directive I had awaited so impatiently. It was from Bob, and it ordered me to report to him at the village of Manoag some thirty miles to the west. Though we would have to go through about fifteen miles of territory still held by the Nipponese, we were so anxious to go that we left at once, not even waiting for nightfall. The dangers were clear, but it isn't every day that a soldier gets an invitation from his own forces to join them after a three-year separation. I rode a horse and fifteen men followed me. As we snaked our way across the countryside through the ricefields, we questioned Filipino civilians closely and repeatedly changed our course. A few times we spotted Japanese in the distance, but if they saw us at all they showed no more interest in us than we did in them.

After some time American artillery began to pound at nothing obvious to me, somewhat ahead and to the south of us. We drifted off northward to avoid it, only to have it move after us. I wondered if we had been spotted and mistaken for the enemy. I dismounted and started to look for a trail around a rice dike that was covered with tall grass. As I turned a bend, I abruptly encountered what was momentarily one of the strangest sights I have ever beheld: three white men, dressed in weird clothing, jumping in and out of a ditch with every artillery burst. They proved to be merely an American officer and two enlisted men garbed in army battle fatigues. They started to deploy against us until their Filipino guide assured them that we were guerrillas. After introductions the officer said he was en route to our headquarters to secure information about the enemy.

In the movies there would have been a joyous and noisy reunion, but we were still in enemy territory where there was a distinct possibility of being fired upon by either the Japanese or the Americans, or both, and with still another enemy, darkness, due to envelop us before we could get to the American front lines. So we forswore celebrating and merely followed the American officer, who was obviously tremendously relieved to be able to abandon his erstwhile mission and head back toward his own army.

During the next few weeks a lot of things happened to me, but one of the main memories I have of those days is that, for the first time, I realized how easy it is to "go native." By that I do not mean that I had forgotten civilized ways but rather how readily I had mixed new habits and attitudes with old, sometimes unconsciously sloughing off much of the old in the process. The degree to which I now needed "re-Americanization" became evident soon after meeting the three Americans in the rice-field.

After we joined forces,we started westward toward the Agno River. It soon became clear that we could not reach it before nightfall, so we decided to spend the night in a cluster of native huts. It was simply too dangerous to walk around after dark into what might become a combat zone at any time. I was still wearing my one-piece khaki suit, my gourd hat, and my crossed bandoliers with their heavy load of ammunition, a getup that must have seemed as strange to my army guests as their battle dress did to me. When we sat down to eat, both sides were happy to exchange food. Our chicken, rice, and Philippine vegetables were relished by the Americans, and I devoured a delicious canned snack called K rations, a commodity I had neither seen or heard of before and so did not know was universally reviled by GIs. My new compatriots then offered me some cigarettes. I took them eagerly, but after smoking a few even the Camels were so insipid it was like tasting air. Though I had not liked them at first, I had long since gotten used to Philippine cigarettes wrapped in black paper and packing at least three times the wallop of any American brand. After we had talked for hours, I said I was going to bed and started inside one of the huts. "Isn't that dangerous?" the lieutenant asked in tones of mild astonishment. I replied that I had been doing it for years; that the natives would be alert and would warn us if anything happened.

At dawn we moved out toward the river, as quickly as we could since some U.S. B-26 light bombers were pasting a village a mile or so to the north and we did not want to get hit accidentally. As we started into the river, some American troops began to ford it coming toward us. Though I had just turned twenty-five, they looked impossibly young and fresh, not to say peculiar as well in their combat outfits. One boy was munching an apple; another winked at us.

When we reached the opposite bank, I stopped and took a long look back. Though it sounds melodramatic to record, this was one of those rare occasions when a man reflects seriously on his past life. Random memories from the preceding three years tumbled over one another in my mind like pieces in a kaleidoscope: thoughts of gnawing, aching hunger; of some ailments that had been merely irritating and others that I had never expected to survive; of never having enough of anything; of perpetual danger and constant anxiety, the foreboding that even momentary lack of vigilance might mean death; all of it mingled incongrously with everlasting uncertainty and interminable waiting. I felt strongly that a bizarre chapter in my life had ended at last. What would come next? I cannot recall having any intuitions about this.

At length I turned away and we continued our march down a dusty road into a small detachment of American troops bivouacked for a rest before pushing on ahead. They all seemed to think I was a Filipino. Finally one of them summoned up sufficient nerve to ask me if I was an American. My temper was often short in those days, and I barked back something like, "What the Goddam hell do you think?" To my surprise, the reply raised immediate cheers and an offer to join them in a meal. The GIs now accepted me, but they simply could not believe that I had been on Luzon for three years. As a matter of fact, the more I talked about it the stranger it sounded to me too. It was like the proverbial awakening from a dream. Some of the newcomers remarked that my eyes darted about constantly. No doubt they did: if I had not long since acquired such a reflex action, I probably would have been dead.[3]

After breakfast the lieutenant in charge of the detachment loaned me a jeep and driver to take me quickly to Twenty-fifth Division Headquarters, Sixth Army. Since the fall of Bataan I hadn't ridden anything faster than a horse or carabao. When the jeep started off, I felt like a Montana sheepherder taking his first ride on the New York subway. I huddled in the back seat and hung onto my gourd hat as the maniacal driver hurtled down the dirt road at what seemed like a hundred miles an hour. Once I looked apprehensively at the speedometer: it read thirty.

When we reached our destination, I was immediately ushered in to meet a general, whose name I have forgotten. He was anxious to get as much information from me as possible and asked me a great array of questions about Japanese numbers, dispositions and plans, the state of Philippine rivers, bridges and trails, the number and condition of guerrilla outfits, and much else. I answered as fully as I could, but to the surprise of both the general and myself, in the middle of a reply I would occasionally lapse into one of the three Philippine dialects I had picked up. I suppose I was just excited. Anyway, each time I apologized, backtracked, repeated my answer in English, and promised to try not to stray again. Finally I had to acknowledge shamefacedly that I couldn't seem to speak anything better than broken English that day. The general smiled broadly and waved off the matter lightly.

With regard to my information, my interrogator was far more serious. He wanted me to get into a plane at once and fly back in broad daylight over the area through which I had just escaped. Twenty miles of the flight would be over territory held by the enemy. I went, of course, but it was the most terrifying flight I have ever taken. Right away there occurred a horrendous explosive roar that shook the plane violently. It was caused by a salvo of U.S. 155mm. cannon being fired directly beneath us. A day or two before I had gone to sleep nonchalantly in a bamboo hut in circumstances that alarmed an American officer unaccustomed to guerrilla existence, but a routine ride in a jeep had frightened me, and now this tempestuous flight back behind enemy lines scared me anew. Courage is a general quality only to a degree: often it is quite specific.

After the flight, which was mercifully brief, my spirits revived rapidly when American officers flocked about me and other guerrillas to ask innumerable questions about roads, rivers, bridges, the Japanese, and the spirit of Filipino guerrillas and civilians. They were not only eager to get information but repeatedly expressed mingled amazement and appreciation that we had seized many villages from the enemy. I remember one tank commander who was especially appreciative because information he had gotten from guerrillas had already enabled him to bottle up sixty-five Japanese tanks.

The next day I finally met Maj. Robert B. Lapham, who had been my guerrilla commander for months but whom I had never seen. Bob was a tall, thin, blond, handsome man who smiled easily and spoke in a soft, even voice. Appearances were deceptive, though. Bob was a fighter to the core and a man who commanded effortlessly through force of character and personality. Every sound, reliable person I knew, who also knew Bob, liked and respected him. We had a drink, or two, or three, to celebrate; and talked at length about our experiences and about how long the odds had been against us. We agreed that God alone had seen us through.

There is a common remark in the army, usually voiced by disgruntled enlisted men, to the effect that there are two ways of doing anything, "the right way and the army way." Like most such acerbic observations, it contains a kernel of truth beneath layers of exaggeration. In my case, nearly three years of highly informal and usually precarious existence had long since led me to say and do whatever I liked without reference to "regulations." Now I began to encounter military red tape once more.

My guerrilla togs occasioned quite a few chuckles, as did my propensity to salute left-handed, the latter having been picked up during the casualness of guerrilla life. Nonetheless, for some time I continued to wear my unorthodox garb, partly because I was used to it, partly because I was too busy to look for more conventional clothing, partly because we were so close to a combat area that few people paid much attention to what anyone wore.

There were always sticklers for regulations, though, and my eccentricities did bother these purists. One day one of them, an MP, stopped Bob Lapham and me as we were entering a command post and asked me if I was an American soldier. When I said I was, he must have concluded that I needed some "shaping up." He proceeded to inform me that my gourd hat, Mexican bandit ensemble, and southpaw salutes constituted being "out of uniform," a violation of regulations. Before I could say a word, Bob grabbed my arm, steered me away, and told the MP to go to hell.

One day when I did at length get around to looking for a more conventional wardrobe, I went into a clothing sales store. I saw a long line, which I did not want to join, so I went directly to a clerk where there was no line. He informed me that only field grade officers were served there. I told him I had been in the field for three years. Having been a mere enlisted man before becoming an ersatz guerrilla captain, I had never learned that "field grade officers" referred to majors or above.

Other imbroglios over regulations followed. One day I went to Sixth Army headquarters to investigate a rumor that the Philippine army was being "reformed." Exactly what "reform" meant was not clear, but it was causing many guerrillas, who had been Philippine army men, to abandon their guerrilla assignments. The first person I encountered was a major whose name I have forgotten and wouldn't want to remember anyway. He wanted to know what rank I had held when the Bataan surrender took place. I told him staff sergeant in the air corps. He then informed me that henceforth he would refer to me as a staff sergeant. I had a short fuse in those days, no doubt made shorter by my experiences. I told him I didn't give a damn what he called me.

The major then changed the subject to back pay. Some months later, in the United States, I was to collect nearly $10,000 tax free, representing forty-six months of accumulated pay, but in February 1945 I hadn't given the subject ten seconds' thought. The major began to explain the system under which I would be paid and returned stateside. At that I blew my cork and told him I had not come to return to the United States but to attend to some business, and that I would like to see his colonel at once. He then ushered me in. I asked the colonel immediately if the Philippine government was in the process of reorganizing its army. He replied "No" with equal abruptness. I thanked him and strode out, still smarting from my encounter with the major.

Unhappily, that was not the end of the pay question. I needed only a small amount of money on a month-to-month basis, but I did need *some*. I had drawn nothing since December 1941 save a $100 partial pay the previous month. Now I went to a finance section and applied for another partial pay. The finance officer informed me that all "recovered personnel" were entitled to only one partial pay: that his only options were to give me all my accumulated back pay, or nothing. I explained that I needed a little money at once but would not be going back to the States for several months. He took refuge in bureaucratic obduracy. I stomped out cursing. I was so disgusted that I signed up on the Philippine army payroll and collected partial pay from it for the remainder of the war. The whole episode was especially galling since I was staying in the Philippines voluntarily.

I had not completely recovered my equanimity from this eminently unnecessary snafu when I came down with recurring fever (malaria) for the first time since 1943. After the initial chills had subsided, I went to an army hospital and requested treatment. There I was bedded down and had glucose fed into my arm. As soon as the treatment was finished, I felt better so I got up and started to leave. A nurse immediately objected that I did not have permission to depart. Perhaps I should note here that only a couple of days before I had met several American nurses for the first time in three years. Of course, I had not forgotten the difference between American women and brown Filipinas; nonetheless, their skins were so white that the first thought that had popped into my mind was that they must be sick. Now this new female paleface was telling me I could not leave. I told her in a few plain words that I *was* leaving. She fled to a doctor, who returned and backed her with some trenchant phrases of his own. To emphasize his point he threatened to report me to my commanding officer. I told him I didn't have one, and walked out the door. I have never had an attack of malaria since.

Of course, I simmered down eventually and began to accommodate myself to military routine once more. I stopped carrying a rifle and discarded the ammunition bandoliers. I contented myself with a nickel-plated mother-of-pearl German Luger 9-mm. pistol in a shoulder holster. Many GIs stopped me to look at this baroque sidearm. One, who had seen General Patton's famous pearl-handled pistol, told me my Luger was much more impressive. Others offered to buy it, even for as much as $500. Generally speaking, I cared little for souvenirs, but I turned down these offers because the Luger was one of the few items I had acquired in the war that I wanted to keep. It never ceased to surprise me how avid so many men were to get Japanese souvenirs, especially samurai swords, sidearms, and flags of the Rising Sun—which by now was becoming the Setting Sun. My Filipino followers were as indifferent to souvenirs as myself, so I often collected much stuff from them and gave it to various Americans. But a wise man once observed that no good deed goes unpunished. One ungrateful rascal, to whom I had given several items, stole my gourd hat, the only thing other than the Luger that I had intended to take home. The samurai sword I had taken off the body of the Japanese garrison commander at the "battle" of San Quintin I still had, though I had thought so little of it that I had used it mostly to cut tobacco and bamboo. Now it occurred to me that some future child of mine might prize it, so, although I had heretofore regarded it as hateful, I had it boxed and mailed home.

After some days of such varied activity I decided that I had to write to my parents. Though it must seem absurd to a reader, soldiers who have been out of all contact with their wives or loved ones for long periods sometimes find it difficult to write anything. So it was with me. Though I had not seen my parents and sisters for six years, nor even heard from them for three years, I had to start several times before I could compose a letter to them and mail it.[4]

Later I discovered something that turned my bewilderment to anger: the American State Department had learned in March 1944 that I was alive and serving with guerrilla forces in the Philippines but for reasons best known to themselves had not reported this to my parents for another eight months. This has always galled me. Of course, when the United States is engaged in a titanic struggle that may determine the character and direction of civilization for centuries to come there are more important things to consider than the forebodings and sorrows of one soldier's family. Still, we are a democratic people who profess to value the welfare and to be concerned with the feelings of each person. Besides, not every individual among the hundreds of thousands employed by the government in Washington was busy every day pondering issues of global significance. Somebody could have spared my family much needless anguish by simply letting them know that I was still alive.

Be all that as it may, my letter soon produced a reply from my father, postmarked March 9, 1945. I picked it up, looked at it, set it down, and picked it up again. Only after several minutes of this did I open it at last, and then I tried to read it all at a glance. Most American soldiers who had much to do with the Japanese regarded Nipponese psychology as hopelessly puzzling—as I have indicated earlier in this narrative. To this I must add that in retrospect I find my own psychology in early 1945 comparably unfathomable. I had hardly been able to read the message telling me the U.S. invasion of Luzon was coming in five days, or to digest its meaning; I had had trouble speaking English to a general in a routine and relaxed interrogation; I could hardly write home; and now I couldn't read the reply. Maybe war does unbalance a person? Maybe, in the last case, I was subconsciously fearful that my father's letter would contain some catastrophic news? Whichever, I finally worked myself up to read it. It was innocuous. A portion went: "We are all well and exceedingly happy. We can only remember you as a strip of a boy. We love you with all our hearts. Your Dad." I felt momentarily drained but immensely relieved.

* * *

While I was gradually becoming an Occidental again, the struggle for Luzon proceeded with unabated fierceness. One of the most heartening features of it was the liberation of many American prisoners of war and civilian detainees from several Japanese prison camps. Though I did not personally participate in any of these operations, one of them was especially gratifying to me because a large detachment of Lapham's guerrillas played an important role in it.

Long before the American landings we guerrilla leaders had devoted much thought to liberating American prisoners, and there were times when we were strong enough to have successfully stormed various camps, but we never made the attempt for the same reasons that other guerrillas on Mindanao far to the south never tried to rescue two thousand American prisoners from the Davao prison camp there. What would we do with the hundreds, perhaps even thousands, of men we would acquire? Some of them no doubt would be overjoyed to swell our ranks, but the majority were sick and weak. We did not have food enough for them; we had no place to hide so many; and they were not up to long marches through jungles and over mountain ranges to the sea, most likely pursued by Japanese troops throughout. Even if we got to the sea, what then? The navy could hardly be expected to risk twenty or thirty submarines to try to take them off. Seaplanes could not land without grave risk of detection. Using a couple of submarines to shuttle prisoners to a ship many miles offshore seemed like the longest of long shots. Thus, many months had gone by, and we had done nothing.

Yet past experience with the Japanese indicated that they might well kill all their American prisoners after an Allied invasion of Luzon. That this dark conjecture was not overdrawn became evident after the war. Then we learned that had U.S. ground forces invaded Japan proper the Japanese would have begun defense of their homeland by killing all the American prisoners there. Those who view the atomic bombing of Hiroshima and Nagasaki as uniquely horrible episodes in human history seem never to have pondered this.

Bob Lapham and Col. Bernard Anderson, a prominent guerrilla leader in Tayabas province to the east, had long been especially concerned about the prisoners. They had pleaded with MacArthur's Headquarters to let them undertake a raid on the infamous prison camp near Cabanatuan in Nueva Ecija province, and had expressed confidence in their ability to get the rescued men to the seacoast. When they met General Krueger in person after the Lingayen Gulf landings, they renewed their entreaties. This time they got the green light, though Lapham was refused permission to take part personally on the ground that his life was too valuable to run the risks involved.[5]

Before the U.S. landings on Luzon, the Japanese had removed most of the stronger prisoners from Cabanatuan and put them on ships destined for Japan. Among those evacuated was my friend Walter Chatham, who had escaped with me on the Death March, spent five months with me in the Fassoth camps, been captured there, and subsequently been consigned to Cabanatuan. As usual, the prison ships were unmarked and so, as usual, several of them were attacked by American planes and submarines. Walter's luck held. His ship made it to Japan. With hundreds of others who landed on Honshu or Hokkaido, he was promptly put to work in a coalmine, from ten to sixteen hours per day, seven days a week. Only about five hundred weak, sick, bewildered men, many hardly able to walk, were left in Cabanatuan by January 1945.

The plan to raid Cabanatuan was worked out by Col. Morton V. White of General Krueger's staff. He got much assistance from Bob Lapham and from Lt. Col. Henry A. Mucci, who was to lead the actual attack by something over a hundred members of the Sixth Ranger Infantry Battalion. The attackers were to be preceded by ten elite Alamo Scouts, who would infiltrate many miles behind Japanese lines twenty-four hours in advance of the main force. The whole venture was to be supported by about four hundred of Lapham's guerrillas, led by two of Bob's

Filipino guerrilla lieutenants, Juan Pajota and Eduardo Joson. Colonel Mucci tried to impress upon his Rangers the extreme gravity of the enterprise by taking them to a church where he briefed them and then asked each one to take a blood oath that he would die rather than allow any harm to come to the prisoners.

The whole venture was planned with unusual skill. When the attack was launched at 7:30 P.M. January 30, 1945, complete surprise was achieved. In twenty minutes it was all over. Every single one of the 225 Japanese soldiers in the camp garrison was killed, and 513 prisoners were freed. The cost was remarkably small: one prisoner died from excitement on the way out; two Americans were killed and seven others were wounded; and about a dozen Filipino guerrillas suffered superficial wounds.

What it cost the enemy is less certain. The author of the most detailed account of the operation says more than a thousand Japanese soldiers in the town of Cabanatuan, a short way north of the camp, heard the firing and rushed to aid their comrades. They ran into a guerrilla ambush set by Lieutenant Pajota and were all slaughtered.[6] I have no reason to doubt the accuracy of this contention, but perhaps it should be viewed in the context of various claims that my own guerrillas killed three thousand Japanese in the five days immediately preceding the Lingayen landings, and that Tom Chengay's battalion alone killed three hundred then. Al Hendrickson, who certainly had as much experience as anyone of fighting all over Luzon throughout the war, thinks all these claims are much exaggerated.[7] Quite likely he is correct, but both my own observation and reports I received from all sides in those days indicate that Japanese were "wall to wall" all over Pangasinan and that a high proportion of them did not live long enough to make it into the mountains.

Aside from saving the lives of five hundred men, the most important aspect of the Cabanatuan raid was symbolic: it showed how much Americans value their own people and the extremes to which we would go to rescue them. In those same weeks Japanese kamikaze attacks were demonstrating how little our enemies valued *any* lives, even their own; how inhuman was their determination to fight on no matter how hopeless the circumstances or how high the cost. The contrast must have helped convince many Americans, if anything further was needed, that *any* measure was legitimate if it could compel the Japanese to surrender and thereby save American lives.

I was overjoyed to learn that one of those liberated from Cabanatuan was my friend and benefactor William J. Fassoth, the civilian sugar planter who had built the "Shangri-la" mountain camps where I had stayed for several months after escaping from the Death March. A year later I felt immensely privileged to write a recommendation that enabled Mr. Fassoth to receive the Medal of Freedom.

It was also heartening to learn in due course that other American troops had successfully raided other prison camps. Some broke into Santo Tomas University in Manila on February 3, 1945, and rescued 3,700 American and Allied civilians. Still others, supported by guerrillas, attacked Los Baños prison camp on Laguna de Bay south of Manila on February 24. There they killed the whole Japanese garrison and rescued 2,100 internees at a loss of only two American dead. These brilliant rescues contrasted starkly with the ghastly fate of 140 American prisoners on Palawan Island. On December 14, 1944, these men were doused with gasoline in an underground shelter, set afire by their Japanese jailers, and then machine-gunned as they tried to break out. Only nine escaped.[8]

Aside from lives saved, fallout from the Cabanatuan raid was mixed. It was appropriate that Colonel Mucci and Capt. Robert Prince should have gotten DSCs for leading the expedition, that the other officers involved should have been awarded Silver Stars, and all the enlisted men and 412 Filipino guerrillas Bronze Stars. But why had two Filipino guerrilla officers, Juan Pajota and Eduardo Joson, been left off the list for Silver Stars when both of them had played leading roles in the rescue?[9] It was an ominous foretaste of the injustice and ingratitude shown to many Filipino soldiers at the end of the war.

One feature of the Cabanatuan raid left a particularly bitter taste in my mouth and, I would gather, in that of Bob Lapham as well. It was the part played in it by the Hukbalahaps, the ancestors of the New People's Army of today. When American forces began to penetrate Luzon, all of us expected to see the Huks disarmed and disbanded. Instead, to our surprise and dismay, and over our protests, the U.S. command elected to give them additional arms and treat them as part of the forces of liberation. Though most of us did not think in ideological terms at that time, and hated the Huks merely because they had consistently opposed and fought us for two years, many American writers were then praising them. The Soviet Union was then regarded as a courageous ally in the common war against Nazi Germany. In the view of contemporary "progressives" there was nothing but nobility to be discovered in anyone or anything Left. I recall becoming enraged on one occasion after reading an article in *Reader's Digest* by some ignoramus who obviously knew nothing serious about Huk activities in the war. They showed their true colors anew during the Cabanatuan raid. Guerrilla Captain Joson, who committed eighty of his men to the rescue operation, had to leave the remaining twenty to guard his own headquarters against a possible treacherous Huk attack. Then, after the rescue had been pulled off, some hundred armed Huks tried to prevent the Americans and guerrillas from taking the liberated prisoners through territory under Huk control.[10]

Because it was decided in the higher echelons of our government that the Huks should be supplied with American arms and equipment, and then left entirely to the attention of the new Philippine government, Huk bullets killed many Americans and Filipinos for years after the war was over.[11] The most notable victims of the murderous scoundrels were Mrs. Aurora Quezon, the widow of the first president of the Philippine Commonwealth, and her daughter, both of whom perished in a Huk ambush. The only beneficent result of this vile deed was that it shocked most Filipinos and deprived the Huks of considerable sympathy and support for a time.

The fate of Japanese soldiers who surrendered in those days was sobering. Now and then one or two would give up and would live long enough to be interrogated by Americans. Occasionally what happened was semi-comic. I have never forgotten one naive prisoner asking during interrogation who was winning the war. He said that if the Americans were winning he wanted to remain a prisoner, but if not he would appreciate it if his captors would return him to his own forces.

Few were lucky enough to voice such sentiments. Not a single Japanese survived either the raid on Cabanatuan prison camp or on the town of Cabanatuan afterward. Almost nobody *tried* to take enemy prisoners, and there were instances of Japanese being shot down in cold blood by American soldiers or guerrillas when they came toward our lines naked, with their hands in the air. Barbarity it was, but the Japanese would not have been treated thus had they not set the tone three years earlier. Even now, near the end of the war, some of them would still booby-trap themselves and feign a desire to surrender in a final desperate effort to kill as many Americans as they could.

Some of the American interrogators of surrendered Japanese were Nisei, American soldiers of Japanese descent who had been imported into the Philippines from Hawaii just before the war to keep the Japanese population of the Philippines under surveillance. They had been trained by the FBI. One could almost feel the hatred between them and the Japanese prisoners. The Nisei tended to be rough questioners.

Generally, those Japanese who were captured and managed to live were meek and cooperative, quite unlike the vicious little beasts they had been in battle. It was this aspect of Japanese psychology that baffled nearly everyone else but which General MacArthur seems to have understood thoroughly when he accepted the formal surrender of Japan and moved about freely in that country at the end of the war, in circumstances that appeared to invite kamikaze attacks.

Years afterward, when World War II came to be seen in a somewhat different perspective, and particularly when I had occasion to make short trips to Japan during the Korean War, my former hatred of the Japanese gradually turned into respect. They were obviously bright, industrious people with a distinctive culture, who were fast clearing away the rubble of the big war and making Japan a clean, beautiful place again. They made no trouble at all for our occupation troops. No doubt my change of mind owed something, too, to the crudeness, poverty, destruction, and general disarray that characterized unfortunate Korea in those years.

12

Back into Action

WHY A PERSON CHOOSES A CERTAIN COURSE OF ACTION AT some crossroads in his life, he often does not know for sure. In war, when personal feelings frequently conflict with what seems to be duty, one is often hard put to explain afterward just what impelled him to do a certain thing and not something else. In January 1945 I could have returned to the United States. I wanted to come home, especially after all the tough experiences I had had, and I remember thinking at the time that I must be crazy to turn down the opportunity.

But turn it down I did. I stayed in the Philippines for another five months, and several times came as close to death as I ever had when a guerrilla. Why did I do it? Perhaps the most elementary reason was that I wanted to stay and see the final defeat of our ruthless enemy. Another consideration was the fate of the Philippines. There were only a handful of us to lead many thousands of guerrillas. If we left our Filipino troops, it was anyone's guess what they might do. Quite possibly they would be overcome by their hatred of the Japanese and would openly go to war with the invaders, a course certain to bring disaster

254

to Filipino civilians. Maybe they would dissolve into twenty antagonistic factions who would fight each other, or the Huks, to determine the postwar political destiny of the islands.

Pride influenced my course too. At first guerrillas were not even included in American plans for the reconquest of Luzon. Then as our contributions as guides, sources of information, guards for bridges and ammunition dumps, and fighters alongside regular U.S. troops became better appreciated, commendations from American officers began to pour into guerrilla headquarters. An American, Colonel Cleland, even asked if he might keep Capt. Tom Chengay and his men indefinitely. This was flattering to both Tom and myself, though I hated the prospect of losing my best officer. Since I knew nothing about the red tape involved in such transfers, I finally told the colonel I would let Tom suit himself. He joined Cleland's unit.[1] I also learned that General Yamashita had remarked that he could regain control of Luzon if he could capture four American guerrilla leaders, one of whom I would like to think was myself. Of course, Yamashita was grotesquely wrong, for by then the American juggernaut was truly invincible, but his observation touched my pride nonetheless.

I also wanted to stay behind because I knew I was needed to coordinate our guerrilla forces with American regulars. I had led my men for many months and so was better suited for this function than any newcomer could be. Simplest of all, my Filipino followers had always been loyal to me, and I considered that I owed them loyalty in return.

Finally, I wanted to do what I could to insure that those who had served faithfully with the guerrillas were properly recognized and rewarded when the war was over. The guerrillas had always fought without official authority, recognition, or pay. Nobody seemed to know anything authoritative about their status, or whether their families would be compensated if they died fighting the enemy. Any guerrilla leader would also know something about

Japanese soldiers and Filipino collaborators who had committed crimes against American and Filipino servicemen, a matter of much conern to American CIC (Counterintelligence).

Developments in the last months of the war were not auspicious in any of these areas. The Philippine government established a pay scale for guerrilla forces that was highly unrealistic and unfair. Officers were to be paid the same as American officers of equivalent rank, but enlisted men were to be paid according to the Philippine scale, a paltry seven dollars per month. Worse, if anything, great numbers of Filipinos were now trying to join guerrilla bands or were claiming that they had been guerrillas all along. No doubt many of them had sympathized with real guerrillas throughout; quite a few had probably aided guerrillas covertly. Now, at last, they felt it safe to indicate their sympathies openly. But it was equally obvious that many were mere eleventh-hour opportunists, rascals who had never risked anything in the whole war but who now wanted to pose as heroes to further their postwar careers, or to claim back pay, or to gain benefits for their families. I have always admired those Filipino men and women who risked their lives to aid us, either with guns in their hands or in less ostenatious ways, but for these eleventh-hour frauds who lacked both valor and shame, and who sought to curry favor and gain honors by trailing in the wake of their dead countrymen, I had, and have, profound contempt.

After my rear area contretemps with doctors, nurses, supply clerks, and officious military police, I came close to ending my career ignominiously—in a jeep accident. One day I went for a ride with a Lt. Harry Lerner, whose name should have been spelled Learner, for he proved to be indeed a novice at driving. We were moving at a good clip along a straight stretch of gravelled road near Santa Maria, Pangasinan, when suddenly a fork in the road loomed ahead. I could see at once that we were going too fast to negotiate it, but this did not prevent Lerner from trying. We would have rolled over for sure had I not grabbed the wheel from him and held it straight ahead. We jumped a large ditch—almost. The front wheels cleared it but the rear wheels didn't. I was catapulted straight up into the air. When I hit the ground, the jeep was ahead of me, stopped dead in a field, its lunatic driver still sitting behind the wheel. I was only shaken up, but after the experience it was almost a relief to get into a combat zone.

Though the fact is not much emphasized in books, the struggle for Luzon was the biggest battle of the whole Pacific war. The Japanese committed more troops there than on any other Pacific island, and the Americans more than in any European campaign save the invasion of northern France. Throughout their defense of the Philippines in general, the Japanese were hampered by a chaotic command structure and by divisions of authority. The Luzon campaign was an exception. Here Gen. Tomoyuki Yamashita was in overall command. He had planned to establish three defensive strongholds on Luzon: one in the mountains east of Manila, another in the mountains west of Clark Field, and the most important one in the mountains and jungle of north Luzon, where he hoped to control the food-producing Cagayan Valley. His last choice was excellent in the sense that this rugged, primitive area, penetrated by only a few poor roads and mountain trails, would minimize the effectiveness of American armor, heavy weapons, and air power, but it had the disadvantages of aggravating his own supply problems and of being highly favorable terrain for guerrilla operations.[2] Thus, the Japanese could control only those areas where they happened to be physically present in considerable numbers. Worse from their standpoint, wholesale sabotage by many guerrilla groups both before and after the U.S. landings had done so much damage to roads, bridges, railways, rolling stock, and trucks that the Japanese could move only a trickle of essential supplies to their defensive positions. Nevertheless, Nipponese soldiers battled on like cornered bulldogs, precisely as Yamashita had expected. It was amazing how long and how well they continued to fight under such adverse conditions. When they were broken as organized groups, they fought on as individuals until they were killed or died from sickness or hunger. Yamashita, in his lair near the top of Mt. Pulog, over nine thousand feet above sea level and about as close to Heaven as he was ever likely to get, had every reason to feel proud of his troops and satisfied with his own efforts. He did indeed give his compatriots in Japan sorely needed time to prepare for the eventual American assault on Nippon proper.

It was into this cockpit that Bob Lapham asked me to go one day in February 1945. I was to serve as liaison officer between the Thirty-second (Red Arrow) Division and the guerrillas attached to them. The Thirty-second was a famous division that had begun the war in the jungles of New Guinea and had been engaged continuously somewhere in the western Pacific for thirty-seven months. Its veterans had climbed so many mountains that some of them said their division insignia should be a mountain goat.[3] Their current task was to try to root the Japanese out of their foxholes along the Villa Verde Trail, a track that wound sinuously upward in a northeasterly direction through the cordillera of Luzon towards Yamashita Ridge, heavily entrenched high ground named for the Japanese commanding general. The trail itself was named after a Spanish priest, Juan Villa Verde, who had long ago passed over this jungle footpath to bring Christianity to the Filipinos in the Cagayan Valley. Although guerrillas were not formally incorporated into the Sixth Army until March 1, 1945, they were being used as front line troops alongside the veterans of the Red Arrow division weeks before that. My main responsibility was to see that they did a good job. The task occupied me continually until June.

Aside from trying to stay alive, my most pressing problem was usually transportation. It seemed to me that I was always on the move, and always on dusty dirt roads. The sweltering heat made me sweat profusely, and the sweat caused the dust to cake on me from head to foot. I spent my last four months of the war with a bandanna tied across my face.

The Villa Verde Trail, a locale where Al Hendrickson had hidden for a time in December 1942, was well named. It was not a road at all but a trail that wound up steep mountainsides and across exposed ridges from near sea level to altitudes of 3,500 feet. U.S. troops had to use bulldozers and graders to widen it enough so trucks and other vehicles could move equipment and supplies along it. Japanese snipers picked off the dozer operators with such disheartening frequency that dozers and graders had to be armorplated. One day I witnessed an episode that I will never forget because it exemplified some of the best qualities of American troops and of the United States itself. I heard an officer order an enlisted man to drive a bulldozer. The man refused, saying it was suicide. For such a reply he could have been executed for disobeying orders in combat, but the lieutenant merely looked at him, climbed onto the bulldozer himself, and went to work. The enlisted man watched silently for a few minutes, then motioned to the lieutenant to stop, and the two traded places without a word.

Fierce fighting along the trail had begun in January when I was still holed up in the foothills east of San Quintin. Progress had been slow. That there had been *any* progress was due mostly to the combat engineers. It is hard to overpraise these men who had to toil under fire to gouge eight-to-twelve-foot roads out of mountainsides so steep that sheer drops of 300–1,500 feet on the outer edges were commonplace. Later, when the rainy season set in, they often had to do their work all over again, since avalanches of mud and water would pour down the mountainsides and wash out the roads. Then the bulldozers would have to wallow in mud sometimes as much as four feet deep and struggle for twelve hours a day to rebuild roads that rose as much as twenty-two feet in a hundred. Many times logs had to be buried in roads to reinforce them. Nobody knows how many hundreds of thousands of sandbags were used to make retaining walls.[4] Merely watching supply trucks go up and down such roads, in the daytime and under fire, with two wheels on the edge of the cliffs, was hair-raising. How ambulance drivers managed it at night I cannot conceive—but they did. Gen. ''Vinegar Joe'' Stilwell showed up once along the trail and said the whole situation was as tough as anything he had seen in Burma.[5]

Life was no more salubrious off the immediate trail. Everywhere on high ground the Japanese had widened and cleared natural caves in mountainsides and along hilltops, and had consolidated them with a vast series of interlocking tunnels, one of them so big it had been made into a hospital with seventy beds.[6] Most of these dugouts were positioned so that the enemy could cover U.S. positions below with machine-gun and mortar fire. Often entrances to the caves and tunnels were on reverse slopes, making them difficult to locate and almost impossible for U.S. artillery to hit. As usual with them, the Japanese were not content merely to sit in these strongholds and await Allied attacks. They sneaked up close to American lines at night, then threw twenty-pound packs of TNT or dynamite into the midst of our troops and tried to set it off with hand grenades. Sometimes they would undertake banzai charges, carrying long bamboo poles with either bayonets or mines on the ends of them. One of their favorite tactics was to infiltrate at night and fight fiercely for springs that had drinkable water.

Combat under these conditions was ferocious. Eventual victory owed a good deal to superior American improvisation. Armored bulldozers took to plowing their way right up to Japanese machine-gun nests. Then tanks would bull in after them and blast the enemy point blank.[7] Tanks would also carry flamethrowers, which terrified the Japanese. When enemy soldiers jumped out of holes to escape the fire, our infantrymen mowed them down. U.S. troops and Filipino guerrillas often dug trenches toward Japanese caves, much as European sappers and miners approached fortifications centuries ago, pushing sandbags ahead of them as they went, until they drew close enough to throw dynamite into the caves and bury the inmates alive. Sometimes machine-gun fire was employed to isolate a cave and keep its Japanese inhabitants down until Allied troops could crawl close enough to toss in TNT or phosphorous bombs. Sometimes Piper Cub planes only 150–200 feet above the ground spotted for artillery, which then plastered a complex of caves with high explosives to prepare the way for our infantry "cleanup" crew with their own explosives and flamethrowers. Some such Japanese strong places were simply bypassed, or surrounded and cut off from food and water, and their inmates left to die. On at least one occasion American troops fell right into a detachment of Japanese underground when a tunnel caved in. They killed all the inhabitants before the latter knew what had happened.[8]

Through I was in the combat zone for several weeks and could easily have been killed any day, at least I did not have to build roads under enemy fire or dig Japanese out of caves. Perhaps what got on my nerves to the greatest degree was our own artillery. The Thirty-second assembled all the 155mm. howitzers they could find and fired them in salvos day and night close to where I slept. The noise was ungodly, and the concussion gave me the feeling of being regularly lifted about a foot off my bunk. I slept little and was consoled only by the fact that the hellish artillery was at least pointed away from me. After a few days of it I comprehended much better the accounts I had once read of soldiers in the trenches on the western front in World War I going mad during intense artillery barrages and rushing into the open to commit suicide.

The savagery of the fighting and the hatreds engendered thereby strain belief. In one place the Japanese launched so many desperate counterattacks that men of the Twenty-fifth Division named it Banzai Ridge.[9] On our side, one day I had to stand aside on a narrow trial to let litter bearers pass as they removed the dead and wounded. On one litter was a boy who had been badly burned by a flashback from a flamethrower he had turned into an enemy cave. Seemingly oblivious to what must have been the excruciating pain of burns over much of his body, he

261

cursed the Japanese hysterically, shouting over and over again, "I got the yellow sons of bitches! I got the yellow sons of bitches!" Sometimes macabre incidents were less serious than this, but no less grisly. One day when I was scurrying along the front I almost stepped on a large stone. When I looked more closely, it was a Japanese head.

More tragic were the inevitable foulups. Many times the air corps was called in to bomb ahead of the advancing infantry. Inevitably, a bombardier's aim would occasionally be faulty or a bomb would fall from the rack too soon, and men would be hit by their own bombs. The second time this happened to one outfit, it buried a few men. The survivors raged at the aviators, cursed them, told them to go to hell, and yelled that the war would be won more easily without them.

Enemy planes took their toll, too. In fact, the last Japanese plane I ever heard or saw very nearly got me. One dark night I was watching an outdoor movie with the Thirty-second Division. The area was not blacked out, and the movie had just ended when a Japanese plane came in low over the mountains, without running lights, unheard, and unseen by radar. Before we knew what happened, the pilot dropped his bombs and strafed the headquarters area. I was lucky: he missed both me and the water wagon I crawled under.

Another time I came even closer to cashing my chips. I was with a Lt. Col. Smith of the Thirty-second. Smith was a mild-mannered officer who had been with the Red Arrow Division through many harrowing battles all the way from New Guinea. Now he was due to go home, but war had not lessened his essential humanity, so he wanted to go to the front lines to bid his men farewell. A friend of his, a major, and I were along when the trail came out onto an open ridge where U.S. troops and some of my guerrillas were dug in. As we came to the front, the major warned us not to walk in the open since there were enemy snipers about who could "give a person a third eye" as a macabre local saying had it. Accordingly, we moved off the ridge. I talked to some of my men and Colonel Smith shook hands with some of his in their foxholes. After goodbyes we went back to the command post down in the foothills, got into a jeep, and started off. Smith's eyes were moist, more at the thought of leaving his men than with joy at the prospect of going home. We had gone only a short way when a Japanese artillery shell plastered an ammunition dump a few yards behind us. Had it come a couple of seconds sooner, Colonel Smith and I would now be names on grave markers.

Many were not so fortunate. One such was a cousin of mine, Warren Corn, of Willow Springs, Missouri. Unknown to me, Warren, whom I remembered only as a small boy, had come to the Philippines as a rifleman in the Twenty-fifth Division of the Sixth Army. He knew I was "missing in action" and had written to his family that he intended to look for me. After landing on Luzon he learned that I was indeed alive, and he informed his family of my good fortune. But I never saw Warren: it was only after I returned to the United States that I learned from his parents that he had been shot through the heart by a Japanese sniper and had been buried at Rosales, Pangasinan.

The Official Army History (Robert Ross-Smith, *Triumph in the Philippines*) mentions that during the spring of 1945 there was a perceptible decline in the morale and combat efficiency of various U.S. regular army units engaged in the reconquest of north Luzon, one evidence of which was a marked increase in psychiatric casualties.[10] It is not hard to understand why, nor to appreciate why the same tendencies existed amid our enemies. If the three F's of combat are "fog, fatigue, and fear,"[11] the latter two deepen visibly near the end of long campaigns or long wars. In the latter stages of the grinding, bloody struggles on the steep mountainsides and honeycombed hilltops of north Luzon, American troops would sometimes hear muffled explosions far underground. They were set off by Japanese troops whose tunnel openings had been sealed by American explosives and who now, sick and despairing, chose to blow themselves up with grenades. American Intelligence wanted us to take prisoners: they even offered riflemen a case of beer for every Japanese prisoner delivered.[12] Most of the prisoners were in a sorry state: wounded, starved, and suffering from beri beri to such a degree that they could no longer fight or retreat, and so drained psychologically that they no longer had the will even to attempt suicide.[13]

With our troops, sagging morale derived from quite different causes. When battle-weary veterans, especially if they were once draftees, think victory is at last in sight there develops among them a marked reluctance to tempt fate and become one of the last casualties. During most of the war I had assumed fatalistically that I would never live through to the end, but now that the end seemed so near, now that true safety at home again loomed as a distinct possibility rather than a utopian dream, the fear of death flooded my imagination remorselessly.[14] Especially poignant were thoughts of my family, so recently filled with elation to learn that I was alive. What a crushing blow it would be to them if I was now killed after all. Every other day I relived all my wartime experiences and prayed that no stray bullet would seek me out so near the end of the trail. So far as I know, I was the only American guerrilla leader actually on the battle line along the Villa Verde Trail at this late stage in the war, though others of Lapham's guerrillas were fighting in the Cagayan Valley.

Some of the great soldiers of history—Alexander of Macedon (356–323 B.C.) and especially King Charles XII of Sweden (1697–1718)—thought war was the grandest and most inspiring of all human experiences. Another such a one, in World War II, was Gen. George Patton. Like most people, I did not share this sentiment. Overall, I thought war was horrible. I was glad when World War II ended, and now I would rather die than relive my experiences during it. Nonetheless, Patton and his spiritual ancestors did have a point. Despite the frightful aspects of war, which are known universally and publicized endlessly, if a person can wrench his imagination away from the issues in a conflict, away from the personal danger involved, away from the *cost* of war,[15] there is no question that for many war is the most vivid of human experiences. Violence has a malign attraction for most of us, as every television advertiser and moviemaker knows. Likewise, if one can persuade himself to view mayhem *strictly as a spectacle,* there are sights in battle that are aesthetically pleasing; "beautiful," Patton would have said. I will never forget the sight of the pale green sea slowly turning red from the blood draining out of a wounded Japanese at Aglaloma Bay. An exploding phosphorus shell, a sudden blossom of white against the sun, is a splendid sight. Planes flying into sunsets, smoke trails against a clear blue sky, multi-colored tracer bullets buzzing through the air like swarms of angry bees, a plane going into a graceful dive preparatory to strafing, the "whoomp" of a bomb hitting the ground followed immediately by a great circular mass of dirt hurtling into the air—all have a certain impressiveness and attraction if one does not think of what gives meaning to them.[16]

Perhaps my anxiety about enduring until the end of the war was quickened by the departure of my longtime friend and compatriot Al Hendrickson. Al had recently had a couple of narrow escapes reminiscent of some of his chilling experiences early in the war. On December 22, 1944, he and some of his men were withdrawing in the face of both Japanese and Huk attacks when his horse slipped while crossing a river and fell on him, breaking his ankle. A month after this mishap Al made contact with American troops in Tarlac and became attached to units of the Eighth Army, then headed for Manila, much as my men and I became attached to the Red Arrow Division. At that time the Japanese were fighting mostly delaying actions in this area since they were expecting major U.S. thrusts elsewhere. This consideration, however, had not yet diminished their habitual ferocity and ingenuity in combat. One of their favorite strategems when retreating was to leave behind an elaborate array of booby traps supplemented by sharpshooters and even an occasional machine gunner. On January 20 they nearly got Al. An isolated and camouflaged machine gunner opened up unexpectedly. Al leaped into a bomb crater and promptly refractured his half-healed ankle. Almost immediately he spotted a Japanese sniper and, with the last bullet in his rifle, shot the man—but only wounded him. The maimed Japanese careened toward him, bayonet fixed. Providentially, a GI happened to be right there and finished off the sniper with a burst from his BAR before Al could be spitted with the bayonet.

That was enough for higher authorities. Al was promptly restored to regular American military status, categorized as disabled, and given orders to return to the United States. I saw him the night before he was to leave and helped him celebrate his departure. After the party was over and Al had said his farewells to many of his guerrilla troops, I drove him toward a camp where he was to be processed for a flight scheduled for the next day. We never got there, or at least I never did. Somewhere along the way we got on a wrong road and arrived at a river. The camp we sought was on the opposite side. Only a railroad bridge spanned the stream. After some consideration we decided to try to drive across the trestle, only to be halted by an American MP. Al, who had had a few additional drinks since the end of his going-away party, inquired belligerently who presumed to prevent us from crossing. The guard replied firmly that his orders came from General MacArthur. Al considered the point briefly, then informed the MP that if MacArthur could retake the whole Philippines singlehandedly, he (Hendrickson) was certainly going to cross "this God-damned bridge." The guard said, "No, sir," but did nothing when Al got out of the prewar Chevy we had commandeered, shook hands with me, shouldered a sackful of souvenirs, and limped off across the trestle, supported intermittently by Lee, his tiny Filipina girlfriend. Every moment I expected to see him fall into the river. When, at length, he reached the other side he turned, waved goodbye, and started down off the trestle. In a moment Lee's head disappeared, then Al's.

My emotions were muddled. I was somewhat jealous of Al, who was going home, and I felt continually remorseful about staying behind and quite possibly getting myself killed, which would utterly dismay my family, who had only recently learned that I was alive and who would surely learn that I could have come home. Yet I still considered it my duty to stay with my guerrillas while the war was going on. But then, after all, I did leave on June 20, 1945, several weeks before the end of the war! So much for logic in human affairs.

13

*Reflections on
the War*

DID GUERRILLAS IN GENERAL, AND WE IN THE PHILIP-
pines in particular, contribute significantly to overall Allied victory? If so, was our contribution worth what it cost
in money, human lives, and intangibles? I cannot say for
certain. Russell Volckmann, both a fellow guerrilla and
an adversary of mine, maintains that neither the British
nor the Americans ever appreciated the potential of guerrillas and consequently never made the best use of them
either in Europe or in the Far East. They were never in-
tegrated into the whole military structure (as they were in
the Soviet Union), never given proper logistical support,
and were usually confined to gathering intelligence. He
considers this to have been one of the lost opportunities
of the war, on the Allied side.[1]

My immediate, emotional response is to agree with Volckmann; yet there is much to be said for the claim of B.H.
Liddell Hart, one of the major military theorists of the twentieth century, that to encourage guerrilla warfare is a mistake
in the long run because its political and moral residues are
almost entirely pernicious and poison civilian society long
after the war is over.[2] There is no question in my mind that

what we guerrillas were able to do in the Philippines was of great value to the American army in the latter stages of the war. Moreover, measured in dollars and cents, it was dirt cheap compared to what the United States spent and got in other parts of the world. Yet so many Filipinos were killed, maimed, despoiled, and brutalized either by guerrillas of the outlaw type or by the Japanese in reprisals that I cannot help but believe that the Filipino people would have been better off had neither any of them nor Americans ever formed guerrilla organizations. Certainly, they would have suffered less, though it would also have taken longer to liberate them. Whether the absence of American resistance in the Philippines would have enabled the Japanese to conquer Australia early in the war and then brutalize *its* people, nobody can know. History cannot record catastrophes that timely action may have averted.

Past history provides little guidance. Without the aid they received from Wellington's army, and lacking the disaster Napoleon Bonaparte suffered in Russia in 1812, the Spanish guerrillas who opposed Napoleon would have been defeated eventually. Their real achievement was political and psychological: they made serious problems for the invaders, prevented them from imposing their will on the whole Spanish people, and provided inspiration to the enemies of Napoleon all over Europe. If one believes the accounts left by Russian partisan leaders who badgered Napoleon on his retreat from Moscow, each one of them defeated him single-handed. Yet the French army in Russia suffered vastly more from heat, cold, and diseases than from military action of any kind. Moreover, Napoleon was not *driven* out of Russia: he decided to attempt an orderly retreat only six weeks after winning the battle of Borodino, and had he begun perhaps three weeks earlier still he would have gotten most of what remained of his army safely out of the country. As in Spain, the greatest contribution of the Russian guerrillas was to keep up the morale of the civilian population.[3]

Much the same was true in Europe during World War II. Guerrillas of a dozen nationalities risked their lives to oppose the Nazis in innumerable ways, yet sabotage on the part of transport workers probably did more real harm to the Axis cause than all the activities of all the partisans combined.[4] Real guerrillas grossly exaggerated their exploits; and after the war so many latecomers, braggarts, and outright frauds talked so grandly of their deeds in the "Resistance" that an outsider might wonder how their homelands had come to be conquered in the first place. Like their predecessors in the Napoleonic era, their chief importance was psychological: their actions and efforts helped clear the consciences of their peoples, and served as a source of national pride when the war was over.

This was fundamentally true in the Philippines too, yet the resistance there did make a more direct and important contribution to eventual victory than anywhere else. Without the deeds of guerrillas the Japanese certainly would have exacted heavier casualties from the American invaders of the Philippines. It was true that there were feuds among American guerrilla leaders; and true that wartime rivalries between Filipino partisan bands often carried over into postwar feuds and gunfights. But, at bottom, nearly all the Americans subordinated their intramural quarrels to the common need to support MacArthur's plans to return; and at bottom a large majority of Filipinos spurned the awkward blandishments of their Oriental conquerors and gave the guerrillas the whole-hearted support without which we could not have operated or even survived. How many casualties and how much damage guerrillas inflicted on the Japanese, and how much they and Filipino civilians suffered in return, will never be determined precisely, but both considerably exceeded European norms. At no time during the war did the Japanese ever devise an effective way to deal with partisans, and near the end of the war General Yamashita lamented that the whole Filipino population had become a vast guerrilla system whose intelligence gathering and sabotage had surpassed all his calculations and fears.[5] Yet it is in no way denigrating to acknowledge that one of the most valuable services we irregulars performed was simply to keep alive the faith of

Filipinos that America had not forgotten them, that our strength would eventually enable us to prevail, that, to paraphrase MacArthur, we would return.

That guerrillas played a vital role in the defeat of the Japanese in Luzon after the Lingayen Gulf landings in January 1945 is unquestioned. What will never be settled is how much was contributed by various groups and whether credit for guerrilla achievements has been distributed equitably. The U.S. Army forces in the Philippines, Northern Luzon (USA-FIP-NL), commanded by Col. Russell Volckmann, have been given the lion's share of the credit. The official U.S. Army history provides a detailed account of how General Krueger originally intended to use Volckmann's guerrillas to gather intelligence, carry out sabotage, raid isolated Japanese units, relieve regular army units on guard duty, and engage in mopping up operations. It adds that all the guerrilla leaders, but Volckmann especially, interpreted orders and directives as broadly as possible and soon expanded their assigned tasks to such a degree that they were performing as regular troops. Some 8,000–18,000 of them blasted bridges, roads, and trails; ambushed Japanese forage parties; picked off enemy messengers and liaison groups; destroyed untold numbers of Japanese vehicles; killed thousands of enemy soldiers; rendered it difficult for the enemy to move anywhere save in large numbers; captured great quantities of Japanese equipment and supplies; and conquered the whole northeast coast of Luzon. All this vastly complicated enemy communications, drained his resources, and reduced the ability of Yamashita's troops to live off the land. Indeed, when the Japanese in north Luzon at last surrendered it was guerrillas who had fought their way within five miles of Yamashita's headquarters, closer than any other Allied unit.[6]

These exploits caused both General Krueger and MacArthur's Headquarters to declare that Volckmann's guerrillas had proved as valuable as a front line division.[7] In his own book Volckmann recounts the deeds of himself and his followers at length, though not boastfully.[8] He does allege that, given the ruggedness of the terrain in northern Luzon, the familiarity of the guerrillas with it, and the nature of the fighting there, it would have taken twice as many regular troops as guerrillas to have duplicated these feats.[9]

That Volckmann's accomplishments were impressive is unquestionably true, but what he and other writers have largely ignored is that the guerrillas of Lapham, Anderson, Hendrickson, myself, and others faced more Japanese in Tarlac, Pangasinan, and Nueva Ecija provinces than his men did in the north and that we cleared out our foes in short order. My own 3,400 highly varied irregulars, scattered all over Pangasinan in groups of 100, 200, or 300 received credit for killing 3,000 of the enemy during the five days immediately prior to the Lingayen landings. Volckmann's forces, by contrast, were engaged against the Japanese in north Luzon for another five months, though admittedly conditions there made military progress much more difficult than in the lowlands where most of our operations took place.

The three thousand dead Japanese credited to my units is an estimate, and it has always been difficult to offer anything better than rough estimates about how many enemy casualties should be attributed to any particular body of guerrillas. There are reasons for this—apart from the general confusion of war. For one thing, General Yamashita had almost three times as many troops in north Luzon in June 1945 as General Krueger supposed.[10] For another, various estimates of both Japanese and Allied casualties are for different groups, different areas, and different periods of time. For example, James gives one set of figures (8,300 American troops and 1,100 Filipino guerrillas killed in combat and 205,000 Japanese deaths in combat) for the whole Philippine archipelago for all of 1945, and another set (400 Americans and guerrillas and 13,000 Japanese killed in combat) for the last six weeks of the war in north Luzon.[11] Volckmann says his guerrilla infantrymen killed more than 4,000 Japanese between January and April 1945, and that all the north Luzon guerrillas inflicted 50,000 casualties on the enemy in the last months of the war.[12] William Manchester asserts that after the fall of Luzon 820 American soldiers were lost while killing 21,000 Japanese in mopup operations.[13] John D. Potter, who admires the military skill of General Yamashita, puts U.S. casualties in the reconquest of Luzon at 10,000 dead, 87,000 in hospitals, and 37,000 "others." He says nothing about Japanese losses.[14] The official army historian gives varying figures for several particular actions.[15] It is all like comparing apples, squirrels, and seashells. It is especially difficult for me, since I was personally involved, to assess the value of Volckmann's guerrilla activity in the context of all Luzon guerrilla operations; doubly so since I had resisted Volckmann's effort to absorb my forces into his command.

Volckmann came out of World War II much decorated by both the American and Philippine governments, and I heard many laudatory comments about his organization in the spring of 1945. Yet their postwar renown unquestionably owed much to the concern of their leader for what would become the historical record. General Whitney, MacArthur's overseer of Philippine intelligence, says Volckmann came to his headquarters only forty-eight hours after the American landings in Lingayen Gulf and delivered a full report on what he and his guerrillas had done during the preceding thirty months, and what they could do henceforth.[16] No other leader of irregulars got there so soon or could report so fully.

A severe critic of guerrillas in Volckmann's locale acknowledges that most of Volckmann's men were able and civilized, and that they fought valiantly; but he denounces a minority among them, some Americans and some Filipinos, as cruel and egotistical scoundrels, drunk with power, who murdered, pillaged, and raped as wantonly as any of the Japanese. He does not accuse Volckmann of approving, much less authorizing, such conduct, but he does maintain that Volckmann did not do enough to restrain these savages.[17]

How much Volckmann knew about the deeds of some of his subordinates, and what he could or could not have done about it, I have no way of determining, particularly so many years after the events. As indicated earlier in this narrative, there were times when I had to swallow the unauthorized and exceedingly distasteful conduct of some of my underlings. Perhaps he did too.

Col. Robert Arnold, who commanded the ill-trained, ill-equipped, and understrength Fifteenth Infantry, had a low opinion of Volckmann's whole operation. He relates that he once visited Volckmann's headquarters where he found some of Volckmann's chief subordinates not merely in good health but positively overweight, and more interested in the good-looking girls who frequented the premises than in anything connected with the war. After a sumptuous dinner a Filipino company commander told him that there were no Japanese within twenty-five miles of the camp and that they had not been bothered by the enemy for months.[18] Yet a few things must be remembered. Arnold had a sour nature; he regarded guerrilla operations as senseless; and when he stumbled into Blackburn's camp in the spring of 1943 he was weak and sick. Blackburn says that after a week or so of rest, good food, and good treatment Arnold's spirits rose visibly.[19]

There are other indications that guerrilla life was not always filled with hardship and danger for Volckmann and his associates. His number one aide, Blackburn, describes supplies of quinine as plentiful, notes that they sometimes received gifts of whiskey, Coca-Cola, and fried chicken, and mentions matter-of-factly that they bought a good deal from an ordinary Philippine grocery store.[20] He says he hated to move out of his own mountain hideout near Ifugao in September 1944 because it was safe: he was surrounded by friendly Filipinos, there was plenty of food, and he dominated all the officials nearby.[21] He relates that Volckmann, who sometimes became depressed, seldom strayed from the heights of virtually inaccessible mountains; but that when he happened to meet him at Tuao in the Cagayan Valley early in 1945, after they had been separated for nearly a year, his superior looked healthy and dapper. A Spaniard gave them a bottle of whiskey, and a Chinese cook fixed them a fine lunch.[22]

All this may be true, but it hardly proves anything note-worthy. Only a fool would live precariously if he could live safely: only saints and mountain climbers actively seek hardship and suffering. Nowhere does the effectiveness of a military organization depend crucially on the standard of living of its commanding officer.

Still, I think Volckmann's achievements have been magnified; or, perhaps more accurately, that those of some of the rest of us have been slighted by comparison. William Estrada justly praises his countryman Tom Chengay as a fearless man and an excellent leader of a band that performed splendidly late in the war,[23] and he praises Lapham,[24] but he says little about any of the rest of us, and in any case his work had an extremely limited circulation. Bob Lapham could have made an outstanding military career for himself by trading on his fame as a guerrilla leader, but he was indifferent to glory or even to credit. In the spring of 1945 he broke his arm, fell sick, resigned his command, and went back to the United States. Thereafter he pursued a civilian career with the Burroughs Corporation. He never wrote anything about his wartime experiences. Lt. Col. Bernard L. Anderson likewise left the army. So far as I know, he wrote nothing about his wartime deeds. I was the only major guerrilla leader in north central Luzon who stayed and fought alongside my men through most of the spring of 1945, but until now I have never published anything, either. Thus, some of the credit for guerrilla achievements in north Luzon in 1945 fell to Volckmann's units by sheer default.

But more was due to foresight. Astute and ambitious, Volckmann seems to have been the only American guerrilla commander on Luzon who kept detailed records, diaries, and rosters of troops. As a result, most of his exploits became part of recorded history. If the rest of us had kept similar records, it would now be much clearer who were authentic guerrillas and who were mere poseurs, which families of fallen irregulars deserved to be compensated, and how much credit ought to have been given to various guerrilla leaders and their groups for their contributions to final victory. But many of us did not keep such records lest they fall into the hands of the enemy, who would not only gain much useful information thereby but would also certainly use them to take murderous vengeance on the families of guerrillas.[25] Yet there is no denying that when decades have passed and memories have failed, "official" history is written from records, and these inflate the importance and immortalize the deeds of those who kept them.[26]

The Philippine government eventually tried to straighten out the historical record but abandoned the effort in the face of insuperable obstacles. Those guerrillas who had once been soldiers in the Philippine army were part of USAFFE, and so their personal records can be found with U.S. military records. As for their compatriots who were civilians, there exist somewhere in Philippine army files official rosters of civilian Filipino guerrillas, but the names thereon may be those of anyone from true partisans to mere rascals who knew somebody important near the end of the war. Whether authentic or phony, few such guerrillas ever got either recognition or financial benefits from the U.S. Army after the war. Most of them simply scattered to their homes and farms in the wake of victory. Soon it became virtually impossible to trace them or to distinguish true from spurious guerrillas. By now the vast majority of them must be dead.[27] Thus, it appears impossible that anyone can ever determine accurately how much which irregular bands contributed to the ultimate triumph of Filamerican forces on Luzon in 1945, and which individuals indubitably served in those bands.

Does it matter? In the grand context of history, not much: to those of us who are still alive and were personally involved, it still burns a little.

In late spring I left the battle zone, moved southwestward to Rosales, Pangasinan, and set up a headquarters there from which to coordinate the activities of my guerrillas. Shortly afterward I went down to Manila for some purpose I no longer recall. While there, I went to see a Filipino writer,

Lt. F.M. Verano, whom I had come to know when he had served as liaison between my headquarters and that of Gen. Manuel Roxas. Verano told Roxas I was in town, and almost immediately we were invited to a party at the house of Roxas's brother. There I encountered one of the most remarkable personalities I have ever known. Manuel Roxas was a politician par excellence. As the thirty or so guests prepared to leave, he called each of us by his right name and spoke to us in a moving, personal manner. He also seemed to me to be an unusually humane man. I once watched tears stream down his cheeks as he listened to tales of the tortures suffered by his countrymen at the hands of the Japanese. Such sentiments can be faked by ambitious politicians, I know, but in Roxas's case I felt sure they were genuine. He was a born leader with an exceptional facility for inspiring others. Though the Japanese had pressured him to serve as president of the Philippine Senate in their wartime puppet government, he did as little as he dared and aided the guerrillas and Allies all he could. At the end of the war he surrendered his military commission and was soon elected president of the Philippine Republic. Though published estimates of Roxas vary markedly, depending mostly on the ideological orientation of the writer, I thought his early death from a heart attack was a grievous loss to the Philippine people.

On this particular occasion Roxas asked me to stay in Manila for a time, but I became impatient and drove back to Rosales. I had hardly alighted from my car when Verano drove up behind me and wanted to know why I had left. He said General Roxas wanted to see me at once, and virtually dragged me into his automobile for the return trip. Back in Manila we met Roxas and rode grandly with him in a chauffeured army car across the wrecked metropolis to the headquarters of General MacArthur. Here I was ushered into the private office of the supreme commander. Already present were fellow guerrillas Lt. Col. Anderson, Majors Lapham, Edwin P. Ramsey, Harry McKenzie, and John P. Boone, and Capt. Alvin Faretta. General MacArthur delivered a short speech. My main recollection of it was that it was not at all of the "I have returned" genre: the general stressed, rather, that *we had remained,* that we had represented our country well by staying on and struggling to erase the stain of the defeats of Bataan and Corregidor. Then he pinned on each of us the Distinguished Service Cross, America's second highest award for valor. My feelings, as was so often the case in those years, were mixed. Naturally, I was pleased and proud, but I was also so taken by surprise that I had to ask someone what the award meant. Moreover, I felt out of place, even faintly foolish, for I was dressed in issue khaki and combat boots, lacked a tie, and had crossed rifles and captain's bars on my collar when I was still officially a staff sergeant in the air corps.

My particular DSC cited me for materially aiding American operations on Luzon; specifically for providing intelligence, raiding the Japanese garrison at San Quintin, and carrying on propaganda work among civilians. Three months later I received the Bronze Star for staying with my troops when I could have gone home. I was also honored by a Philippine congressional citation. I heard a story that I had been recommended for the Philippine Distinguished Star, an award equivalent to our congressional medal of honor, but if so nothing ever materialized. It was probably just the nine millionth "latrine rumor" of the war. The anomaly of my rank was clarified a few days after the audience with General MacArthur. I was appointed a captain AUS from USAFFE headquarters, with rank from December 11, 1943.

Of the many guerrilla organizations in the Philippines, Bob Lapham's was the only one whose officers were not reduced in rank at the end of the war. The highest rank in the whole outfit was Bob's own: major. That we were not reduced seemed to me proper recognition of our accomplishments, but not less an acknowledgment of Bob's sense of proportion. Some other outfits had as many backwoods "colonels" as rabbits have descendants.

The saddest memories I retain from World War II are those related to our postwar treatment of Filipinos. Seldom in history have one people been so loyal to another or suffered so much for another as the Filipinos did for Americans. We had built no serious defenses in the Philippines when the war began, yet throughout the struggle the Filipinos shared our hardships, fought beside us, and risked their own and their families' lives for us. Those of us in the central plains of Luzon could not have survived at all without regular aid from local civilians. Many such civilians lost everything they had for trusting us too much. We owed them protection and defense, yet when the war was over we expected them to be grateful to us for having at length rescued them from further disasters of our making, disasters that had already cost them perhaps a million dead from battle casualties, internecine slaughter, the bloody oppression of civilians, and the merciless scourges of disease and starvation. Yet, despite it all, most ordinary Filipinos were overjoyed when the American army returned.

What ought we have done? In my opinion, we should have made the Philippines a forty-ninth state. Contrary to most of what is written in books, contrary to everything "progressive" people are supposed to believe, I am convinced that in a free election most ordinary Filipinos would have voted to retain or strengthen their ties with America.[28] Of course, this was not true of those prominent Filipinos who hoped to become the rulers of an independent nation. Sadly, it is also a fact that race and nationality consciousness are the foremost mass passions of our century, and that in every part of the world ambitious politicians have been able to inflame multitudes by clamoring for "freedom" and "independence." Perhaps they would have done so in the Philippines too had we retained our control there. But at least we could have offered our wartime allies a choice.

After the war our government was remarkably stingy in its treatment of U.S. guerrillas. The War Claims Act provided that prisoners of war or civilians who had been held by an enemy government and not fed up to standards prescribed by the Geneva Convention should be paid $1 for every day spent in captivity, plus an extra $1.50 per day if they had been treated inhumanely or forced to perform unpaid labor in violation of the Geneva Convention. Al Hendrickson tried for ten years to persuade Congress to amend the act to include guerrillas, with the money to be taken out of Japanese war reparations. He got nowhere. Leon Beck battled in U.S. courts for twelve years to finally keep $992 which our government claimed had been wrongly paid to him as compensation for being a prisoner of war, because he had spent only thirteen days as a prisoner before escaping on the Death March, after which he had been a guerrilla for nearly three years. James P. Boyd, whose personal hegira resembled Beck's, was less successful. He was officially classified as a prisoner of the Japanese for only one day, April 9, 1942, after which he escaped, and so he was sent a check for one dollar—which he still cherished, uncashed, in 1984![29]

Such treatment of American guerrillas was grotesque. That we never properly compensated many of those Filipinos who served with us, or the families of those who died doing so, was truly shameful. To be sure, obstacles in the way of justice were numerous and daunting, and some effort was made to cope with them. For instance, Bob Lapham went back to the islands early in 1947 as a consultant to the Guerrilla Affairs Section of the U.S. Army. He stayed about six months, working with his own guerrilla officers and with American regular officers to reconstruct records and rosters that would be as complete and accurate as possible for Tarlac, Pangasinan, Nueva Ecija, and Nueva Vizcaya provinces. He tried to secure back pay and military status for deserving men and to insure that some assistance would be forthcoming to the families of those who had died fighting alongside ourselves against our common enemy. Sorting out the legitimate claims from the more numerous false ones was always difficult and often impossible. Bob said afterward that he believed something approaching justice had been done for most of his men,[30] an estimate more optimistic than most. For me the whole business has always been intensely disheartening.

It has often been alleged that Filipinos came out of World War II demoralized. I have always found this hard to accept, since the vast majority of those whom I saw or dealt with were elated, jubilant at the return of American troops and the prospect of imminent victory. But save for the brief trip to Manila to be decorated, described above, I was always out in the hinterlands. The demoralization was said to have been much worse in cities, and especially in Manila. That it existed cannot be doubted, since it has been attested to by numerous American and Filipino writers of several ideological persuasions. They also agree that some of it was inevitable and some was not; and for that which was not, responsibility is divided between Americans and Filipinos themselves.

The descent commenced right at the beginning of the war. The U.S. Army threw open its storehouses in Manila to let Filipino civilians carry away what they could rather than allow it to fall to the invaders. Not satisfied, the recipients plundered Chinese shops and grocery stores for good measure. The police could do nothing since they were too busy elsewhere, they had had their firearms taken away a couple of days earlier, and too many people were involved anyway.[31] The wholesale looting of Manila followed. This set the pattern for the future. Before long agriculture broke down, food shortages developed, prices of everything soared while wages remained low, and poor people starved to death in the streets while profiteers and collaborators lived grandly. Under such pressure gangsters and rascals of every stripe flourished. Some were spectacularly shameless. There were Filipino doctors who sold quinine and sulfa drugs at high prices while Filipino survivors of the Bataan Death March died from want of such medicines. Some rascality was bizarre. Graves were robbed to steal fancy clothes and to knock the gold teeth from the mouths of the dead. Some thievery was incredible in its boldness. One robber lifted a Japanese officer's sword in a theater; another stole a machine gun off a Japanese truck parked in front of a restaurant.[32]

Japanese occupation forces soon contributed heavily to the economic and moral debacle. They elbowed their way into every Philippine industry of any consequence and manipulated the currency in ways that steadily drained the country of its raw materials and movable wealth.

To avoid starvation and to survive the counterpressures

on them from the Japanese on one side and competing bands of guerrillas on the other, ordinary Filipinos were forced into the sort of moral compromises their political leaders faced when serving in the Japanese-sponsored "Philippine Republic." Everybody stole from everybody else, both to live and to sell the loot to the Japanese. It soon seemed that any noteworthy transaction required an agent, a go-between, or some "sharpy" taking a cut.

Black marketeering flourished; "protection" was routinely sold to railway shippers; hijacking became commonplace; ticket scalping proliferated; ersatz foods multiplied; dogs and cats in various guises appeared on restaurant menus; local government broke down to such a degree that garbage and even unburied corpses lay in the streets of tropical cities for days on end; and shortages of everything were so bad that if one went to a hospital he had to bring his own bandages and medicines. At the war's end stevedores systematically looted American ships at temporary piers, and the streets of Manila teemed with hawkers of everything salable.[33]

Worst of all was the growth of eleventh hour "heroes" and of violence, especially in 1945. Many who had done nothing save pray that MacArthur would return soon now swaggered about carrying .45s. They talked loudly about what fearless guerrillas they had been, shouted orders at civilians, and confiscated food in the name of "military law." They kidnapped and robbed or murdered the wealthy, or merely the unlucky, on the ground that the victims were "collaborators."

During the war thoughtful Filipinos, viewing current destruction and what they knew was certain to come, and knowing that eventual reconstruction would be difficult, expressed the hope that when the war was over America would not forget Filipino bravery in the common struggle and would provide the aid the Philippines would need so sorely.[34] Things hardly turned out thus. In 1945–46 hordes of American soldiers flooded into the Philippines, many of them interested primarily in un-Christian living. Filipinas flocked to them, and venereal disease rates soared. Though Bob Lapham thought the American officers with whom he worked to investigate Filipino guerrilla war claims were generally conscientious, others have portrayed them as preoccupied primarily with playing golf or "investigating the anatomy of local women."[35] Perhaps worst of all, a swarm of "fast buck" types followed a-pace, taking advantage of wartime privations and general disorder.

Such irresponsible conduct indicated a fundamental inadequacy: in 1945–46 the U.S. government had no clearcut Philippine policy. While Washington did follow through on the highest level of *general* policy, in that independence which had been promised to the Filipinos in 1934 was granted on schedule in 1946, when it came down to particular deeds the islands were treated with a mixture of muddle and neglect. In Manila, meanwhile, members of the new Philippine Congress, not to be outdone in either folly or venality, voted themselves back pay even though their national treasury was empty. In Washington years passed, senators and congressmen grew older, memories of the war receded, and interest waned in either Philippine claims or American obligations. With that strange perversity that seems to overcome us periodically, we adopted the policy that some Europeans have described wryly as "treating neutrals like friends, enemies like neutrals, and friends like enemies." Filipinos could never understand why their idol, General MacArthur, went off to promote and preside over the recovery of Japan rather than the Philippines; why in the first year after the war their country received only about $3 million in UNRRA aid while Yugoslavia got $300 million;[36] or why Americans seemed more solicitous about the condition of Nisei in the United States than that of ex-allies.

Small wonder that so many in the Philippine generation that has grown up since 1945 have become anti-American. They never experienced the warm comradeship of Americans and Filipinos in the war years. Their memories are, rather, of stolen war property, American and Filipino profiteers, endless squabbles over veterans' benefits, and those tawdry features of our civilization that so often impress foreigners more than American qualities of which we can justly be proud. Those Filipinos, old now, who do remember the war years have been saddened by these developments. I have received letters from some I knew and some I did not, and clippings from Philippine newspapers, referring to me as a "grateful American" and praising me in terms that are embarrassing, all because I have done such small things as keep in touch with some wartime Filipino associates or refer to Filipinos favorably in occasional letters to American magazines.[37]

How little we, as a people, appreciate the intangibles in human affairs; how heedlessly we threw away so much good will in the Philippines that could have been preserved merely by curbing a small number of swine among our own people and by treating more generously those who struggled and suffered with us. A remark attributed to the German chancellor Konrad Adenauer seems apropos here: "If God saw fit to limit human intelligence, it hardly seems fair that He did not also limit human stupidity."

Few important things in life go smoothly; certainly few things in the army do. A week after I had received my DSC I said goodbye to all my friends and put in for air transportation home. At once I hit a snag. I was informed that everyone in my category (Project J, "Recovered Personnel") had long since been flown out and that only seagoing transportation was now available. I protested that this policy was both absurd and unfair since I had remained in the service for additional months of my own volition. Was I now to be penalized for it?

I got nowhere with the middle-range military bureaucrats who deal routinely with such matters, so I asked to see Major Gen. Charles A. Willoughby, MacArthur's G-2. The next day I was leaning over a desk in his outer office writing something when a massive man came up alongside me and asked if I was Captain Hunt. Momentarily startled, I gazed upward at the giant who loomed over me and then downward as his huge hand engulfed mine. General Willoughby then asked how old I was.

When I told him I was twenty-five, he said he had read some of my dispatches when he was in Australia and from them had envisioned me as a much older man. Then he asked me what he could do for me. I told him my troubles. He said he thought I should take an ocean liner; that three weeks or so of lounging in deck chairs with attentive nurses about struck him as an especially pleasant way to travel for someone who had been in a war zone for three years. I replied that I had not seen any of my family for more than six years and would like to get home as soon as possible. He shrugged at what clearly seemed to him my invincible irrationality. Then he wrote me an endorsement for air transportation, phrased so generously that it might have served as a commendation, and wished me well.

Two days later I boarded a C-54 at Nichols Field, where I had been at the outbreak of the war. My earthly possessions consisted of a couple of GI uniforms, some underwear, a few toilet articles, and my ornate 9mm. German Luger. Looking over my shoulder through the window of the plane, I watched the shores of the Philippines gradually disappear into the trackless sea. I had seen the whole war on one of those islands, and by the grace of God I was still alive. It seemed improbable.

Now, long after, I seldom think about the war or my part in it, save for the recollection and study that were essential to write this book. Its composition has been, for me, an emotional experience. I undertook it with several hopes: to add a bit to the historical record of World War II; to apportion credit a little more equitably among Americans and Filipinos who struggled and endured so much together; and to pay a final tribute to the many Filipinos who did so much for me.

When the book is finished, I shall read it and then put the war behind me, but I will never forget the lessons World War II taught me. When I look now at fields, trees, birds, mere clouds in the sky, I see beauty and feel content. It seems so easy to imagine that henceforth peace will engulf the earth because that *ought* to be the case.

Yet, on the intellectual level, I have to agree with Margaret Utinsky, who endured worse things at the hands of the enemy than I ever did. She points out that people do not change much. We Americans read history, if we do so at all, as if it had no relation to us, no messages for us. The same terrible things—war, starvation, torture, execution—continue to happen, as they have for ages past, and each time we act surprised. Years pass, people visit places where ghastly crimes were once committed and shameful indignities inflicted, but where museums now stand. They pay admission, acquire a few superficial impressions, and learn nothing from having seen one more "historical shrine."[38] Perhaps there truly is an unbridgeable gulf between different kinds of human experiences and different categories of knowledge. When men contend with material substances, inanimate objects, and natural forces, each generation can build on what has been achieved by its predecessors, and we witness humanity's visible progress in engineering, medicine, agriculture, the natural sciences, and the multiplication of wealth. Yet in such realms as the relationship of individuals to each other, of individuals to governments, and of governments to other governments, areas where people are on both sides, domains where human vanity, obstinacy, and ambition prevail, knowledge seems noncumulative. Here, each generation seems doomed to repeat the crimes and follies of its predecessors, and we still wrestle with most of the same problems that vexed the ancient Greeks.

Notes

For complete information on works cited, see the Selected Bibliography beginning on page 246.

1: *The War Begins*

1. There are good descriptions of both the material and the psychological unpreparedness in the United States and the Philippines in Forbes J. Monaghan, S.J. *Under the Red Sun,* pp. 12–13; Theodore Friend, *Between Two Empires,* pp. 169–71, 192–95; Marcial P. Lichauco, *"Dear Mother Putnam"* pp. 6–7; and Manuel Buenafe, *Wartime Philippines,* pp. 26–39. A particularly pungent condemnation of stupid and irresponsible Western "intellectuals" of that era, of American "bunglers" in the Philippines, and of assorted "sons of bitches" in Washington is delivered by Robert H. Arnold, *A Rock and a Fortress,* pp. 75–76, 109. Like myself, Arnold spent much of the war as a guerrilla on Luzon.

2. Samuel Grashio and Bernard Norling, *Return to Freedom,* p. 8.

2: *The Struggle for Bataan*

1. Samuel Grashio, in Grashio and Norling, *Return to Freedom*, p. 2.

2. What training and service were like in the Imperial Japanese Army is related unforgettably in a novel by a perceptive man who served in that army in China in the 1930s. See Hanema Tasaki, *Long the Imperial Way.*

3. John Toland, *But Not in Shame*, p. 183.

4. Samuel Grashio, personal communication to the author (B.N.).

5. Russell W. Volckmann, *We Remained*, pp. 158–59.

6. Clark Lee, *One Last Look Around*, pp. 271–76. Lee remarks that the air corps especially detested ground support assignments and never surrendered its official corporate faith that the war could be won by strategic bombing alone.

7. John Deane Potter, *The Life and Death of a Japanese General*, a biography of Gen. Tomoyuki Yamashita, describes many similar instances.

8. Lichauco, *"Dear Mother Putnam,"* pp. 164–65.

9. Saburo Sekai, with Martin Caidin and Fred Saito, *Samurai*, p. 46. See also pp. 72–74.

10. Teodoro A. Agoncillo, *The Fateful Years*, 2: 896–98.

3: *The Bataan Death March*

1. The best brief discussion of the whole question is in Stanley Falk, *Bataan*, pp. 194–98.

2. Monaghan, *Under the Red Sun*, p. 124.

3. The last opinion is that of Monaghan, ibid., p. 108. For other interpretations of the character and motivation of the Japanese, see Bert Bank, *Back from the Living Dead*, pp. 52–53; Robert Considine (ed.), *General Wainwright's Story*, pp. 203–4; 257; Philip Knightley, *The First Casualty*, pp. 292–94; Gregory Boyington, *Baa! Baa! Black Sheep*, pp. 361–62; Quentin Reynolds (ed.), *Officially Dead*, pp. 15, 35; James Bertram, *Beneath the Shadow*, p. 104; Agnes Newton Keith, *Three Came Home*, pp. 3–13, 231–33, 294, 306–14, 317; Sidney Stewart, *Give Us This Day*, pp. 82–83, 97, 104–5, 173–74; Falk, *Bataan*, especially pp. 227–30; Clark Lee, *They Called It Pacific*, pp. 280–82; Ernest Miller, *Bataan Uncensored*, pp. 366–71; Edgar Whitcomb, *Escape from*

Corregidor, p. 267; and Ernest Gordon, *Through the Valley of the Kwai*, p. 53. Bank, Wainwright, Boyington, Smith, Bertram, Keith, Stewart, Miller, Whitcomb, and Gordon were all prisoners of the Japanese at one time or another.

Agoncillo, a Filipino who survived the Death March and later became a historian, says that even though he did not face up to it at the time he eventually came to realize that mortality on the march owed more to the sickness and weakness of the prisoners than to the deliberate brutality of the guards (*The Fateful Years*, 2: 901–2). All I can say is that there was plenty of both.

4: *In and Out of the Fassoth Camps*

1. Vernon Fassoth, personal communication to the author (B.N.).

2. On September 14–16, 1984, I (B.N.) attended a meeting of the Indiana Oral Military History Association in Indianapolis. Also present were about twenty veterans of Bataan, Corregidor, and Luzon guerrilla life. Several of them had been in the Fassoth camps at one time or another. At the meeting a poster was displayed which listed by name all those known to have been in the Fassoth camps. There were 104 names on it. Nobody present proposed either to add or delete names.

3. Monaghan, *Under the Red Sun*, pp. 133–40.

4. Volckmann, *We Remained*, pp. 62–70.

5. Philip Harkins, *Blackburn's Headhunters*, pp. 58–62.

6. Henry Clay Conner, "We Fought Fear on Luzon," p. 74.

7. At least this was the opinion of Blackburn (Harkins, *Blackburn's Headhunters*, p. 58). Fassoth's third camp was raided by the Japanese on February 22, 1943, a development that might have produced added inducement to surrender.

8. Conner, "We Fought Fear," p. 72.

9. Walter Chatham, personal communication to the author (R.H.).

10. Donald Blackburn relates that, in circumstances not unlike mine, he and Russell Volckmann owed their lives to a Filipino named Guerrero. The man sheltered the pair for a month when they were nearly dead from sickness and star-

vation. Mr. Guerrero found them places to hide, had his daughters feed them, procured a doctor to treat them, paid the doctor himself, found guides to lead them northward, and even paid for the guides, all at great risk to himself and his family, and when he had little money. Harkins, *Blackburn's Headhunters,* pp. 50–56. Like me, Blackburn had a wound, in his case an infected heel, that troubled him most of one spring. Treatment was unavailing, so he just walked on it anyway. Eventually it healed (Harkins, *Blackburn's Headhunters,* p. 164). I doubt that I would have been as lucky.

Like Blackburn and myself, Clay Conner owed his life to Filipinos who operated miniature camps like that of the Fassoths, and who taught him how to catch shrimp and eels in rivers ("We Fought Fear," p. 71).

11. We (R.H. and B.N.) are indebted to Mrs. Ann Petrites, the sister of William Fassoth's daughter-in-law, for making available to us a copy of Fassoth's unpublished account of the origin, construction, operation, and demise of his three camps. I (B.N.) am grateful to William Fassoth's son, Vernon, for allowing me to use his own taped recollections of what happened in the camps.

I (R.H.) am also obliged to Walter Chatham for numerous personal recollections of the life he shared with me in Fassoth's second camp. Some of them corrected my uncertain memory. On the question of how many of us escaped from the camp, however, I believe my memory has been more accurate than his.

5: *Daily Life with Filipinos*

1. Robert Lapham, personal communication to the author (B.N.).

6: *Early Guerrillas of Luzon*

1. An excellent account of guerrilla operations through the centuries, shorn of contemporary mythology and replete with examples of irregular operations all over the world, is Walter Laqueur, *Guerrilla.* For a brief critique of partisan warfare as seen by professional soldiers, see Michael Howard, *The Causes of Wars,* p. 88.

2. A lurid account of the bloody excesses of Luzon guer-

rillas, both American and Filipino, is given by Ernesto R. Rodriguez, Jr., *The Bad Guerrillas of Northern Luzon.*

3. Ira Wolfert, *American Guerrilla in the Philippines*, p. 142.

4. Trevor Ingham, *Rendezvous by Submarine*, p. 45.

5. Edward F. Dissette and H. D. Adamson, *Guerrilla Submarines*, p. 30.

6. There is considerable information about Fenton's background, character, and eccentricities in Charles A. Willoughby, *The Guerrilla Resistance Movement in the Philippines*, pp. 264–65; and also in Ingham, *Rendezvous by Submarine*, p. 160; Allison Ind, *Allied Intelligence Bureau*, pp. 135–42; Agoncillo, *The Fateful Years*, 2: 735–37; and Jesus A. Villamor, *They Never Surrendered*, pp. 89, 106–9, 218. A particularly scathing account is provided by Manuel F. Segura, *Tabunan*, especially pp. 181–202.

7. Fenton's unpublished diary is in the possession of Morton J. Netzorg, proprietor of the Cellar Bookshop in Detroit and of an excellent private research library of materials relating to the Philippines.

8. Arnold, *A Rock and a Fortress*, pp. 200–201.

9. Lichauco, *"Dear Mother Putnam,"* p. 84.

10. Albert C. Hendrickson, personal communication to the author (B.N.).

11. Rodriguez, *The Bad Guerrillas*, pp. x–xi, 38–48, 57–98, 115–25, 130–32, contains gory descriptions of the crimes and vices of various northern Luzon guerrillas. The quotation is from p. 38. Agoncillo relates some of the charges against Escobar *(The Fateful Years*, 2: 755).

12. William L. Estrada, *A Historical Survey of the Guerrilla Movement in Pangasinan, 1942–1945*, p. 33.

13. Volckmann, *We Remained*, pp. 36–39.

14. Al Hendrickson says Nakar got his radio from Warner (personal communication to the author [B.N.]). For varied accounts of Nakar's activities and fate, see Courtney Whitney, *MacArthur*, pp. 128–29; Charles A. Willoughby and John Chamberlain, *MacArthur, 1941–1951*, p. 210; Dissette and Adamson, *Guerrilla Submarines*, p. 31; and Agoncillo, *The Fateful Years*, 2: 655.

15. The whole idea may have been suggested to MacAr-

thur by "Chick" Parsons, later to gain renown as the supreme commander's director of submarine contacts with Philippine guerrillas. Dissette and Adamson, *Guerrilla Submarines,* p. 12.

General Wainwright, who formally surrendered all Allied troops in the Philippines when Corregidor fell, did not share MacArthur's enthusiasm for guerrillas, perhaps because their very existence complicated his own problems. He called them "hotheads."

16. Of several lists of Thorpe's entourage that I (B.N.) have seen, no two are the same. *According to a sympathetic biographer,* Ferdinand Marcos, who had been in the thick of the Bataan campaign and who long after the war became the controversial and embattled ruler of the Philippines, was responsible for slipping most of these men through chinks in the Japanese forward wall. The Japanese eventually found out about this, arrested Marcos, and tortured him atrociously in Fort Santiago, but he could not tell them anything because he did not know where any of the men had gone afterward. Hartzell Spence, *For Every Tear a Victory,* pp. 142, 156–58.

17. Personal communications with William H. Brooks (R.H.), Robert Lapham, Vernon Fassoth, and Donald Blackburn (B.N.). See also Conner, "We Fought Fear," p. 74.

18. Estrada, *Historical Survey,* p. 50. Brooks describes the ambush Thorpe set for the Japanese convoy (William H. Brooks, personal communication to both R.H. and B.N.). It seems virtually certain that Brooks's memory failed him about "McIntyre." The index to General Willoughby's *Guerrilla Resistance Movement,* p. 572, lists a James McIntyre who was active as a guerrilla, but on Mindanao, hundreds of miles to the south. Thus, the dynamiter with Thorpe must have been Capt. Ralph McGuire, who was killed by Filipinos in the Zambales Mountains in the following year, 1943.

19. Ind, *Allied Intelligence Bureau,* p. 9.

20. Ibid., p. 118; *Intelligence Activities in the Philippines,* p. xi, gives the date as November 4, 1942. This is typical of the differences among sources in these chaotic times.

21. Whitney, *MacArthur,* pp. 130–31.

22. Yay Panlilio, *The Crucible,* pp. 337–46; Willoughby, *Guerrilla Resistance Movement,* pp. 112–13.

23. Arnold, *A Rock and a Fortress*, pp. 17–39, 75–76.

24. Ibid., pp. 17–39, 184–88.

25. Agoncillo, *The Fateful Years*, 2: 655–66.

26. Conner, "We Fought Fear," pp. 70–87, describes his exploits at length.

27. Albert C. Hendrickson, personal communication to the author (B.N.). Volckmann provides a long description of Walter Cushing and his activities (*We Remained*, pp. 26–36), as does James Dean Sanderson, *Behind Enemy Lines*, pp. 196–218. On one of his trips to Manila, Cushing persuaded high Filipino officials to give him three sets of identity papers showing him to be (1) a Filipino of Spanish extraction, (2) and Italian mestizo, and (3) a priest. This was probably the source of the allegation, made by many writers, that Walter Cushing and his brothers Charles and Joseph were mestizos. See Sanderson, *Behind Enemy Lines*, p. 214.

28. Robert Lapham, personal communication to the author (B.N.).

29. Willoughby, *Guerrilla Resistance Movement*, p. 418.

30. Volckmann, *We Remained*, pp. 82–90, describes the journeys and adventures of Moses and Noble, and Blackburn describes the variegated, often ragtag, outfits they "unified." See Harkins, *Blackburn's Headhunters*, pp. 96–100. About the latter, Robert Arnold observes that while many American guerrillas put personal rivalry and political ambition above other considerations, at least they did not shoot at each other as their Filipino counterparts did (*A Rock and a Fortress*, p. 201). Filipinos were not above settling personal feuds by turning each other in to the Japanese.

31. Harkins, *Blackburn's Headhunters*, pp. 94, 100.

32. Volckmann, *We Remained*, p. 139; Albert C. Hendrickson, personal communication to the author (B.N.).

33. Dissette and Adamson, *Guerrilla Submarines*, pp. 39, 233, for example. Jesus Villamor turned in a similar official report to USAFFE headquarters in Australia in 1943. See Willoughby, *Guerrilla Resistance Movement*, pp. 263–75.

34. After the war both Volckmann and Blackburn left long accounts of their tribulations, both before they managed to get to northern Luzon and while they were building guerrilla

organizations there; see Volckmann, *We Remained,* and Harkins, *Blackburn's Headhunters.*

35. Harkins, *Blackburn's Headhunters,* pp. 87–88; Robert Lapham, personal communication to the author (B.N.).

36. Wolfert, *American Guerrilla,* p. 157.

37. Donald Blackburn, many of whose experiences and problems paralleled my own, came to the same conclusion I did about drinking when one of his guerrilla liaison men, bearing the sadly appropriate name of Fish, was caught by the Japanese while drunk. Harkins, *Blackburn's Headhunters,* p. 174.

38. Ibid., p. 131.

39. Estrada, *Historical Survey,* pp. 28–29.

40. Harkins, *Blackburn's Headhunters,* p. 101.

41. Margaret Utinsky, *Miss U.,* pp. 129, 137.

42. Ingham, *Rendezvous by Submarine,* pp. 107–8.

7: Hukbalahaps and Constabulary

1. Most of the debts of peasants were incurred not to improve their lands and to increase their incomes but to finance weddings, funerals, and fiestas, and to bet on cockfights. Spence, *For Every Tear a Victory,* p. 230.

2. A good brief account of the rise of the Philippine Communist Party is given by George E. Taylor, *The Philippines and the United States,* pp. 92–97.

3. More than twenty years after World War II, when Taruc was still in prison, he wrote *He Who Rides the Tiger,* with assistance from Douglas Hyde, an Irish ex-Communist. In it, Taruc chronicles his gradual disillusionment with communism, a process spread over some twenty-five years. At first he resented chiefly communist discipline. Then he gradually became aware that the Philippine communists were using resistance to the Japanese to serve the ends of the international communist movement, just as other communists employ local discontents for this purpose anywhere. Once these realizations became clear, he was more quickly alienated by their ruthlessness, inhumanity, dogmatism, and self-seeking, which he saw as destroying all the goodness that had infused their original common effort. Taruc, *He Who Rides the Tiger,* especially pp. 17–18, 20–22, 30–31, 34, 50–53, 79, 167–68.

Long before, Taruc had written another book, *Born of the People*. In *He Who Rides the Tiger* he says that José Lava, general secretary of the Philippine Communist Party, wrote a lot of doctrinaire Marxism in it that did not truly reflect Taruc's own state of mind at that time (pp. xiii, 7). William Pomeroy, an American communist, later claimed that he wrote all of *Born of the People* for Taruc. See Morton J. Netzorg, *The Philippines in World War II and to Independence*, p. 151.

4. Teodoro A. Agoncillo, in *The Fateful Years* (2: 674), argues that Thorpe's capture and execution by the Japanese were important factors in the breakdown of cooperation between USAFFE guerrillas and the Huks. Blackburn says Thorpe (whom he chooses to call "Crabtree") ruined any chance for concerted action by behaving in a stupid and arrogant fashion toward the Huks. Harkins, *Blackburn's Headhunters*, p. 79. Clay Conner, William H. Brooks, and Al Hendrickson, all of whom had considerable experience with the Huks, think the political differences between the two groups would have precluded cooperation in any case. Conner, "We Fought Fear," pp. 73–75, 78; Albert C. Hendrickson, personal communication to the author (B.N.); William H. Brooks, personal communication to the author (R.H.).

5. Among many examples of this view of things, see David J. Steinberg, *Philippine Collaborators in World War II*, p. 93; Teodoro A. Agoncillo and Oscar M. Alfonso, *A Short History of the Philippine People*, pp. 514–17; Usha Mahajani, *Philippine Nationalism*, pp. 459–60; Benedict J. Kerkvliet, *The Huk Rebellion*, especially pp. xv, 67, 69, 71–79, 105–18, 255–67; Jules Archer, *The Philippines' Fight for Freedom*, pp. 179ff.; and Hernando J. Abaya, *Betrayal in the Philippines*.

6. Conner, "We Fought Fear," p. 76.

7. The phrase is that of Monaghan in *Under the Red Sun* (p. 144) but the sentiment is mine.

8. For a good summary of how Marxist irregulars proceeded in this manner in Europe, see Laqueur, *Guerrilla*, pp. 223–38; in China and the Philippines, see ibid., pp. 256–93. See also Taylor, *The Philippines and the United States*, pp. 96–97.

9. Even Kerkvliet, so understanding toward all Huks, acknowledges this (*The Huk Rebellion*, pp. 50–51). When Vincente Lava left Manila hurriedly in January 1942 just ahead of the Japanese, he left on his desk plans for a village defense corps identical to those drawn up by Chinese communist guerrillas in 1937 after the Japanese invasion there (Taylor, *The Philippines and the United States*, p. 95). What USAFFE headquarters in Australia knew and surmised about the Huks during the war is summarized in Willoughby, *Guerrilla Resistance Movement*, pp. 453–57.

10. Monaghan, *Under the Red Sun*, p. 144.

11. Agoncillo, *The Fateful Years*, 2: 668, 672.

12. *Intelligence Activities*, October 23, 1944, no. 81, pp. 3–4.

13. For other estimates see Taylor, *The Philippines and the United States*, pp. 121–22; Abaya, *Betrayal*, p. 219; Spence, *For Every Tear a Victory*, pp. 211–12; and Kerkvliet, *Huk Rebellion*, pp. 87, 93–94. Spence notes that the Huks themselves claimed to have killed thirty thousand Japanese in "1,200 pitched battles."

14. Robert Lapham, personal communication to the author (B.N.).

15. Russell Brines, *Until They Eat Stones*, pp. 48–51.

16. Buenafe, *Wartime Philippines*, pp. 226–28.

17. Willoughby, *Guerrilla Resistance Movement*, p. 363. Marcial Lichauco, a law partner of Manuel Roxas, says he asked a Constabulary patrolman late in 1943 what he would do if American and Filipino troops landed some day and the Japanese put him on the firing line. The man replied that he and several of his friends had put the same question to their commanding officer. He had told them that every man would have to decide for himself, and that he wished all of them well. Lichauco, *"Dear Mother Putnam,"* pp. 136–37. It was well known among Constabularymen that General Francisco's sentiments were similar. See Teofilo del Castillo and José del Castillo, *The Saga of José P. Laurel*, p. 304.

8: *Guerrilla Life*

1. Allison Ind, *Allied Intelligence Bureau*, p. 116.

2. Harkins, *Blackburn's Headhunters*, pp. 223–26. Ar-

nold, in *A Rock and a Fortress,* p. 192, also alludes to his plight then.

3. Panlilio, *The Crucible,* p. 111.

4. Ibid., pp. 239, 248–49.

5. Panlilio acknowledges that for all the trouble she and Marking had with their guerrillas, much of their time was spent a good deal like most of ours. She said Marking himself was the only doctor they had, and his knowledge came from a correspondence course in nursing he had once taken. She learned some from him, and everyone learned from experience. Marking's guerrillas were often close to Manila. There many of them posed as civilians and got jobs on the Manila docks, where opportunities for sabotage were much greater and more diversified than they ever were for our men. *The Crucible,* pp. 56, 58, 110.

6. Blackburn says *Enoch* French was killed by a Filipino subordinate who thought French had given him too little Japanese military scrip for his wedding; that the killer surrendered to the Japanese, who then let him join the Philippine Constabulary; and that one of French's officers ambushed him on a patrol soon after. Harkins, *Blackburn's Headhunters,* p. 175. I think this is a reference to the same person and the same incident, and that either Blackburn's recollection of the details, or mine, is faulty, but it is impossible to be certain so long after the events. Conceivably, there were two different persons and two separate events. Either way, the moral is the same: one could never be entirely sure of the loyalty of even his closest associates.

7. Panlilio, *The Crucible,* p. 185.

8. Blackburn relates that he once let a Filipino subordinate ambush a Japanese patrol just to keep up everyone's spirits, only to have the man botch the job. Harkins, *Blackburn's Headhunters,* p. 201. My luck was better.

9. Laqueur, *Guerrilla,* cites many examples of guerrillas' efforts to cope with bandits, going back as far in time as the Spanish resistance to Napoleon, 1808–13. See especially pp. 36, 95.

10. Vernon Fassoth, personal communication to the author (B.N.).

11. Laqueur believes that one of the main reasons for the

effectiveness of Russian guerrillas in World War II was that they were in regular radio communication with their general staff and thus were never burdened with a feeling of isolation and abandonment (*Guerrilla,* p. 212).

12. Ibid., p. 21.

13. For a thoughtful survey of the problems and dilemmas of the Japanese, see Steinberg, *Philippine Collaborators,* pp. 56–58.

14. Monaghan describes such an episode that took place in Tayabas province early in the war (*Under the Red Sun,* p. 147).

15. This particular ruse seems to have been commonest around Manila. See Panlilio, *The Crucible,* p. 192.

16. Willoughby, *Guerrilla Resistance Movement,* p. 247. Rufino Baldwin, a north Luzon guerrilla, was captured in 1943 when his ex-fiancée learned that he had acquired a new girlfriend and turned him in to the Japanese. They tortured him every day for two weeks in Baguio, then sent him to the infamous Fort Santiago in Manila, from which he never emerged. Harkness, *Blackburn's Headhunters,* pp. 158, 175.

17. This particular barbarity was even inflicted on women, one being the Filipina wife of Fish, Blackburn's liaison man who had been taken by the Japanese while drunk. Fish himself was flogged into unconsciousness before being executed. Harkins, *Blackburn's Headhunters,* p. 184.

18. Panlilio, *The Crucible,* pp. 206–7.

19. Aubrey S. Kenworthy, *The Tiger of Malaya,* pp. 61–62.

20. This was done to Jack Langley, who had commanded a small guerrilla outfit before he was captured. Harkins, *Blackburn's Headhunters,* p. 182.

21. Ingham, *Rendezvous by Submarine,* p. 40.

22. Conner, ''We Fought Fear,'' p. 75.

23. For instance, Agoncillo and Alfonso, *Short History,* p. 466.

24. Wolfert, *American Guerrilla,* p. 147.

25. Ibid., pp. 184–85. Appalling atrocities of this genre were commonplace in irregular operations in centuries past. Wars between Balkan peoples and the Turks in medieval and early modern times were notoriously savage and bloody. Rus-

sian partisans harrying Napoleon's army on its retreat from Moscow were extremely cruel. One village elder asked a partisan leader if he knew a new way to kill a Frenchman: all known methods had already been tried. Laqueur, *Guerrilla*, pp. 15–18, 46, 61.

26. Panlilio, *The Crucible*, pp. 196–98.

27. Ibid., 218; Harkins, *Blackburn's Headhunters*, pp. 179, 184, 194; Ingham, *Rendezvous by Submarine*, pp. 124–25.

28. Volckmann, *We Remained*, p. 107. Though I subsequently had considerable trouble with Volckmann (see chapters 10 and 13), his assessment of these knotty problems is virtually identical with my own. Volckmann, pp. 125–26, 131.

29. Panlilio, *The Crucible*, pp. 158–59, 218.

30. Monaghan, *Under the Red Sun*, p. 142.

31. Ibid., p. 223.

9: The Plight of the Filipinos

1. Willoughby and Chamberlain, *MacArthur*, pp. 213–14.

2. For an extended analysis of Japanese policy in the Philippines, see Agoncillo, *The Fateful Years*, 2: 74–150. For brief synopses, see Robert S. Ward. *Asia for the Asiatics?*, especially pp. 56–58; and Ingham, *Rendezvous by Submarine*, p. 162.

3. These facets of Filipino psychology are discussed in Steinberg, *Philippine Collaborators*, p. 26; and Theodore Friend, *Between Two Empires*, pp. 24–31.

4. Harkins, *Blackburn's Headhunters*, p. 139. For an excellent discussion of what constitutes treason on both the intellectual and the practical levels, though mainly in a European context, see Margaret Boveri, *Treason in the Twentieth Century*.

5. Elliot R. Thorpe, *East Wind, Rain*, p. 163.

6. For a consideration of traditional Philippine policy in trying circumstances, see Steinberg, *Philippine Collaborators*, pp. 13, 60; Friend, *Between Two Empires*, pp. 182–83; and Mahajani, *Philippine Nationalism*, p. 433. That Quezon urged other Filipino politicians to cooperate with the Japanese when they had to in order to spare the Filipino people

is claimed by Antonio M. Molina, *The Philippines through the Centuries*, p. 335; by Castillo and Castillo, *Saga of José P. Laurel*, pp. 118–19; as well as by all those prominent Filipinos who did collaborate with the conquerors or appeared to do so.

James K. Eyre, Jr., *The Roosevelt-MacArthur Conflict*, pp. 55, 76–102, claims that rivalry between the American president and the famous general was more bitter than is usually recognized, that MacArthur and his entourage regarded presidential military strategy as virtual betrayal of themselves and their forces, and that MacArthur not merely saw to it that information about Quezon's rages and threats made its way to Washington but used Quezon's outrage to pressure Washington to send more support to his forces in the Far East.

7. Archer, *The Philippines' Fight for Freedom*, p. 177.

8. Ricarte's actions are defended by two fellow Filipinos of quite different philosophical orientation: Lichauco, *"Dear Mother Putnam,"* pp. 15–16, and Agoncillo, *The Fateful Years*, 2: 918–19.

9. Information about all these groups, their antecedents, sponsorship, and activities may be found in Taylor, *The Philippines and the United States*, p. 106; Agoncillo, *The Fateful Years*, 2: 918–19; Ingham, *Rendezvous by Submarine*, pp. 163–64; Brines, *Until They Eat Stones*, pp. 73–75; F.C. Jones, *Japan's New Order in East Asia, 1937–1945*, p. 367; Panlilio, *The Crucible*, pp. 26, 43–44; José P. Laurel, *War Memoirs*, pp. 25, 64, 301; and Castillo and Castillo, *Saga of José P. Laurel*, p. 93.

10. For instance, Abaya, *Betrayal*, especially pp. 35–40.

11. See Steinberg, *Philippine Collaborators*, pp. 23–24, 73–84, 87–95, 98–99; and, more briefly, Mahajani, *Philippine Nationalism*, pp. 440–41; and Friend, *Between Two Empires*, p. 244. Ironically, Laurel was himself an indecisive man. See Buenafe, *Wartime Philippines*, p. 216.

12. Apologies for Laurel are his own *War Memoirs* and Castillo and Castillo, *Saga*. Other sympathetic considerations of his plight and intentions are provided by Lichauco, *"Dear Mother Putnam,"* pp. 112, 124, 182–83; Agoncillo, *The Fateful Years*, 2: 912–15; and Spence, *For Every Tear a Victory*, pp. 172–73, 297, 303.

13. See Peter Calvocoressi and Guy Wint, *Total War*, for an extended description of Japan's administrative deficiencies (pp. 673–710, 721–22, 783–89, especially pp. 703–5).

14. One of the most unbridled condemnations of all the "collaborators" was delivered in Abaya, *Betrayal in the Philippines*, for which Ickes wrote a foreword. See especially pp. 9–11, 21–33, 50–53, 86–91, 104–8, 151–62. The quotation is from p. 102. More moderate variations on the same theme are Taruc, *He Who Rides the Tiger*, pp. 144–47; Kerkvliet, *Huk Rebellion;* Thorpe, *East Wind, Rain*, pp. 152–53, 156–58, 163; and Archer, *The Philippines' Fight for Freedom*, pp. 193–95.

15. Laurel, *War Memoirs*, pp. 40–41.

16. Castillo and Castillo, *Saga*, pp. 3–4.

17. See Lichauco, *"Dear Mother Putnam,"* p. 119, for Vargas's ambition to become president of the Republic; p. 77 for the anecdote about the apples.

18. Steinberg, in *Philippine Collaborators*, discusses Filipino collaborators, their problems and intentions, exhaustively. See especially pp. 37–38, 60–69, 115, 131–66.

19. Ibid., pp. 160–62.

20. See Archer, *The Philippines' Fight for Freedom*, pp. 194–95; Eyre, *The Roosevelt-MacArthur Conflict*, pp. 173–93; and, most vehemently, Abaya, *Betrayal*, pp. 9–11, 22–33, 59–76, 84.

21. D. Clayton James, *The Years of MacArthur*, vol. 2, *1941–1945*, pp. 691–93.

22. Panlilio, *The Crucible*, pp. 177, 188–92.

23. Elinor Goettl, *Eagle of the Philippines*, pp. 181–82, 188, 194.

24. Ind, *Allied Intelligence Bureau*, p. 153; Spence, *For Every Tear a Victory*, pp. 173–75; Willoughby, *Guerrilla Resistance Movement*, pp. 39, 45–61, 205–6, 285, 340, 383, 387, 390–97. Lichauco, Roxas's prewar law partner, presents the same favorable picture of his colleague's purposes and activities (*"Dear Mother Putnam,"* pp. 19, 92, 113–14, 134). A further indication of Roxas's true colors is that the Kempeitai recorded his name as head of the American spy network in the Philippines, *Intelligence Activities*, p. 78.

25. Taylor points out that the Huks were avid to punish

collaborators because they knew it would divide the country, but adds that true nationalist guerrillas like Confessor and Tomas Cabili also wanted them punished from patriotic motives (*The Philippines and the United States*, p. 112). Archer notes (*The Philippines' Fight for Freedom*, p. 195) that it was difficult to hold trials because the Japanese had destroyed so many official records. Abaya, *Betrayal*, pp. 110–15, grumbles that the most prominent defendants were to be tried by judges whom they had earlier appointed rather than by "resistance" judges, as in Europe. At the Nuremberg War Crimes Trials the same parties acted as both prosecutors and judges.

Steinberg, in *Philippine Collaborators*, pp. 131–66, and especially in a lengthy description of the Sison case, pp. 134–41, examines all the arguments from constitutions and laws, both American and Philippine, from precedents and circumstances, from the habits of peace and the exigencies of war, that bear on accusations of collaboration.

26. Taylor, *The Philippines and the United States*, pp. 101–2.

27. Gen. Jonathan Wainwright, who had surrendered Corregidor, was later given the Distinguished Service Cross and the Congressional Medal of Honor, reportedly over the disapproval of MacArthur.

28. Taylor, *The Philippines and the United States*, p. 99.

29. Reprinted in H. de la Costa, S.J., *Readings in Philippine History*, pp. 279–80.

30. Taylor, *The Philippines and the United States*, pp. 110, 119, thinks this almost certainly would have been the case. Of course at this writing (1986) the communists, now styled New People's Army (NPA) rather than old Huks, appear once more to have a chance to come to power.

31. Spence, *For Every Tear a Victory*, particularly pp. 100–200, recounts Marcos's exploits in war and peace. The tone of the book is laudatory. A reader's skepticism is aroused, though, by the author's carelessness about details: e.g., putting the Sierra Madre Mountains on the wrong side of Luzon, locating the province of Nueva Ecija on the Pacific coast when it is in the middle of Luzon, and having Marcos make preparations to meet Walter Cushing at a time after Cushing was dead. See pp. 166–67.

32. For example, Primitivo Mijares, *The Conjugal Dictatorship of Ferdinand and Imelda Marcos*. Mijares was once Marcos's top public relations man. He disappeared somewhere on a flight between Guam and Manila. Officially, no one knows what happened to him.

33. See, for Instance, *Newsweek*, Feb. 3, 1986, pp. 24–25; and, in greater detail, *Philippine News* (published in San Francisco), Jan. 29-Feb. 4, 1986, pp. 1, 4–5.

34. There are two documents that bear my signature and that call for the arrest of unauthorized guerrilla organizers in Pangasinan. Both are dated October 9, 1944. One of them, hereafter referred to as Annex B, is brief and is addressed to "All Sector Commanders, P.W.A., 2 Military District." It reminds recipients that the only authorized command in that part of Luzon is the one headed by Major Lapham, and orders the arrest of all organizers not working under that command. It is signed with my full name, and it is unquestionably genuine.

The other document, hereafter referred to as Annex A, is much longer, is written on paper with a printed letterhead rather than a typed one, and even though it bears the same date as Annex B it was clearly written on a different typewriter. It is addressed to a particular individual identified only as "I.C." A postwar Filipino congressman, Cipriano S. Allas, who identifies himself as a captain and former head of the intelligence division of Marcos's Maharlika guerrillas, says "I.C." is Captain Crispulo Ilumin. I never heard of Ilumin and cannot imagine any reason why I might ever have written to him, much less given him orders about anything. Annex A also calls for the arrest of Ferdinand Marcos "specially," which I would have written "especially," even had I singled out Marcos, which I almost certainly did not do. At that time I did not know him well or attach any particular importance to him. Finally, Annex A is signed simply "Ray," a practice I did not follow when issuing formal orders. For all these reasons I think Annex A is a forgery, most likely invented after the war to bolster claims for back pay by supposed followers of Allas and Marcos.

The forgery thesis is supported by another letter, written by Allas in 1947 to "The Commanding General, Philippine

Ryukyus Command." In it Allas, who is clearly trying to secure official recognition of claims that Marcos's Maharlika forces and his own intelligence unit were well established by 1943, says that some of his men joined my unit in May or June of 1943, when in fact I did not get my own command until June 1944. He adds that there were different guerrilla units in eastern Pangasinan, when only my own were there. Finally, he alleges that Maharlika guerrillas actively supported American regular troops along the Villa Verde Trail in the spring of 1945, though I was there at the time and do not recall seeing any. Thus, I am not impressed by "Captain" Allas's concern for accuracy.

35. One of the documents secured from the National Archives and reprinted in the *Philippine News* (Jan. 29-Feb. 4, 1986, p. 5), with a letterhead that reads "Headquarters Philippines-Ryukyus Command," dated March 24, 1948, and sent from Capt. E.R. Curtis to Lt. Col. W. M. Hanes, says that I arrested Marcos in December 1944 "for illegally collecting money to construct an air field near Baguio for the purpose of rescuing General Roxas," and that I would have held Marcos permanently had not Roxas appealed to Lapham to have him released. All I can say, forty-one years later, is that I have no recollection of this. In a long article devoted to these matters, the *Philippine News* implies strongly that, far from being heroes, both Allas and Marcos were engaging in black market sales to the Japanese. The *Philippine News* is decidedly hostile to Marcos. It supported his opponent, Mrs. Corazon Aquino, in the election campaign of early 1986.

36. Willoughby, *Guerrilla Resistance Movement*, p. 488.

37. Al Hendrickson regards with profound skepticism all claims that Marcos commanded large numbers of guerrillas. Personal communication to the author (B.N.).

38. Robert Lapham, personal communication to the author (R.H.).

10: *I Get My Own Command*

1. Ingham, *Rendezvous by Submarine*, especially pp. 20, 38–39, 51–52. General Willoughby expresses his appreciation of Parsons's talents and achievements *(Guerrilla Resistance Movement*, p. 101).

2. See chap. 9 herein for the Cruz mission. For an account of the expeditions of Parsons, Villamor, and Smith, see Willoughby and Chamberlain, *MacArthur*, pp. 215–18, 231.

3. William Manchester, *American Caesar*, pp. 378–79. Eyre, in *Roosevelt-MacArthur Conflict*, pp. 168–69, calls Whitney an undiplomatic and belligerent racist.

4. Ingham, *Rendezvous by Submarine*, p. 131; Dissette and Adamson, *Guerrilla Submarines*, pp. 69–70. It is worth noting that General Willoughby, who knew Whitney well, calls him a "brilliant executive" and praises him warmly. Willoughby, *Guerrilla Resistance Movement*, p. 101; Willoughby and Chamberlain, *MacArthur*, p. 214.

5. Uldarico S. Baclagon, *Philippine Campaigns*, pp. 238–43, 251–54.

6. Villamor, *They Never Surrendered*, pp. xiii–xv, 134–35, 200, 207, 215–17, 232–33, 235–36, 264, 272, 284. Villamor wrote most of this memoir but died before it was finished. The book was completed from Villamor's notes by Gerald S. Snyder.

7. Panlilio, *The Crucible*, pp. 249–54, 285; Ingham, *Rendezvous by Submarine*, p. 15.

8. Panlilio, *The Crucible*, p. 165.

9. Whitney himself describes this evolution in considerable detail in *MacArthur*, pp. 91, 132–43, 146–47. That he does not exaggerate his own role is indicated by similar though briefer descriptions by James, *The Years of MacArthur*, pp. 509–10; and Beth Day, *The Philippines*, p. 104. Neither writer is a partisan of Whitney. Willoughby, *Guerrilla Resistance Movement*, p. 194, and Robert Ross-Smith, *Triumph in the Philippines*, pp. 26–27, also describe Whitney's accomplishments.

10. Blackburn describes all the trouble early guerrillas had trying to rig up some kind of transmitter that would work even part of the time. Their single most persistent problem was keeping batteries charged. Harkins, *Blackburn's Headhunters*, pp. 142–45, 151–63, 170–71.

11. Blackburn says this was a misapprehension that arose, possibly, from the consideration that most of Volckmann's guerrillas were not former soldiers but ex-stevedores, litter bearers, guards, informers, and supply carriers, all men who

might routinely carry bolos. Harkins, *Blackburn's Headhunters*, p. 251. Blackburn also says that, when Volckmann first tried to organize all the north Luzon guerrillas under his command in November 1943, the move was welcomed by all save Capt. Ralph Praeger (ibid., p. 189). Since Lapham did resist such an effort, and since Praeger had been captured by the Japanese in August 1943, Blackburn's memory is clearly faulty on this point. It is yet another example of how difficult it is even to reconstruct events accurately in the wartime Philippines, much less interpret everyone's actions and motives fairly.

12. Baclagon, *Philippine Campaigns*, p. 237.

13. Donald Blackburn, personal communication to the author (B.N.).

14. Villamor, *They Never Surrendered*, p. 183.

15. Harkins, *Blackburn's Headhunters*, pp. 1–15.

16. Ibid., pp. 166–68, 172.

17. Volckmann, *We Remained*, p. 118.

18. *Intelligence Activities*, appendix 5.

19. Whitney, *MacArthur*, p. 147.

20. Arnold, *A Rock and a Fortress*, pp. 194–95.

21. Wolfert, *American Guerrilla*, p. 278.

22. Activities of this sort were undertaken at the same time by Volckmann's guerrillas farther to the north. See Volckmann, *We Remained*, pp. 168–75; Whitney, *MacArthur*, pp. 183–84.

23. Conner, "We Fought Fear," p. 86; Frank Gyovai, personal communication to the author (B.N.); Panlilio, *The Crucible*, pp. 258–59.

11: The Americans Return

1. Potter, *Life and Death*, describes Yamashita's plans. See especially pp. 61, 69, 106, 126, 129, 141.

2. *Intelligence Activities*, no page given.

3. Conner acknowledged similar awkwardness on both sides after he and several of his men ran into American soldiers after three years in the jungle. "We Fought Fear," p. 87.

4. Samuel Grashio experienced comparable inability to

write to his wife in circumstances not unlike mine. Grashio and Norling, *Return to Freedom*, p. 140.

5. A lengthy description of plans for liberating the prisoners, and all the problems and misgivings involved, are in Forrest Bryant Johnson, *Hour of Redemption*, especially pp. 139–40, 163, 208–10, 227, 255–56.

6. Ibid., p. 346.

7. Albert C. Hendrickson, personal communication to the author (B.N.).

8. James, *The Years of MacArthur*, pp. 642–43.

9. That I am not exaggerating the contribution of the guerrillas to the success of the raid is indicated by the remark of a Filipino historian: "In this rescue the guerrillas covered themselves with well deserved glory." Buenafe, *Wartime Philippines*, p. 253.

10. Johnson, *Hour of Redemption*, pp. 210, 337–38.

11. Lapham recalls General Krueger's attitude, typical of so many Americans at all times, that all that mattered was defeating the enemy quickly and that anyone who would fight the Japanese was to be welcomed. Lapham discussed the Huk menace with Philippine President Sergio Osmeña and with Carlos Romulo, but they felt powerless to interfere with Allied military operations. Robert Lapham, personal communication to the author (B.N.).

12: *Back into Action*

1. I am grateful to Tom Chengay for writing a moving commendation of me to General MacArthur. Tom stayed in the Philippine army long after the war. I lost contact with him for many years and rediscovered his address only in 1983. I wrote to him then and looked forward keenly to seeing him once more, or at least corresponding with him, only to receive from his wife the disheartening news that he had become completely incapacitated. He died April 17, 1984.

2. One of the lessons the Huks learned from the war was the defensive strength of these mountain fastnesses in northern Luzon. The present (1986) headquarters of the reconstituted Hukbalahap movement is in this wild region.

3. John M. Carlisle, *Red Arrow Men*, pp. 34–35.

Notes

4. Carlisle gives vivid descriptions of road construction under these conditions. Ibid., pp. 77–81, 108–11.

5. H. W. Blakeley, *The 32nd Infantry Division in World War II*, p. 248.

6. William de Jarnette Rutherfoord, *165 Days: The 25th Division on Luzon*, p. 137.

7. Ibid., pp. 113–14.

8. Carlisle, *Red Arrow Men*, p. 144. General Blakeley covers the whole subject of combat problems and how they were overcome along the Villa Verde Trial, briefly but capably and in a measured tone, in *The 32nd Division in World War II*, pp. 220–49. Carlisle, a war correspondent for the *Detroit News*, writes in a fashion at once thickly patriotic and reminiscent of the famous war correspondent Ernie Pyle. The 32nd Division is "the best in the world"; all the officers are fearless and inspire their troops by staying in the front lines; all the enlisted men are "great guys," well-trained Gary Cooper types, even braver than usual if wounded; they write sticky letters to Super Girls back home; et cetera. Even so, Carlisle provides much specific information about the struggle for north Luzon in the spring of 1945. Rutherfoord's book, *25th Division on Luzon*, is essentially a collection of drawings, accompanied by a brief running commentary, by an infantryman who fought along the Villa Verde Trail. It is both more informative and more analytical than one would expect.

9. Rutherfoord, *25th Division on Luzon*, p. 118.

10. Ross-Smith, *Triumph in the Philippines*, pp. 394, 398, 503–4, 511.

11. An apt characterization by Rutherfoord, *25th Division on Luzon*, p. 106.

12. Though I did not actually see this, Carlisle mentions a number of such instances. See *Red Arrow Men*, pp. 27, 57–60.

13. Rutherfoord, *25th Division on Luzon*, p. 159.

14. As in so many instances during guerrilla life in the Philippines, Donald Blackburn's experiences and thoughts about them were remarkably similar to my own. See Harkins, *Blackburn's Headhunters*, pp. 312–13.

15. On this point Rutherfoord offers one of his typically pithy aphorisms: "You cannot realize the cost of war until

you start collecting your own dead." *25th Division of Luzon*, p. 46.

16. Once more Blackburn was struck by the same thought as I. One day in December 1941 when everything connected with the war was going catastrophically for the Allies, he watched the Japanese cruise in a leisurely, arrogant way along the Luzon coast, and move men and equipment ashore, while planes rose unhurriedly from carriers. "The scene [he said] had a contradictory quality of beauty, the ugly beauty of naval power massed for a death blow." Harkins, *Blackburn's Headhunters*, p. 19.

13: *Reflections on the War*

1. Volckmann, *We Remained*, p. 226.
2. Liddell Hart, *Strategy*, pp. 379–82.
3. These instances are discussed by Laqueur, *Guerrilla*, pp. 41, 48–49.
4. Ibid., p. 230.
5. Kenworthy, *The Tiger of Malaya*, pp. 20–21. Agoncillo offers some thoughtful estimates of the importance and limitations of the Philippine guerrillas, as seen by a professional historian twenty years after the event. *The Fateful Years*, 2: 760–61, 775–77.
6. Trevor N. Dupuy, *Asian and Axis Resistance Movements*, p. 32.
7. See Ross-Smith, *Triumph in the Philippines*, pp. 421–22, 458–78, 540–78; James, *The Years of MacArthur*, pp. 683–90; Whitney, *MacArthur*, pp. 183–84.
8. Volckmann, *We Remained*, pp. 175–97.
9. Ibid., p. 216.
10. Ross-Smith, *Triumph in the Philippines*, pp. 573–78.
11. James, *The Years of MacArthur*, p. 690.
12. Volckmann, *We Remained*, p. 197.
13. Manchester, *American Caesar*, p. 430.
14. Potter, *Life and Death*, p. 152.
15. Ross-Smith, *Triumph in the Philippines*, pp. 421–22.
16. Whitney, *MacArthur*, p. 184.
17. Rodriguez, *Bad Guerrillas*, names names and specifies offenses. See pp. 115–42, 185.
18. Arnold, *A Rock and a Fortress*, pp. 209–10, 216.

19. Harkins, *Blackburn's Headhunters*, pp. 223–24.

20. Ibid., pp. 178–93.

21. Ibid., pp. 206–7.

22. Ibid., p. 278.

23. Estrada, *Historical Survey*, p. 55.

24. Ibid., p. 50.

25. Such fears were not imaginary. One major kept a diary in which were the names of all those who had harbored him. When the Japanese captured him, they also got the diary and proceeded to kill all the kind-hearted people listed in it. Monaghan, *Under The Red Sun*, p. 142.

26. Leon O. Beck, who travelled about among several guerrilla bands on Luzon, says it was common for guerrilla leaders to keep records but that these were usually buried in bottles to prevent their seizure by possible Japanese raiders. Beck, personal communication to the author (B.N.). Perhaps some others did this, though I doubt it; certainly I (R.H.) never did. Hendrickson says he kept *some* rosters. Albert C. Hendrickson, personal communication to the author (B.N.).

27. For a more detailed consideration of the matter see Estrada, *Historical Survey*, p. 37; and Johnson, *Hour of Redemption*, pp. 350–54.

28. Many a Filipino guerrilla wanted to buy U.S. war bonds with the pittance he was paid intermittently during the war. Ingham, *Rendezvous by Submarine*, p. 170.

29. Leon O. Beck and James P. Boyd, personal communications to the author (B.N.).

30. Robert Lapham, personal communication to the author (B.N.). Things weren't much different elsewhere. War correspondent Clark Lee relates that shortly after the war he asked someone he knew in Bangkok how many Siamese guerrillas there had been. The man answered that he estimated 10,000 at the end of the war but that he expected to see at least 25,000 in a parade the following Tuesday. Lee, *One Last Look Around*, p. 196.

31. Lichauco, *"Dear Mother Putnam,"* pp. 11–12.

32. Ibid., pp. 80–81.

33. These conditions and the circumstances that gave rise to them have been dissected by many writers. The following are a sampling. Lichauco, *"Dear Mother Putnam,"* pp. 11–

12, 105, 148, 153, 169–70, 192–94; Day, *The Philippines,*
pp. 123, 223–24; Monaghan, *Under the Red Sun,* pp. 271–
79; Agoncillo, *The Fateful Years,* 2: 545–91, 759, 853, 886;
Castillo and Castillo, *Saga,* pp. 224–26, 298–99; Taylor, *The
Philippines and the United States,* pp. 119–20; Eliseo Quirino, *A Day to Remember,* pp. 130–49.

34. Lichauco, *"Dear Mother Putnam,"* p. 23. The passage was written in his diary February 7, 1942.

35. Robert Lapham, personal communication to the author (B.N.). Villamor, *They Never Surrendered,* p. 286, de-
livers the scathing characterization. Villamor had become
acidly anti-American by the time he got around to writing his
memoirs, a generation after the war.

36. Molina, *Philippines,* p. 377.

37. Bernardo M. Morada to Ray Hunt, October 14, 1983;
Manila Courier, August 7, 1983, p. 5.

38. Utinsky, *Miss U.,* p. 92.

Selected Bibliography

Abaya, Hernando J. *Betrayal in the Philippines*. New York: A.A. Wyn, 1946.

Agoncillo, Teodoro A. *The Fateful Years: Japan's Adventure in the Philippines*. 2 vols., Quezon City: R.P. Garcia, 1965.

Agoncillo, Teodoro A., and Oscar M. Alfonso. *A Short History of the Filipino People*. Manila: Univ. of the Philippines Press, 1960.

Alip, Eufronio M. *Political and Cultural History of the Philippines*. 2 vols. Manila: Alip & Sons, 1958.

Archer, Jules. *The Philippines' Fight for Freedom*. New York: Macmillan, 1970.

Arnold, Robert H. *A Rock and a Fortress*. Sarasota, Fla.: Blue Horizon Press, 1979.

Baclagon, Uldarico S. *Philippine Campaigns*. Manila: Graphic House, 1952.

Bank, Bert. *Back from the Living Dead*. Tuscaloosa, Ala.: privately printed, 1945.

Bertram, James. *Beneath the Shadow*. New York: John Day, 1947.

Blakeley, H.W. *The 32nd Infantry Division in World War II*.

Madison, Wisc.: 32nd Infantry Division History Commission, n.d.

Boveri, Margaret. *Treason in the Twentieth Century.* London: Macdonald, 1961.

Boyington, Gregory. *Baa! Baa! Black Sheep.* New York: Putnam, 1948.

Brines, Russell. *Until They Eat Stones.* New York: Lippincott, 1944.

Buenafe, Manuel. *Wartime Philippines.* Manila: Philippine Education Foundation, 1950.

Calvocoressi, Peter, and Guy Wint. *Total War: Causes and Consequences of the Second World War.* New York: Penguin, 1979.

Campbell, Arthur. *Guerrillas.* London: Arthur Books, 1967.

Cannon, M. Hamlin. *Leyte: The Return to the Philippines. The U.S. Army in World War II.* Vol. 2, part 5, of *The War in the Pacific.* Washington, D.C.: Department of the Army, 1954.

Carlisle, John M. *Red Arrow Men: Stories about the 32nd Division on the Villa Verde Trail.* Detroit: Arnold Powers, 1945.

Castillo, Teofilo del, and José del Castillo. *The Saga of José P. Laurel.* Manila: Associated Authors, 1949.

Conner, Henry Clay, Jr. "We Fought Fear on Luzon," *True,* August 1946, pp. 69–87.

Considine, Robert, ed. *General Wainwright's Story.* Garden City, N.Y.: Doubleday, 1946.

Day, Beth. *The Philippines: Shattered Showcase of Democracy in Asia.* New York: Evans, 1974.

de la Costa, H., S.J. *Readings in Philippine History.* Manila: Bookmark, 1965.

Dissette, Edward F., and H.C. Adamson. *Guerrilla Submarines.* New York: Ballantine, 1972.

Dupuy, Trevor N. *Asian and Axis Resistance Movements.* New York: Franklin Watts, 1965.

Dyess, William E. *The Dyess Story.* Edited by Charles Leavelle. New York: Putnam, 1944.

Estrada, William L. "A Historical Survey of the Guerrilla Movement in Pangasinan, 1942–1945." Master's thesis. Manila: Far Eastern Univ., 1951.

Eyre, James K., Jr. *The Roosevelt-MacArthur Conflict.* Chambersburg, Pa.: Craft Press, 1950.

Falk, Stanley. *Bataan: The March of Death.* New York: Norton, 1962.

———. *Liberation of the Philippines.* New York: Ballantine Books, 1971.

Friend, Theodore. *Between Two Empires: The Ordeal of the Philippines, 1929–1946.* New Haven: Yale Univ. Press, 1965.

Goettl, Elinor. *Eagle of the Philippines: President Manuel Quezon.* New York: Messner, 1970.

Gordon, Ernest. *Through the Valley of the Kwai.* New York: Harper, 1962.

Grashio, Samuel, and Bernard Norling. *Return to Freedom.* Tulsa, Okla.: MCN Press, 1982.

Harkins, Philip. *Blackburn's Headhunters.* New York: Norton, 1955.

Hartigan, Richard Shelley. *The Forgotten Victim: A History of the Civilian.* Chicago: Precedent, 1982.

Howard, Michael. *The Causes of Wars.* Cambridge: Harvard Univ. Press, 1983.

Ind, Allison. *Allied Intelligence Bureau.* New York: McKay, 1958.

Ingham, Trevor. *Rendezvous by Submarine: The Story of Charles Parsons and the Guerrilla Soldiers in the Philippines.* Garden City, N.Y.: Doubleday, 1945.

Intelligence Activities in the Philippines during the Japanese Occupation. Vols. 1–2. Intelligence Series. General Reference Branch. Tokyo: General Headquarters, U.S. Armed Forces, Pacific, Military Intelligence Section, 1948. (Microfilm.)

James, D. Clayton. *The Years of MacArthur,* Vol. 2, *1941–1945.* Boston: Houghton Mifflin, 1975.

Johnson, Forrest Bryant. *Hour of Redemption: The Ranger Raid on Cabanatuan.* New York: Manor Books, 1978.

Jones, F.C. *Japan's New Order in East Asia, 1937–1945.* New York: Oxford Univ. Press, 1954.

Karig, Walter, Russell L. Harris, and Frank A. Manson. *Battle Report: Victory in the Pacific.* 5 vols., vol. 5. New York: Rhinehart, 1949.

Keith, Agnes Newton. *Three Came Home*. Boston: Little, Brown, 1947.

Kenworthy, Aubrey S. *The Tiger of Malaya: The Story of General Tomoyuki Yamashita*. New York: Exposition Press, 1953.

Kerkvliet, Benedict J. *The Huk Rebellion: A Study of Peasant Revolt in the Philippines*. Berkeley: Univ. of California Press, 1977.

Knightley, Philip. *The First Casualty*. New York: Harcourt Brace Jovanovich, 1975.

Laqueur, Walter. *Guerrilla: A Historical and Critical Study*. Boston: Little, Brown, 1976.

Laurel, José P. *War Memoirs*. Manila: Lyceum Press, 1962.

Lee, Clark. *One Last Look Around*. New York: Duell, Sloan & Pearce, 1947.

———. *They Called It Pacific*. New York: Viking Press, 1943.

Lichauco, Marcial P. *"Dear Mother Putnam": A Diary of the War in the Philippines*. No place, publisher, or date.

Liddell Hart, Basil H. *Strategy*. 2nd rev. ed. New York: Praeger, 1972.

Luvaas, Jay, ed. *Dear Miss Em: General Eichelberger's War in the Pacific, 1942-1945*. Westport, Conn.: Greenwood Press, 1972.

Mahajani, Usha. *Philippine Nationalism: External Challenges and Filipino Response, 1565-1946*. St. Lucia, Queensland: Univ. of Queensland Press, 1971.

Manchester, William. *American Caesar: Douglas MacArthur, 1880-1964*. Boston: Little, Brown, 1978.

Mijares, Primitivo. *The Conjugal Dictatorship of Ferdinand and Imelda Marcos*. San Francisco: Union Square Publications, 1976.

Miller, Ernest. *Bataan Uncensored*. Long Prairie, Minn.: Hart Publications, 1949.

Molina, Antonio M. *The Philippines Through the Centuries*. 2 vols. No place given: U.S.T. Cooperative, 1961.

Monaghan, Forbes J., S.J. *Under the Red Sun*. New York: Declan X. McMullen, 1946.

Moody, Samuel B., and Maury Allen. *Reprieve from Hell*. Privately printed, 1961.

Morison, Samuel E. *The Liberation of the Philippines*. Vol.

13 of *U.S. History of Naval Operations in World War II*. Boston: Little, Brown, 1959.

Netzorg, Morton J. *The Philippines in World War II and to Independence (December 8, 1941–July 4, 1946): An Annotated Bibliography*. Ithaca: Cornell Univ. Press, 1977.

Newsweek, February 3, 1986.

Panlilio, Yay. *The Crucible*. New York: Macmillan, 1950.

Petillo, Carlos M. *Douglas MacArthur: The Philippine Years*. Bloomington: Univ. of Indiana Press, 1981.

Philippine News, January 29–February 4, 1986.

Potter, John Deane. *The Life and Death of a Japanese General*. New York: New American Library (Signet), 1962.

Quirino, Eliseo. *A Day to Remember*. Manila: Benipayo Press, 1958.

Reel, Frank A. *The Case of General Yamàshita*. Chicago: Univ. Of Chicago Press, 1949.

Reynolds, Quentin, ed. *Officially Dead: The Story of Commander C.D. Smith*. New York: Random House, 1945.

Rodriguez, Ernesto R., Jr. *The Bad Guerrillas of Northern Luzon*. Quezon City: J. Burgos Media Services, 1982.

Ross-Smith, Robert. *Triumph in the Philippines. The U.S. Army in World War II*. Vol. 2, part 16, of *The War in the Pacific*. Washington, D.C.: Department of the Army, 1963.

Rutherfoord, William de Jarnette. *165 Days: The 25th Division on Luzon*. Privately printed, 1945.

Sekai, Saburo, with Martin Caidin and Fred Saito. *Samurai*. New York: Bantam, 1978.

Sanderson, James Dean. *Behind Enemy Lines*. New York: Van Nostrand, 1959.

Segura, Manuel F. *Tabunan: The Untold Exploits of the Famed Cebu Guerrillas in World War II*. Cebu City: M.F. Segura Publications, 1975.

Smith, Bradley F. *The Shadow Warriors: The O.S.S. and the Origins of the C.I.A.* New York: Basic Books, 1983.

Spence, Hartzell. *For Every Tear a Victory: The Story of Ferdinand E. Marcos*. New York: McGraw-Hill, 1964.

Steinberg, David J. *Philippine Collaborators in World War II*. Ann Arbor: Univ. of Michigan Press, 1967.

Stewart, Sidney. *Give Us This Day*. New York: Norton, Popular Library ed., 1947.

Taruc, Luis. *He Who Rides the Tiger*. New York: Praeger, 1967.

Tasaki, Hanema. *Long the Imperial Way*. Boston: Houghton Mifflin, 1950.

Taylor, George E. *The Philippines and the United States: Problems of Partnership*. New York: Praeger, 1964.

Thorpe, Elliot R. *East Wind, Rain*. Boston: Gambit, 1969.

Toland, John. *But Not in Shame*. New York: Random House, 1961.

Utinsky, Margaret. *Miss U*. San Antonio: Naylor, 1948.

Villamor, Jesus A., as told to Gerald S. Snyder. *They Never Surrendered*. Quezon City: Vera-Reyes, 1982.

Volckmann, Russell W. *We Remained*. New York: Norton, 1954.

Ward, Robert S. *Asia for the Asiatics? The Techniques of Japanese Occupation*. Chicago: Univ. of Chicago Press, 1945.

Whitcomb, Edgar. *Escape from Corregidor*. Chicago: Regnery, 1958.

Whitney, Courtney. *MacArthur: His Rendezvous with History*. Westport, Conn.: Greenwood, 1977.

Willoughby, Charles A. *The Guerrilla Resistance Movement in the Philippines*. New York: Vantage Press, 1972.

Willoughby, Charles A., and John Chamberlain. *MacArthur, 1941–1951*. New York: McGraw-Hill, 1954.

Winslow, Walter G. "Escape from Bataan." In Timothy Clark (ed.), *The World Wars Remembered*. Dublin, N.H.: Yankee, Inc., 1979, pp. 138–45.

Wolfert, Ira. *American Guerrilla in the Philippines*. New York: Simon & Schuster, 1945.

Index

319

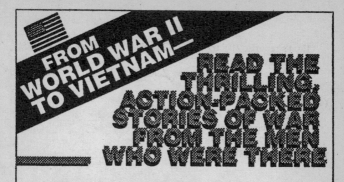

FROM WORLD WAR II TO VIETNAM—

READ THE THRILLING, ACTION-PACKED STORIES OF WAR FROM THE MEN WHO WERE THERE